COLLECTING

MUSCLE CAR Model Kits

TIM BOYD

CarTech®

CarTech®

CarTech®, Inc.
838 Lake Street South
Forest Lake, MN 55025
Phone: 651-277-1200 or 800-551-4754
Fax: 651-277-1203
www.cartechbooks.com

Edit by Bob Wilson
Layout by Connie DeFlorin

ISBN 978-1-61325-395-3
Item No. CT624

Library of Congress Cataloging-in-Publication Data

Names: Boyd, Tim, author.
Title: Collecting muscle car model kits / Tim Boyd.
Description: Forest Lake, MN : CarTech, [2018]
Identifiers: LCCN 2017042374 | ISBN 9781613253953
Subjects: LCSH: Muscle cars–Models–Collectors and collecting. | Automobiles–Models–Collectors and collecting. | Motor vehicles–Models–Collectors and collecting.
Classification: LCC TL237.2 .B692 2018 | DDC 629.22/1207 5–dc23
LC record available at https://lccn.loc.gov/2017042374

Written, edited, and designed in the U.S.A.
Printed in China
10 9 8 7 6 5 4 3

DISTRIBUTION BY:

Europe
PGUK
63 Hatton Garden
London EC1N 8LE, England
Phone: 020 7061 1980 • Fax: 020 7242 3725
www.pguk.co.uk

Australia
Renniks Publications Ltd.
3/37-39 Green Street
Banksmeadow, NSW 2109, Australia
Phone: 2 9695 7055 • Fax: 2 9695 7355
www.renniks.com

Canada
Login Canada
300 Saulteaux Crescent
Winnipeg, MB, R3J-3T2 Canada
Phone: 800 665 1148 • Fax: 800 665 0103
www.lb.ca
Phone: 2 9695 7055 • Fax: 2 9695 7355
www.renniks.com

Table of Contents

Dedication

This book is dedicated to two people: the late Roger Harney and author/historian Pat Ganahl.

Roger Harney joined Monogram Models soon after high school graduation in 1957 as an entry-level junior draftsman. By the early 1960s, Roger had progressed to become a kit designer and engineer (he took the lead in developing the Big T kit that became a Monogram best seller that inspired a full-sized copy). His responsibilities continued to increase and he became model shop manager in the 1970s, and then a member of Monogram's senior management team later that decade. Roger eventually became a vice president, as Monogram later merged with Revell and went through seven more changes of ownership. As you might imagine, Roger was also the consummate car enthusiast, from his high school 1950 Olds 88 coupe, to his cherished 1963 Corvette roadster in recent years. Roger had planned to retire from Revell in 2014 after an incredible 57-year career in service of model car builders and kit collectors, but he passed away unexpectedly in January of that year. If you have ever purchased a Monogram kit (or a Revell kit introduced after 1986), chances are that Roger had a hand in its creation. There are a number of influential executives and leaders who have made great contributions to the model car hobby, but no one can match the dedication or longevity of Roger Harney. Godspeed, Roger.

Pat Ganahl is well known to anyone who has followed the hot rod and custom car hobby since the mid-1970s, through a career as editor at various times of *Street Rodder, Hot Rod, Rod and Custom*, and *Rodder's Journal* magazines, and through his many best-selling automotive book titles. Today, "too tall" Ganahl is acknowledged as the hobby's premier historian. However, his role here is a little more personal. When he was editor of *Street Rodder* magazine in 1977, Pat agreed to a proposal from a college student in Michigan who wanted to author a monthly column in his magazine on the topic of hot rod and custom model cars and kits. Pat helped the aspiring writer to develop the proposal and his writing style. He even taught the writer how to photograph the model cars that were to be featured in the column! The "Modeler's Corner" feature was an immediate success and eventually became one of the most popular recurring features of the magazine. As you may have guessed by now, I was that college student and aspiring car writer. I have now written and published 500+ articles and features in more than 30 magazines worldwide, including slightly more than 200 "Modeler's Corner" columns for *Street Rodder* during the last 40 years. None of this would have happened without Pat's acceptance, counsel, and encouragement. Thanks, Pat!

—Tim Boyd, September 2017

Acknowledgments

At the top of my list of acknowledgments is Mark Budniewski, who is in my judgment the hobby's single most knowledgeable kit authority these days. Mark agreed to my request to review the text for possible errors and omissions, and on very tight turnaround timing, too. Thanks to Dennis Doty, Chuck Helppie, and Tom Woodruff, who each stoked my interest in model car kit history and collecting back in my college days. The information in this book would be far less precise if not for the efforts of Bob Shelton and Bill Coulter, who collectively researched, compiled, and published the hobby's definitive guide of model car kit offerings and their values. Now in its seventh revision, their guide is an indispensable reference for anyone considering the purchase of old, out of production model car kits.

I wanted to include a Scale Showroom section in several chapters of this book, to show readers who are not familiar with the hobby, or built their last kit back in the heyday of model kit building in the mid-1960s, just what is possible when the kits in this book are constructed by adults with care and precision. At the top of this list are Mike Hanson, a full-sized car restorer and contract model car constructor based in Arizona, and Dean Milano, a model car journalist and historian who opened a model car kit museum in the suburbs of Chicago in the early 2000s. Mike photographed many of his model cars and commissions for your viewing enjoyment here. Dean agreed to my request to visit with him and spend a day photographing his many built kit examples. Several fellow model car builders and journalists also contributed their works, including Bill Coulter and Bob Downie. Equal thanks to those who exhibited their built models at major model car events during the last 25 years, as I went through my photo archives and chose some of the best cars they built and I had photographed to show you here.

On the publication side, a big thanks to the team at CarTech Books, especially my editor Bob Wilson who first approached me with the idea for the book and then served as an endless cheerleader and confidante as the project developed. I also want to thank all the magazine editors I have worked with through the years, and especially so four longtime former magazine editors, who each worked with me for many years: Geoff Carter and Tom Vogele of *Street Rodder* magazine, Gary Schmidt of *Scale Auto Enthusiast* magazine, and Jim Haught of *Scale Auto* magazine.

Resources

Books

Coulter, Bill, and Bob Sheldon. *The Directory of Model Car Kits 1/24-1/25 Scale, Seventh Edition.* For purchase information, contact Bob Sheldon via email at: thedirectory@cinci.rr.com or via mail at 3116 W. Montgomery Road #C, Maineville, Ohio, USA, 45039.

Forums

Spotlight Hobbies at board2.spotlighthobbies.com
Model Cars at modelcarsmag.com/forums/

Vintage Kit Specialists

Spotlight Hobbies at spotlighthobbies.com
Model Roundup at modelroundup.com
Model Empire, Inc. at modelempireusa.com

Collectible Toy Shows

Old Toyland Shows at oldtoylandshows.com

Model Car Events

Scale Auto at scaleautomag.com
Model Cars at modelcarsmag.com/forums/calendar/

Introduction

Combine fads, toys, and the 1960s and several things immediately come to mind. Frisbees. "Sting Ray" Schwinn bicycles. Hula-hoops. Batman. Silly monsters. Silly Putty. Secret agents and spies. Slinkys. And model car kits.

If you were a boy or a young man (or perhaps a young woman) in the 1960s, chances are that you bought and built model car kits. You loved trips to your local five-and-dime store. You studied myriad kit boxes to decide which kit deserved your allowance or hard-earned odd-job money. You rushed home, broke the seal, opened the box, and then explored the instruction sheet and parts. You had to decide which of the three kit versions to build before piecing the model together; then, with or without paint? You admired the finished result and maybe even entered it in the local hobby store's model car contest. Or, maybe you blew it up in the backyard with your favorite form of fireworks.

Several societal and manufacturing developments coincided to make this happen. First, by the 1960s, the children of the post–World War II baby boom had grown old enough to have hobbies. Second, the United States was in the midst of an automotive craziness that (sadly) has not been repeated. Finally, improved toy production techniques, specifically moldable styrene plastic and three-piece sliding molds, made one-piece model car kit bodies possible (and affordable). All of these together made model car building one of the most popular fads of the early to mid-1960s.

Yes, model car kits were a big deal then. A portion of each subsequent generation has gone through similar experiences with these kits, although not to the all-consuming levels of the 1960s.

While most 1960s fads faded away to the history books and cable channels, model car kits and model car building have endured. Certainly, it is not nearly as popular now as it was in the formative years, but more than a few of those young model kit builders have continued to buy and build kits through the years, or more likely, have returned to the hobby as their adult lives progressed. Others have discovered and joined the hobby in more recent years.

With this book, I hope to document the model car hobby, specifically the portion of it that addressed (and continues to address) the world of muscle car model kits. I want to reacquaint those now-aging baby boomers with the kits they built as kids, and document all the other kits that were made but that they never saw or built. For those who are younger or until now unaware of the subject, I want to expose you to what is one of the most enduring hobbies extant and perhaps one that you might want to consider participating in yourself. And for the many readers of this book who love the real muscle cars of this world, I hope to open a view to a part of the muscle car hobby you may not have known about: collecting kits of your favorites from the muscle car era.

What Is a Model Car Kit and Which Ones Are Covered?

Since the advent of the modern model car kit in 1958, tens of thousands of kits were introduced throughout the following six decades. These range from 1/87th scale all the way up to 1/8th scale and have been produced by companies from all over the world. Obviously, some way to draw realistic boundaries around all of this is essential. As we say in the auto industry, we're going to scope the project.

Here are some guidelines for the coverage. First, the most popular scales for model kits are by far 1/24th and 1/25th the size of the real cars. Second, with just a few exceptions, the best kits of American cars come from American model kit manufacturers. I've focused on the kits from AMT, Revell, JoHan, Monogram, MPC, IMC, Lindberg, and their successor companies. Also included are a couple of newer companies, Polar Lights and Moebius. Third, the emphasis is on unassembled model car kits. Within the last 20 years, pre-assembled die-casts have become very popular, but they are an entirely different category and merit coverage elsewhere.

Many model kits have seen 5, 10, or even more subsequent "reissues" with new box art and minor changes. The primary focus here is on the first version of each kit that was brought to market. Reissues are occasionally shown, but the priority is the "original issue" of each kit.

What Is a Muscle Car?

That's a subject for debate among most automotive enthusiasts. For a book on a subject as broad as muscle car model kits, I had to settle on a definition of muscle car early on. That was no problem, as I personally developed my own definition for the term many decades ago.

The first part is the easy part. Back in the 1960s, cars like the GTO were called supercars, not muscle cars. Supercars were intermediate-sized cars with big V-8s, exciting styling, and (ideally) the imagery to go with it. They were offered from 1964 to

1971, with a few select products continuing through the 1974 model year with their credentials relatively intact. What constitutes a supercar's "big engine" is a little less clear. The traditional definition was a displacement of 400 ci or larger, but many would include the 389-powered GTOs and 383-powered Road Runners, and possibly even the 390-powered Fairlane and Comet GT/GTA big-engined supercars. I personally added the small-block intermediates that performed equal to or better than their big-block equivalents, for instance, the 340 and E58 360 powered B-Body Mopars and the W-31 Cutlasses, to my supercars definition.

But what about the Boss 429, Z-28, Duster 340, Impala SS427, and the two-seat domestic sports cars? They aren't supercars by the above definition, but these days most enthusiasts would agree that they should be included in any discussion of performance cars from the mid-20th century.

Accordingly, I've adopted a broad muscle car definition of any 1960s to 1974 American manufactured V-8 car, with 4-barrel carbs, dual exhausts, tuned primarily for performance attributes, and presenting design and image attributes to match the performance. And a published quarter-mile elapsed time (in pure factory-stock form) of mid-15 seconds or quicker. Extra credit is ensured if the car had a successful record in sanctioned competition.

Therefore, that's what I've used to guide the coverage and organization of this book. Finally, while not muscle cars in the traditional sense, there are several 1950s to early 1960s cars that set the precedent for the muscle car era, and I've included these as well to set the stage for what happened next.

Interestingly, while perusing my automotive library during the development of this book, I ran across an article in the magazine *2009 MuscleCar Milestones*. In it, well-respected muscle car authority Greg Rager addresses the subject in the sidebar "Muscle Car: Defined?" He makes some of the same points I do about how broad the muscle car market really was, back in the day. In the end, he suggests "each car should be judged on its own merit compared to whatever else was available at that particular point in time." He then mentions the Twin-H Hudsons of the early 1950s as an example of a car that was a great success at NASCAR and on the street, and concludes that it *was* a muscle car. Needless to say, I fully agree with Greg's muscle car rationale. By the way, I've included that Twin-H Hudson in this book, too.

How This Book Is Organized

Using the above as a guideline, I begin by discussing the advent of the modern model car kit and laying out some basic model car terminology and a way of rating the desirability of old model car kits.

I'll continue with the model car kits of the post–World War II cars that set the stage for the muscle car era. Then I'll cover the true supercars model kits in individual chapters devoted to each major corporation. The GM contingent is split into two chapters: one on Chevy and the other on Buick/Olds/Pontiac; AMC is included with Chrysler.

Next, I cover the junior/compact muscle cars as a group, and the family-size muscle cars as another group. Domestic sports cars, and 1960s tuner cars (think: Shelby, Yenko, etc.) also each rate their own chapters.

I'll wrap up with advice if you decide you want to join (or rejoin) the ranks of today's adult model car kit collectors, plus some thoughts about the future.

What to Expect in Each Chapter

Given my broad definition for muscle car, chances are you will see more than a few of your favorites in kit form. Many of the kits shown originated in the 1960s or early 1970s. However, there have been three additional "waves" of newly produced muscle car kits in the following decades, and I'll cover those as well.

At the end of most chapters is Scale Showroom. This shows how some of the kits covered in that chapter look when assembled by experienced adult modelers using currently available materials and techniques.

A number of sidebars throughout the book explain some of the inside events that have taken place in the world of model kit development and manufacturing. Some of these secrets have remained unknown to even the most dedicated model car hobbyists and collectors until now.

I'll also provide some advice regarding which are the best kits and which should be avoided. For the model car companies, I'll address future kit opportunities at the end of each chapter in a section called Missing in Action.

A Word about Accuracy and Images

Ask all of the editors I've ever worked for, and they will tell you that I am a stickler for accuracy. Accuracy makes a statement about your values and character, and, as a writer, it is your duty to pass along the most accurate and correct information you can secure.

To set the stage for our discussion of model kits, I have first provided a summary of some of the key information about the real muscle cars that formed the inspiration for these kits. Like many of you, I have an entire library composed of six decades of muscle car reference books, magazines, and reference material, and I consulted it repeatedly in preparing this text. Though I've provided the best and most current information available to me, it is more than likely that some of this information is now considered out of date or incorrect. In those few (I hope) cases, please accept my apologies in advance.

As far as accurate information on the model car kits, the history of model car kits during the last couple of decades is best summarized as "never say never." Just when you think you know the whole story of model car kit history, new and contradictory information turns up. Again, I've made every effort to be as accurate as possible, but mistakes are possible. If you see one, please let me know via CarTech Books, Inc., but understand in advance that I'll need to see photographic and other supporting evidence. Corrections will be included if there are future printings of this book.

Finally, as you look through the images of model car boxes in this book, you'll see some that are, well, pretty beat up. Many of the boxes in this book are leftovers from someone (myself or others) who actually built the kit that was in that box. Some modelers saved the boxes as remembrances, others repurposed them for collections of model car engines or parts, and some were nearly thrown out before being saved at the last second. I've chosen to include these well-worn artifacts in order to tell, and illustrate, the whole story of muscle car model kits. I hope you'll be able to look upon them with the same appreciation that is now bestowed upon barn-find muscle cars.

Model Car Kits: A Great Hobby Then and Now

Model cars have been a part of my life since age eight and I attribute much of my personal and professional success to my involvement in this hobby. They are, of course, the reason that you are reading this book.

My fondest hopes are that with this book, I may bring a smile to your face, perhaps a recollection or two of a fun time in your own past, and maybe even a desire to engage (or re-engage) on some level with a hobby that is among the most fun and enduring hobbies of this era of American history.

Are you ready? Then let's get going and dig deep into the world of muscle car model kits.

In the Beginning

Chapter 1

The Origins of the Model Car Kit Hobby

In the beginning, most model car kits were derived from the same tooling used to produce 1/25th-scale new car dealer promotionals. These were factory-assembled and molded in colors, but omitted the engines, detailed chassis, and building options found in model car kits. Promotionals shown here, clockwise from the upper left, are the 1960 Dodge Dart and 1965 Plymouth Fury (produced by JoHan), 1969 Ford Galaxie XL (produced by AMT), 1966 Charger, and 1970 GTO (produced by MPC).

The model car kit phenomenon developed quickly in just a few years, starting in the late 1950s. As is so often the case, this growth and progress occurred in several major steps. Promotionals, sliding molds, 3-in-1 kits . . . they all played a role in the rapid development of the model car hobby. Let's take a look at these developments as I lay the groundwork for the coverage of muscle car model kits later in this book.

They Came First: 1/25th-Scale Promotionals

The popularity of promotional dealer-giveaway toys grew following World War II and continued through the 1950s. One of the earliest recognized promos was a very basic aluminum-based 1948 Ford miniature from a company not surprisingly named Aluminum Model Toys. Yes, this was the start for a company that later led the development of model car kits, later using the new name AMT.

Promos became available for many of the 1950s cars, usually rendered in 1/25th scale. Each year, the car companies would contract with a manufacturer of promotionals for replicas of their best-selling cars. Eventually two companies, AMT and JoHan (joined later by MPC), became the primary sources for these promotionals. The material used for these "toys" was typically an acetate that allowed a reasonable level of detail, but was unfortunately prone to moderate to severe warping over time.

One-Piece Bodies and Sliding Molds

A huge step ahead in scale authenticity occurred with the invention of three-piece sliding molds, an accomplishment credited to then-AMT engineer George Toteff. These sliding molds produced three-dimensional, one-piece bodies for promotional models. A further achievement was when AMT began molding its promotionals in a more rigid material that did not distort. This material was called Cycolac, and AMT made the switch during the 1961 promotionals run (while JoHan stuck with acetate bodies through the 1963 model run).

1/25th-Scale Assembly Kits with One-Piece Bodies

Model car kits of varying detail, quality, materials, and scale size had been produced for several years, but these kits were compromised in many ways. Unlike the acetate or Cycolac promos, these car kits were usually made from styrene pellets that, when heated, could be injected into a mold and rapidly cycled, allowing mass production. Styrene parts could also be assembled together by the modeler using, well . . . styrene glue.

By the mid-1950s, styrene hobby kits were becoming more common, but these kits all suffered from the need to glue the body together from separate pieces forming the sides, front, rear, hood, trunk, and top. The finished product clearly showed the joints of these multi-piece bodies, along with the attendant glue smears and misshapen assemblies that could result. Typical of these kits were a series of 1/32nd-scale car replica kits from a Revell-AMT joint branding project starting in 1955.

Starting with the 1958 model run, AMT decided to use its sliding mold tooling to produce unassembled versions of its 1/25th-scale promotionals, using styrene as the molding medium. These "kits" were then packaged for sale directly to the public via department stores, hardware stores, drug stores, and hobby shops. With the new one-piece bodies and easily glued parts, these AMT model car kits, which later became known as annual kits, were perfectly timed for the automotive-centric climate of the late 1950 United States.

AMT's 1958 annual kit debut included the Buick Roadmaster, Edsel Pacer, Fairlane 500, and Pontiac Bonneville. Another company by the name of SMP, very closely related to AMT, offered a Chevy Impala and Chrysler Imperial. The above kits were manufactured in convertible and (except for the Imperial) two-door hardtop form. Needless to say, these kits were a huge hit with boys, teens, and young adults back then.

For 1959, the AMT/SMP lineup grew with replicas of the Corvette, Thunderbird, Lincoln Continental, and Mercury Park Lane joining the latest Buick Invicta, Impala, Imperial, Edsel, Galaxie, and Bonneville kits. Another promotionals manufacturer joined the unassembled kit fray when JoHan introduced kits of the 1959 Dodge Custom Royal, Cadillac Fleetwood, Oldsmobile 98, and Plymouth Fury. A year later, JoHan's offerings added a 1960 Chrysler New Yorker and DeSoto Adventurer to its kit catalog. Revell, an early pioneer of assembly model kits who had previously offered a few 1/25th-scale kits with multi-piece bodies in the late 1950s, joined the 1/25th-scale annual kit competition in 1962. Its kit lineup replicated nearly the entire Chrysler Corporation lineup, including the Plymouth Fury and Valiant, Dodge Dart and Lancer, and Chrysler Newport and Imperial; this time these kits included the now-expected one-piece bodies.

The breadth of 1/25th-scale kit coverage of the American Automotive Marketplace grew each year through the mid-1960s, with AMT and JoHan leading the charge. A new company, MPC, founded by George Toteff, the same engineer who created AMT's three-piece sliding kit molds, introduced its first kit in 1964. By 1968, MPC was producing kits of many of the

These are among the first modern-era 1/25th-scale model car kits. Shown are examples of the 1958 (upper left), 1959 (center and lower left), and 1960 (center column) annual kits from AMT. On the right are 1960 and 1961 annual kits from AMT's primary annual kit competition in the early years, JoHan Models. Note the "SMP" labeling on some of the AMT boxes.

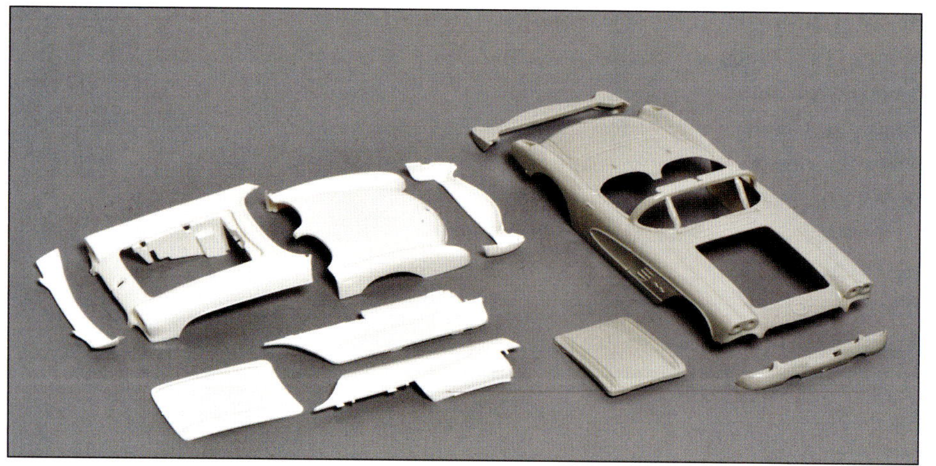

Until AMT began producing model kits using its multi-piece sliding tool molds, most model kits were made up of separately molded front, rear, top, and side pieces that retained easily visible seams even if assembled with exceptional care. Here a Revell multi-piece Corvette body is compared to the AMT one-piece Corvette body. While far more expensive to engineer, these new kits with one-piece bodies fueled the exploding popularity of model car kits starting in the late 1950s.

auto industry's most desirable nameplates, including the new GTO and Charger. Meanwhile, Revell's 1962 kit lineup was not a success, so it did not return to annual kits until 1969 with a new kit of that year's Mustang hardtop and convertible.

The 3-in-1 Customizing Kit

Beyond the pure appeal of being able to build a very accurate replica of your favorite showroom spectacular, AMT's new 1958 model kits included another feature that would become tremendously important to the growth of the model car kit hobby. Each kit offered *three* different ways to be built by the hobbyist. In addition to the showroom stock version, parts were included for a mild custom and a race car version. (Note: SMP actually pioneered the 3-in-1 idea one year earlier in 1957, with kits of the current year Chevy Bel Air and Pontiac Star Chief, but these were packaged as bagged kits and sold in much smaller quantities than the AMT 1958 kits.)

At first, these additional 3-in-1 parts were very generic and limited in scope. But by the mid-1960s, each model 3-in-1 model car kit now included highly developed and application-specific custom and race versions, often replicas of the latest brand name parts from the rapidly developing hot rod, custom, and racing parts business. AMT's 3-in-1 versions were frequently credited to the leading builders of the custom car movement, including George Barris, Bill Cushenberry, the Alexander Brothers, Gene Winfield, and Dean Jeffries.

This 3-in-1 feature engaged the model-building public, allowing each hobbyist to become his or her own "car designer." Model car kit coverage became very prominent in national magazines including *Rod and Custom* and *Car Craft*, and soon several magazines dedicated solely to the model car hobby debuted. Contests recognizing the builders who crafted miniature masterpieces from these 3-in-1 kits became commonplace, eventually reaching a series of national competitions that at their height awarded real cars to the national champions!

Opening Hoods with Engines

Starting in 1957, Revell's very limited series of 1/25th-scale kits with multi-piece bodies had also included opening hoods with rudimentary representations of engines.

For its 1960 lineup of annual kits, AMT revisited the idea by adding opening hoods combined with its one-piece bodies, placing replica engines underneath. First announced in three kits (the Buick Invicta, Thunderbird, and Corvette convertibles), and also added to the Chevy and Ford pickup kits that year, by 1961 engines and opening hoods were expanded to many of AMT's annual kits, including all nine convertible kits.

For 1962, every single AMT annual kit except for one (the Valiant) included parts for engines. (It should be noted that in some cases, primarily the slower selling compact car kits, the engines were to be displayed separately alongside the model, rather than under the hood as with most kits.) Engines quickly became the base expectation for purchasers of 1/25th-scale kits from that point forward.

This AMT sell sheet from 1962 was targeted at hobby shop owners and model kit distributors, and explains the consumer appeal of the 3-in-1 format of its 1962 annual kits' lineup. Typical 3-in-1 kits featured parts to build models in showroom stock, competition, and custom versions. Note the paragraph at the lower right, which reads "All builders of AMT 3-in-1 customizing kits are assured the latest ideas and innovations in the field of customizing by Car Craft *magazine and George Barris (King of the Kustomizers), Consultants to AMT."*

These AMT 1960 and 1961 convertible annual kit sell-sheets convey the added appeal of scale engines. The 1960 catalog (left) calls out its three "1960 Special Edition convertibles . . . with engine and operating hood." The 1961 catalog (right) states, "Now – Each [convertible] kit contains a completely authentic and detailed engine just waiting to be customized to fit the car the way you want to build it."

AMT's Trophy Series and Revell's Speed and Show Kits

In late 1959, AMT took an additional step with a new 1/25th-scale model kit lineup that proved the appeal of model car kits stretched well beyond Detroit's current model year lineup. AMT's 1932 Ford Roadster 3-in-1 Trophy Series kit became a monstrous hit. AMT is reported to have sold 5 million copies of this kit in just its first five years on the market. Starting the following year in 1960, AMT rapidly expanded its Trophy Series kit lineup through the next eight years. Beyond the appeal of the varied kit subjects, these kits featured a greater level of detail throughout than the annual kits, typically including detailed chassis with separately molded suspensions, expanded engine compartment detail, and multi-piece interior assemblies.

Following AMT's lead, Revell debuted its Speed and Show kits starting in late 1962, expanding the level of detail even further to include operating doors and trunks and complex chassis/suspension designs. Revell also quickly grew its kit lineup, with models of Tri-Five Chevys and Ed Roth's latest creations being among its best sellers. With its more popular kit topics and much greater detail, Revell's Speed and Show kits enjoyed far better success than its ill-fated 1962 annual kit lineup. Monogram's newest car kits were also full-featured in the same manner as those of AMT and Revell.

Given the marketplace response to these new AMT and Revell kit categories, their greater level of detail and complexity soon migrated to the yearly kits replicating Detroit's latest showroom offerings. The result? By the mid-1960s, certain annual kits like AMT's 1965 Ford Galaxie 500 XL and 1967–1968 Mustang GT included intricate detailing that matched the best of AMT's Trophy Series lineup.

AMT's new Trophy Series kits were more detailed than its typical annual kits. Shown are three of its most successful early Trophy Series offerings: a 1932 Ford Roadster, a 1940 Ford coupe, and a double kit of a 1929 Model A Roadster and the famous Barris Ala-Kart*. Revell's speed and show kits were also very popular; pictured here are its 1956 Ford Pickup, Mickey Thompson's* Challenger 1*, and Ed Roth's* Tweedy Pie*. The overwhelming success of these kits prompted a higher level of detail to be added into the annual kit lineups from America's kitmakers.*

Box Art That Emphasized Fun and Provoked the Imagination

At first, AMT and JoHan's 1/25th-scale kits were merchandized in generic boxes with no more personalization than the subject of the kit contents ink-stamped in a small white rectangle at the lower end of the end panels. However, with the growth of the hobby kit business and the competition created by multiple kitmakers, box art soon grew more specific to each kit's contents. By the mid-1960s, the annual kit lineups from

Drag racing a C2 Stingray, or being the first to own a miniature of the all-new 1968 Corvette; towing your A/FX-style 1965 Fairlane match racer to the strip or admiring your just-completed SOHC 427 Mustang racer. What hobby shop customer wouldn't be enticed by the high-quality commercial art seen on these mid- to late 1960s annual kit boxes?

AMT and MPC were sold in boxes that featured the very best in contemporary commercial art.

Not only were these illustrations finely rendered commercial art in the best tradition of the full-sized carmakers' advertising agencies, these illustrations spoke clearly to the target audience. The illustrations sparked the imagination of modelers and were key to the continued success and growth of the model car hobby kit industry. (This is in part why I will place such an emphasis on showing these box tops throughout this book.)

Why Should Muscle Car Owners, Collectors, and Fans Care about Model Car Kits?

Great question!

Beyond the obvious appeal of revisiting something that brought you much fun and joy at an earlier part of your life, the reasons for having an interest in model car kits are many.

First and right up front, next to the real cars themselves, model car kits comprise a very complete historical record of any given muscle car. They're highly detailed, three-dimensional representations of the real thing. Sure, looking at pictures in an old brochure, and reading about your favorites in a book, magazine, or website is interesting, but this offers nowhere near the level of information provided by a well-designed model car kit.

Running your hands over the flanks of a miniature 1969 Z-28 body provides far more tactile and visual information than the two-dimensional printed image. Model kits reveal detailed information such as the shape of the engine fuel pump, the engraved pattern of the rear-seat quarter-panels, and the configuration of the differential and suspension. These are things you might miss in other information sources. Assembling a Boss 302 engine in 1/25th scale really is next best to building the real thing in your garage (and let's be honest, in many cases these days many folks are instead paying a professional to assemble that real engine!).

Today, historical accuracy is a goal of most car collectors. As Day 2–type muscle cars continue to grow in popularity, the annual model car kits of the 1960s and early 1970s become a great source of historical information about the exact type and name brand of Day 2 and Day 3 parts and modifications that were used back then. These 3-in-1 kits included the latest in customizing and performance accessories in each box. They were like a scaled-down SEMA show, decades before SEMA grew to the size and popularity it enjoys today.

Granted, many muscle car owners collect die-cast replicas. But while today's die-cast replicas are continually improving in accuracy and detail, the limitations of a metal replica manufactured in such a small scale are many, and a close inspection often reveals a distinct lack of accuracy in body proportions and lifelike appearances. The technologies and materials used in 1/25th-scale styrene model kits avoid the die-cast accuracy issues.

Moreover, if you build up your model car kits, you can often spec them out exactly as you would have back in the day, right down to the exact same factory paint color and powertrain configuration of your choice. That's a whole lot easier than spending months or years finding a real muscle car that meets your own preconceived factory order specs!

Then there's the whole thing about maintaining a real muscle car collection. The ongoing expenses associated with storage, insurance, maintenance, plus the risks of having to search out and replace rare components because of an accident, can be headaches for the real muscle car collector. Most of these expenses are nonexistent, and the cost is at most a mere fraction of what it would be, if you collect 1/25th-scale kits. Indeed, it's a great way to stay involved in the muscle car hobby for those who have decided to downsize their real car collections for one reason or another.

Of course, nothing replaces the thrill of starting up and taking off down the street or strip in a real original muscle car. Model car kits are a fine way to experience some of the same joy, albeit on a much smaller scale!

Revell's 1969 Z-28 kit produces a spectacular 1/25th-scale replica of the real car that every Chevy muscle car enthusiast would love to have in his or her collection. The kit even includes the Chevy parts counter Z-28 dual-quad carb cross-ram intake manifold and the factory dual chambered exhausts. (The model shown here also shows Day 2–style wheels and tires, sourced from a well-stocked model parts box.)

Nobody Knew Back Then . . .

Veterans of Detroit's 1960s and early 1970s muscle car wars often comment that few back then realized the significance and future collectability of these cars. They were our transportation, our entertainment, a key enabler of our lifestyle, a source of our dreams, and, for a fortunate few, a means of livelihood. They were modified, raced, and eventually sold or run into the ground (or for those of us in the northern states, they rusted away!). That is in part why they are so hard to find in original form these days and so expensive when located.

Likewise, no one realized the potential future collectability of model car kits back then. They were built (often in one sitting), showed around, run across the floor, and often eventually blown up in the backyard. It follows that the few remaining unbuilt model kits of the muscle car era are also valued possessions and collectibles today. Throughout the rest of this book, I'll celebrate both the cars and the kits that replicated them, all the while remembering what they meant back then, and what they represent today.

A Brief History of Model Car Kitmaker Lineage

Throughout this book you'll find references to AMT, AMT-Ertl, Monogram, Revell, Revell-Monogram, and so forth. What's up with all this?

If you were a model car builder in the 1960s or 1970s, you probably remember the names AMT, Revell, Monogram, Aurora, and later on, MPC. You probably also heard of Lindberg, but quickly learned that many of its kits didn't live up to your expectations. Today, one company, Round 2, owns the brand names AMT, MPC, and Lindberg. Hobbico owns the Revell and Monogram brand names; they are used interchangeably by a single organization producing kits under both names.

So how did we get from there to here? What follows is a brief historical recap of each major model maker's corporate evolution from the 1960s to today.

AMT

At one time the largest kitmaker in the world, AMT began as Aluminum Model Toys after World War II, soon shortening its name to AMT. A big break came in 1958, with its introduction of one-piece bodies formed of styrene and its merchandising of the resulting unassembled promotionals as 3-in-1 model car kits. AMT thrived into the mid-1960s, but as the decade progressed its focus on the model kit business was diffused by unsuccessful forays into the AMT Model Car Turnpike, Dynamic Slot Cars, and a spinoff Speed and Custom division based in Phoenix, Arizona, with the goal to develop and market accessories for real cars. AMT also developed a prototype of a Corvair-based real car called the Piranha; it was to be built of the same Cyclolac material used for AMT's promotionals. (AMT even became a supplier to the automotive industry with several contracts to manufacture parts such as taillamp lenses and side reflector lamps.) Meanwhile, AMT's core business of 1/25th-scale promotionals and model car kits started losing key promotional and kit contracts to now-competitor MPC.

As a result, AMT faced some financial difficulties in the late 1960s, but recovered in the early 1970s, credited partly to a best-selling lineup of 1/25th-scale semi-truck kits and the business-focused recovery actions of a new company president, Tom Gannon. It again ran into trouble in the late 1970s, with unresolved issues with its unionized labor force and the truck kits having run their course of popularity. AMT eventually closed its Troy, Michigan, headquarters and factory; it consolidated at a second facility in Baltimore, Maryland. It was then acquired by the British toymaker Lesney, the famous maker of Matchbox toys. After further difficulties, the Ertl Company, a very successful maker of 1/16th-scale die-cast farm toys and replicas, purchased the entire AMT tool bank and brand assets. The company was renamed AMT-Ertl.

Revell

Also started in the 1940s, Revell was based in Venice, California. It produced a broad range of model kits of all types, with cars being a portion of, but not the primary source of, its sales volume. Revell is credited with producing the first accurate model car kits, including the Highway Pioneers series starting in 1951. Revell's 1955 kit lineup introduced several 1/32nd-scale car assembly kits in boxes co-branded with AMT. Starting in 1957, it produced several 1/25th-scale car kits with multi-piece bodies. It became AMT's main competitor in the 1/25th-scale car kit marketplace in the early 1960s, while continuing a broad range of other non-automotive kit topics including airplanes, boats, and spacecraft. Revell was acquired by a French kit company in the early 1980s, and then sold to Odyssey Partners in 1986 to be joined with the Monogram lineup.

Monogram

Yet another toy and kitmaker with origins in the post–World War II U.S. business environment, produced a wide range of hobby kits, and later expanded into the 1/24th- (not 1/25th) and 1/8th-scale car kit business in the late 1950s and early 1960s. Its late 1960s acquisition by Mattel resulted in a broad lineup of show-car kits, often developed in association with designer Tom Daniel. Following its successful recruitment of AMT's then-president Tom Gannon, Monogram returned to a focus on realistic car replica assembly kits. Monogram was eventually joined with Revell in 1986 as part of the Odyssey Partners acquisition event.

JoHan

Some sources suggest that JoHan models was a side business owned by John Haenle, who reportedly ran a tool and die business aligned with the automotive manufacturing environment in Detroit. JoHan was primarily a producer of 1/25th-scale promotionals that expanded into the model kit business in 1959. JoHan's models were renowned for crisp detail, superb body proportions, and overall accuracy. As the model kit business fundamentally changed in the early 1970s, JoHan's new offerings were scaled back, with the last new kit being a promo-type 1979 Cadillac DeVille. Several others later attempted to revive the JoHan lineup but ultimately failed. It is presumed that most of its model tooling is permanently lost or scrapped.

IMC

Industro-Motive Corporation, or IMC, was an automotive supplier that expanded into the model kit business around 1964. It hired away AMT's spokesperson and model car guru Budd "the Kat" Anderson, who proceeded to design a series of kits targeted at the advanced model car builder. Heavily weighted to Ford products, concepts, and race cars, these kits contained many operating features and advanced ideas, but also had a reputation for being difficult to assemble. The last new tooling from IMC was around 1970. Some of its kits were later reissued under the Testors and Union (Japanese) brands, and a few resurfaced in the 1990s under the Lindberg trade name.

Aurora

For much of the 1960s and early 1970s, Aurora was the largest kitmaker in the world. Its kits were focused primarily on subjects other than automotive. Aurora almost acquired AMT in the summer of 1964; the pending deal was reportedly squelched by the intervention of the U.S. Federal Trade Commission. Nabisco later acquired the company, but a period of mid-1970s difficulties resulted in Nabisco dissolving the company. Monogram acquired most of its automotive kit tools.

MPC

In 1963, George Toteff (the AMT vice president credited with creating the three-piece sliding mold technology that enabled one-piece model car bodies) departed that company along with one of his key lieutenants. They set up Model Products Corporation (later MPC) in Detroit's northeast suburbs. By 1968, MPC had grabbed many of the most desirable promotional and kit topics, and many hobbyists considered it the hottest kitmaker. General Mills purchased MPC in 1971 and it remained a very competitive kit producer until eventually being sold to AMT-Ertl in 1986.

Lindberg

This northeastern U.S. kitmaker offered a wide range of toy kits, including some 1/25th- and 1/32nd-scale car assembly kits. Serious car modelers largely dismissed Lindberg because its kits were not at the level of the best domestic competition. The Lindberg name resurfaced in the early 1990s when MPC's former president, George Toteff, led the development of a new series of 1/20th-, and then later, 1/25th-scale car kits. These newest kits were fully competitive with the best of the competition and earned new respect for the Lindberg brand. Round 2 recently acquired Lindberg.

Ertl

A well-known maker of die-cast farm toys and replicas, Ertl entered the hobby market in 1973 with a series of well-conceived 1/25th-scale semi-truck, farm tractor, and construction equipment kits that reflected a good deal of fresh thinking. It eventually produced more than 40 different kits before purchasing the assets of AMT from Lesney-Matchbox in 1982.

AMT-Ertl

Created when Ertl acquired the AMT lineup, AMT-Ertl became one of the top two car kitmakers in the late 1980s and continued in that role for at least the next decade. In 1998, Racing Champions, a highly successful producer of licensed die-cast racing replicas, purchased AMT-Ertl. In an ill-advised move, the new owner began dismissing the AMT-Ertl kit development staff, completing a layoff of all remaining staff in May 2000. In January 2007, then-owner RC2 announced plans to discontinue the entire AMT-Ertl kit lineup. Shortly thereafter, Round 2 acquired the rights to produce AMT-Ertl kits in 2008, and later completed a purchase of all AMT-Ertl brand and tool assets in December 2011.

Revell-Monogram

In 1986, Odyssey Partners acquired the Monogram and

Revell product lines and brands. While production was consolidated at Monogram's Morton Grove, Illinois, plant, product development and sales staffs remained separated at first. After a number of ownership changes, including a period of ownership by Binney & Smith, the maker of Crayola products, hobby conglomerate Hobbico purchased Revell-Monogram in 2007.

Galaxie Limited

Best known as the former editor and owner of *Scale Auto Enthusiast* magazine (and also a muscle car collector of note), Gary Schmidt formed the model car kit company Galaxie Limited. It has produced a limited portfolio of superb 1/25th-scale model cars and fifth-wheel/tow-behind trailer kits. Although none of these kits are muscle cars, there is the hope that its kit range might expand in that direction in the future.

Polar Lights

Starting in 1995, a new company headed by Tom Lowe produced a series of toy kits that largely replicated the Aurora kit range of the 1950s and 1960s. It then produced several all-new 1/25th-scale car kits. Racing Champions, and then Round 2 eventually acquired Polar Lights.

Round 2

Tom Lowe resurfaced as the owner of a new company, Round 2, which acquired the production rights, and soon thereafter the full ownership of all tooling for the AMT, AMT-Ertl, MPC, Lindberg, and Polar Lights product ranges. Round 2 has implemented an aggressive reissue program, including often-spectacular box art and the recreation of almost-original issue versions of numerous kit topics.

Moebius Models

Another new kitmaker has surfaced within the last decade; its product lineup includes new 1/25th-scale car kits of topics that have never been produced before in that scale. Owner Frank Winspur has directed a kit lineup including a series of 1950s Hudson Hornet kits that set numerous new standards for car kits.

Model King

This concern primarily markets limited-edition short production runs from tooling owned by other kitmakers. It has recently developed a close relationship with Moebius Models, introducing exclusive kit derivatives from its tooling that feature famous racing topics.

All the Others

Other companies producing 1/24th- and 1/25th-scale styrene model kits of this era include such makers as Hubley, ITC, Palmer/PSM, PMC, Pyro and SMP. Generally, their products are either of marginal quality or they produced fine kits but only of a few specific subjects. Most collectors view these makers as footnotes rather than main participants in the model car kit business.

Round 2 currently owns and produces kits under the AMT, MPC, Lindberg, Ertl, and Polar Lights brands. Recently, Round 2 has reboxed a number of modern-era kits that were engineered by AMT-Ertl during the late 1980s to early 2000s, using newly created box art (shown here) that is reminiscent of AMT's original 1960s to early 1970s annual kits.

The Four Waves of Model Car Kit Evolution and the Envy Factor

You don't have to be a kit expert to make sense of what is to come here, but it will definitely help if I at least define a few basics. There are a number of terms that have developed during the roughly six decades of the modern kit era that I'll use throughout this book, so I'll tackle that subject first.

Then I need to cover the basics of why some of your favorite muscle car kits of the 1960s were never reissued, while others seem to reappear at regular intervals. Next I'll define the four generations (or waves) of model car kit development. Then there's the subject of collectability. Which kits are most desirable and why?

Shall we get started?

Key Model Car Kit Terms Defined

To help your understanding of the kits discussed, it will be helpful to define some of the terms you'll see throughout this book.

1/1-Scale

This is the term that model car builders and collectors use to refer to the real car that is being duplicated by the model. Most model cars are 1/25th the size of the real car, while the real car is 1/1 the size of the real car!

1/24th Scale, 1/25th Scale, or the Popular Scales

The vast majority of muscle car model kits have been produced in 1/25th scale (that is, 1/25th the size of the real car). Most remaining kits have been produced in 1/24th scale. Together, these are called the popular scales, or bi-scale.

While a built 1/25th-scale model will be slightly smaller in size than the same topic rendered in 1/24th scale, most kit collectors view them as the same in terms of desirability, and they display them together. (A few muscle car model kits have been produced in other scales, including 1/8th, 1/12th, 1/16th, 1/20th, 1/32nd, 1/43, and 1/48th the size of the real cars; for the sake of brevity, these kits are not discussed in this book.)

Annual Kit

This refers to the yearly production run of model car kits that duplicated the current model year offerings in the dealer showrooms of America. By the mid-fall of each year, 1 to 2 months after the debut of real cars, convertible kits of the current crop of 1/1-scale cars became available at the local hobby store, drug store, hardware store, or department store. A month or two after that, the hardtop kits appeared on the store shelves.

Promotionals

These are the preassembled and pre-painted (or molded in color) "toys" that were typically given away by auto dealers back in the day. Promotionals were the first new scale cars to hit the market each year, often coinciding with the dealer's annual new car showing week. In some years, friction models were also available at the local toy store; these were promotionals with an added flywheel mechanism that allowed the kits to be rolled across a floor.

Unlike model kits, promotionals did not offer multiple building versions and omitted opening hoods with engines. The same tools (or modifications to these tools) later produced the unassembled annual kit versions that are the primary subject of this book. Promotionals were typically produced in a sturdier Cycolac plastic versus the styrene used in assembly kits.

3-in-1

Most annual model car kits contained parts to construct the kit in one of three versions. These versions were usually showroom stock, custom (mild and/or wild "advanced custom"), and competition (drag, rally, or oval track racing). When these kits were new, most builders constructed them in the custom or racing versions, not the showroom stock configuration.

Reissue

A new release of a previously issued model car kit. A reissue will usually include fresh box art, and often will include a few details that differ from the original release or the most recent previous reissue.

Tool

A large, liquid-cooled metal mold that produces injection molded styrene model car kits. Tooling is a major investment for a model car company. Once engineered and produced, it can be used over and over again (more than a few of the hobby kits at your local store today are produced on tooling originally created 5 to 6 decades ago!), or it can be modified to create a different kit product.

Master

Up until the last two decades, model kits were developed by first fabricating the parts, including the body itself, as 1/10th-scale wood masters. These masters were then used via the pantograph method to engrave the 1/25th-scale parts into the tool base used to produce the final kits. (Today, 1/10th-scale masters are no longer used in kit development, replaced by computer-aided design (CAD) and epoxy-based castings.)

A good example of a 3-in-1 kit is AMT's vintage 1966 Cyclone GT annual kit. The box top displays the then-popular A/FX match racer-inspired drag version. The box ends (far left and far right) illustrate the custom version, in this case a design credited to customizer/show-car builder Gene Winfield. On one side panel is the factory stock Cyclone GT, while the other side panel illustrates some of the optional parts and features of the custom and drag versions.

These are two examples of 1964½ Mustangs. The promotional on the left is a factory-assembled toy that came in a ready-to-use form, and was generally available through new car dealers. The AMT annual kit on the right came in unassembled form (shown here in a mocked-up, partially assembled status), thereby allowing the builder to paint and customize the final product to his or her desire.

The Mechanics of Kit Reissues

Many of the most valued and desirable models are the annual kits from the 1960s and early 1970s. Some of these kits have seen many subsequent reissues, while others never returned to the market after their initial few months of being on sale. "Why is that?" I am often asked.

As is often the response in the world of model car kits, the answer is not a simple one. First, it helps to understand that the model car kit world is primarily a business, as such the kit manufacturers were looking to maximize the financial return on their kit tooling investment. This basic premise often guided the evolution and ultimate fate of a given annual kit.

The heyday of the 1/25th-scale annual kit was in the mid-1960s. Here you see a nearly complete set of AMT's 1966 annual kits. (Missing is the Corvair, Impala SS convertible, Mustang hardtop/convertible, and Barracuda). Note the consistent merchandising/package design approach of the box art. While following the same graphic theme, varied colors and illustration themes allowed each kit to stand on its own while still being part of the AMT 1966 annual kit family.

Reasons Why a Given Annual Kit Was Never Reissued

With many original annual kit tools, the configuration of the tooling was modified to replicate the changes in the next year's offering from the car makers. Thus, during the summer of 1964, AMT's 1964 GTO kit tool was permanently altered to replicate the upcoming 1965 GTO. Likewise, AMT's 1967 Mustang GT annual kit tool was updated to produce the 1968 Mustang GT, and still later, the 1968 Shelby GT500. What does this mean? The chances of seeing reissues of the AMT 1964 GTO or the AMT 1967 and 1968 Mustang GT annual kits are just about zero. This is particularly the case when Round 2 is still able to successfully sell reissues of its existing 1965 GTO and 1968 Shelby GT500 kits, which remain the last and still current evolutions of the original tooling for these kits.

Another frequent reason that your favorite original annual kit has never been reissued is that the tooling was irretrievably modified into some other subject. As an example, AMT's 1966 Mustang GT 2+2 fastback annual kit has never been reissued. The reason is that the body tooling was heavily modified to produce an altered-wheelbase, A/FX-style kit. The interior and chassis tooling migrated to yet another kit, a replica of the Mach 1 Mustang show car/concept from the 1966–1968 Auto Show circuit.

In fact, many annual kit toolings were subsequently changed to bring competition/race-themed kits to the market. In most cases, the new kits were either oval track or drag racing topics. To produce accurate replicas, the annual kit bodies were heavily modified (particularly around the wheel openings), and most of the original body trims and badging were removed. As an example, AMT recycled a number of its old annual kit tools for a series of oval track–style Modified kits in 1970–1972. In most cases, given the amount and degree of changes to the body tooling, it was either impossible or unaffordable to return the tooling to showroom stock condition. In those few cases where this *was* attempted (such as the AMT 1965 GTO and MPC 1970 GTO kits), the resulting product was noticeably compromised versus the original annual kits.

Finally, in some cases, the original annual kit tooling was scrapped (destroyed) when doing so would provide an advantageous tax write-off benefit to the owner of the tooling. Thus, your chances of seeing the AMT 1963 Meteor kit reissued went out the door when this tooling was scrapped, most probably during the late 1960s and very early 1970s when AMT was facing financial difficulties.

Reasons Why a Given Annual Kit Has Seen Multiple Reissues

Why then wasn't AMT's 1965 GTO tool changed for the 1966 GTO? That would be the case because the promotionals contract for the 1966 GTO transferred from kitmaker AMT to crosstown rival MPC. This means that AMT didn't get to see blueprints of Pontiac's updates for the 1966 GTO. In addition, MPC planned an assembly kit derived from its new GTO promotionals tooling. Thus, it would be unlikely that both AMT and MPC would have offered kits of the same 1966 topic, especially when an AMT kit would have hit the market months after the MPC kit. Therefore, AMT (again looking to maximize its tooling investment) simply re-boxed its existing 1965 GTO tool as a Trophy Series kit, and then continued to reissue that kit for the rest of the decade.

As a corollary to the above, an annual kit tooling of the final evolution of a real car generation just prior to a major new platform change makes it much more likely to remain available as a reissue. Thus, when Chevrolet introduced its Impala for 1965 with its all-new body and chassis, AMT had to produce all-new tooling for its 1965 Chevy kits. This allowed the company to retain and reissue its previous 1964 Impala kit tooling for decades to come.

Many individual cases exist that are more involved than the basics discussed above, but if you are wondering why your favorite muscle car kit has never been reissued, it's probably at least partially because of these considerations.

The following depicts the life cycle of AMT's original 1964 Pontiac A-Body tool. It began as a Le Mans convertible (top left) and then underwent minor changes to become the 1964 GTO annual kit (bottom left). The tool was then revised to become the 1965 GTO annual kit (top center). When AMT lost the 1966 GTO contract to MPC, AMT reissued their 1965 GTO with new Trophy Series box art (bottom center). The tool was later modified into a Modified Production racer (not shown), and then underwent a flawed attempt to return the kit to a factory stock form (top right). Further refinements followed (bottom right), but the latest version still falls short of the original annual kit.

Beginning in the late 1960s, AMT began reissuing some of its outdated annual kit tooling with new box art. Some were straight reissues (such as the 1967 Vette, center left); but more often they were packaged as part of a themed catalog grouping. Shown are reissues from the Elegance Series (center and bottom left), Wild Flower Series (top right), and a couple with a south-of-the-border theme (center and lower right) kit series.

Some of the most desirable annual kits underwent irrevocable changes to their tooling after the current year production run was completed. For instance, AMT's 1966 Mustang GT 2+2 body tooling was altered to a shortened wheelbase configuration and joined with new interior and chassis tooling to create an AWB/early-style funny car kit. Meanwhile, the 1966 Mustang GT 2+2 kit's interior/chassis/engine tooling was repurposed to create a new kit of the Ford Mach 1 Concept Vehicle.

More changes to highly desirable original annual kit toolings are shown here. AMT's 1968 Mustang GT was converted to a Shelby GT500. MPC's 1966 Mustang GT body tooling was modified to become the body of MPC's Ohio George Gasser kit. AMT's 1966 Skylark GS, Revell's 1962 Dodge Dart, MPC's 1969 Camaro, AMT's 1970 Mustang, and AMT's 1971 Torino GT toolings were all modified to create the competition-themed kits shown here. It's unlikely you'll ever see the original factory stock kits reissued.

The Four Waves of Model Car Kit Development

For each model car kit pictured in Chapters 3 to 13, I'll include a note as to the "wave" of the kit. Quite simply, this refers to when the kit was first designed and produced, and gives you some idea of the level of detail and accuracy of the resulting kit. Here is the definition for each wave.

Wave 1

These are kits that were engineered in the first wave of the modern model kit, which is also the primary period in which annual kits were introduced each year. For purposes of this book, Wave 1 kits were first introduced in 1958 through 1976. Most of these kits replicated the newest Detroit offerings, and were developed from factory blueprints of the real cars. A significant number of these Wave 1 kits are still in production today, and the majority of kits shown in this book are Wave 1 kits.

Wave 2

Wave 2 kits were mostly introduced from 1977 to 1986 or so. This means that these Wave 2 kits were developed anywhere from 5 to 20 years or more after the real cars were first introduced. In addition, unlike the 3-in-1 configuration of most Wave 1 and Wave 2 kits generally could be built in one, or at most, two versions. Factory blueprints of muscle cars were generally no longer available to kit developers, and the expertise need to accurately capture the delicate contours of body shells varied across the kit production base, which means that some Wave 2 kits have bodies that are poorly proportioned.

These Wave 2 kits were sometimes simplified versus Wave 1 kits (containing fewer parts and thereby allowing expedited assembly). On the other hand, some Wave 2 kits produced more accurate, specific muscle car models. For example, Monogram's Wave 2 1970 Boss 429 kit precisely duplicated the real car, whereas the original Wave 1 kits often did not replicate a specific factory muscle car version in terms of engines, wheels, exterior graphics, and trim.

Wave 3

Wave 3 kits originated during the period of 1987 to 1999. This was the period when the adult model car builder became a primary target of the hobby kit manufacturers, and the kits produced during this period were highly detailed and exceedingly accurate in order to meet the expectations of the serious adult builder. While these kits were generally manufactured outside the United States, the kit design still took place in the United States and the tooling was usually created at one of two highly experienced Canadian tooling houses.

Wave 4

These kits were first introduced in the years 2000 and beyond. By this point, kit engineering and production was moving overseas, mostly to East Asia and China. Wave 4 kits generally show incredible detail and engraving and superb fit and finish. Surprisingly, though, these kits often contain minor body inaccuracies resulting both from the inability of the tooling sources to actually see the real car they are replicating and from the adoption of computer-aided design to replace the previous practice of developing 1/10th-scale wood masters. The possible use of digital scans of the real car being modeled could largely solve this issue, but the model companies generally state that they cannot afford this added expense given the relatively low sales volume of today's kits versus those produced in earlier decades.

Also, keep in mind that in referring to the Wave of each kit, I am referencing the first production date of the original tool the kit was based upon. Thus, Revell's 1969 Shelby GT500 convertible, first introduced in 2013, is a Wave 2 kit (rather than Wave 4) because it is derived from the original Monogram 1970 Boss 429 kit introduced in 1982.

The Envy Factor

The envy factor is a different way to define the collectibility of muscle car model kits. When my editor and I first talked about producing this book, we agreed right away that it was not a good idea to list a dollar value for the old, out of production kits shown in this book. There is no single source of irrefutably accurate pricing data, and the prices paid for collectible kits can widely vary depending on how badly the buyer wants the kit and how anxious the seller is to move the kit along and be paid for it. Values change over time, too.

These are mid- to late 1960s Mopar B-Body kits from each of the four waves of kit development. JoHan's 1964 Polara/Fury, AMT's 1965 Coronet, MPC's 1968 Coronet R/T, and JoHan's 1969 Road Runner kits were annual kits introduced when the cars were new, making them Wave 1 kits. Monogram's 1969 Super Bee kit hit the market in 1983, soon followed by a 1970 GTX, making them Wave 2 kits. Revell's 1967 GTX and Coronet R/T, Lindberg's 1964 Belvedere, and AMT/Ertl's 1968 Road Runner were introduced in the late 1980s to mid-1990s, representing Wave 3 of kit development. The Polar Lights 1965 Coronet, and Moebius's superb 1965 Satellite kits came with the last decade and a half, marking Wave 4 of kit design and development.

Instead of providing a price range, I have devised an asterisk rating of one (*) up to five (*****) to reflect the overall desirability of the kits I'll show in Chapters 3 to 13. Think of this as an indication of the "whoa!" or envy factor. That is, a reflection of the reaction that a knowledgeable model car kit enthusiast or collector would have if they saw this kit sitting on a shelf in your garage, basement, attic, or hobby room. Stated simply, the more envious the sigh of the observer when they see your kit, the higher the asterisk rating it deserves.

The following are factors in determining the asterisk count for each kit.

- How desirable is the kit topic? In a simple example, a 1964 GTO kit is more desirable to most collectors than a 1963 Tempest kit.
- How hard is it to find an original, mint condition version of the kit available for sale?
- If you could find a mint original, what is the price you'd have to pay to acquire it, relative to other model car kits?
- How accurate a replica can be constructed from the kit?
- Have kits of the same muscle car topic been produced by other kitmakers? If so, are they easy to locate, and do they produce a more accurate replica when built? (If the answers are yes, this will make the kit on your shelf less have less of an envy factor.)
- For reissued kits, is the box art of the kit on your shelf preferred to other releases of the kit, and/or is the box art a rare version?

The majority of the kits pictured in this book are assigned an asterisk rating of one (*). This is because many kits have seen numerous reissues through the years, and/or that a given 1/1-scale muscle car topic has often seen multiple kits produced by different manufacturers. Bottom line, these kits are generally easy to locate and do not command a premium price.

Very few kits are assigned ratings of ***, ****, or *****. Particularly for these last two ratings, be prepared to pay into the three-digit dollar range for a pristine, mint original. The good news is that, even today a ***** kit will rarely, if ever, approach a four-digit selling price. (It is probably worth noting here that while model kit prices haven't traversed the $1,000 barrier, in a few cases promotionals derived from the same kit body tooling have sold for as much as $1,500 or more).

In the end, the asterisk rating assigned to each kit is a simple judgment call. Take it as a relative indication (but far from a scientific or ironclad statement) of a given kit's envy factor. The most definitive guide of current dollar value of a given kit is best found in the latest edition of the *Directory of Model Car Kits* book described in Chapter 14.

Now, on to the Fascinating World of Muscle Car Model Kits

With these basics now out of the way, it's time to delve deeply into the subject of this book. Grab a cool one and sit back as I take you on a journey through the world of muscle car model kits.

*As you would expect, under the above definition, kits with an envy factor of four to five asterisks (**** to *****) are rare bears indeed. Pictured here are **** and ***** kits representing a cross section of General Motors, Ford, and Chrysler intermediate supercars. Add any of these to your personal collection and you'll draw the attention of any knowledgeable model car kit collector!*

Laying the Groundwork for Muscle Cars

The Pre–Supercar Era

Put yourself in the place of a new car buyer during 1949 to 1963; that is to say, before the introduction of supercars, as they are known today.

If you were looking for a new car that prioritized rapid acceleration and a higher top speed than most cars of the era, what would you have purchased? Oh yeah, let's add a few more qualifiers. You needed space for a family or friends, so that ruled out a sports car. Whether your wallet allowed it or not, the idea of driving a big, heavy, chrome-festooned luxury barge was also out of the question. Moreover, you wanted a car that was eye-catching, while still in good taste. If that car had a successful competition record in sanctioned automotive racing, it was also a big plus. What, then?

Most automotive historians consider the 1949 Oldsmobile 88 to be the first car that meets the broad definition of a muscle car as I've adopted it for this book. The power of the new Rocket V-8, developed for the larger 98-series Olds, delivered a very powerful performance envelope when placed in the lighter GM A-Body normally used in the lower 76-series Oldsmobile. The result was called the Oldsmobile 88, and it quickly developed a reputation as a hot car. This was followed by the 1951–1954 Hudson Hornet with its Twin-H-Power High-Compression 6, fast cars on the street and winners at the racetrack. Then came the legendary Chrysler 300, and on a more accessible level, the 1955 Chevy with its small-block 265 Power Pack V-8.

As the 1950s progressed, Chevys with a fuel-injected V-8, 1957 Fords with a factory-supercharged V-8, and even a 1958 Mercury with a 400-hp rating were tops for any factory-assembled car that year. Desoto, Dodge, and Plymouth followed the Chrysler 300 recipe to varying degrees on a more affordable scale with the Adventurer, D500, and Fury/Sport Fury, respectively. Some would claim that the 1957 Rambler Rebel also fit in this category.

Things quieted down with the recession of 1958 and the holdover impact in 1959, plus the return of fuel economy and practicality as prime buyer motivations, combined with the excitement surrounding the introduction of domestically produced compacts from the big three. But with the new decade, Chrysler was back in the muscle market with its ram induction V-8s: 1961 brought out the 409 Chevy, 1962 the 406 FE Ford and the hot (if questionably styled) Chrysler B-Bodies with its Max V-8s, and so on. The trend only gained further steam in 1963 and 1964.

So, which of these cars actually found themselves the subject of a 1/24th-1/25th–scale model car kit? Evenly as recent as 10 to 15 years ago, the answer would have been very different. But today, thanks in no small measure to both a longtime model kit industry stalwart (Revell) and a totally new entry in the hobby kit marketplace (Moebius), the answer is that nearly all of the cars listed above have at one point or another seen a popular scale model car kit.

This collage just hints at the wide range of scale replicas of influential post–World War II performance-themed cars that helped set the stage for the muscle car era that began in earnest with the 1964 model year.

Oldsmobile 88

Starting with the 1949–1950 Oldsmobile 88, there were at least two, and perhaps three, attempts to bring a model of this car to market before the final product appeared in 2013. In the mid-1960s, Revell had started development of a 1949–1950 Olds kit, but then heard that Monogram had a kit of the exact same car underway, so Revell killed that project. (Little evidence has subsequently surfaced that Monogram actually had such a kit under development).

More than three decades later, the AMT-Ertl brand, then under the ownership of Racing Champions (a pre-assembled die-cast replica maker) announced to the hobby trade its plans for 1950 Olds 88 and 1949 Studebaker kits. Later, it was discovered that these were nothing more than trial balloons. With kit topics being dictated by the buyers of the large discount chains and big-box stores back then (instead of the core model car hobbyist), both ideas flopped, and the kits never appeared.

Meanwhile, throughout the first decade of the 21st century, a 1950 Olds was on Revell's list of potential kit topics, and it finally made its way to the top in time for a 2013 introduction of a superb 1/25th-scale kit. Revell pulled out all the stops to accurately replicate the intricate body shape of this car, including some very expensive die work to achieve the correct underbody roll of the rear fenders. A second Olds custom kit added typical period upgrades including a J2-style tri-power V-8 with headers and dual exhaust, and modestly lowered front and rear suspension. Revell's late VP of Engineering, a 57-year employee of the company, owned a 1950 Olds 88 coupe as a young adult. Maybe that is one reason why the kit came out so well.

It's taken nearly 50 years, and the possible involvement of up to four different kitmakers (counting Revell under two different ownerships), but now an absolutely first-class kit series of the 1950 Oldsmobile 88 (Wave 4/) is available. The Olds Custom kit is really outfitted like an early to mid-1950s mild street coupe and is typical of what performance enthusiasts might have driven back then.*

Hudson Hornet

The Olds 88 was a very successful product in the early NASCAR years. However, the Hudson Hornet soon replaced its position at the front of the oval racetracks. It seems strange to think of a six-cylinder–powered car as being a performance leader in the early 1950s, but that's what happened.

That leads me to the topic of a Hudson Hornet model kit. It was a topic frequently seen in model car magazine reader polls of new kit ideas, but I never, ever dreamed such a kit would materialize. Eventually it *was* produced as a kit, but it took a new model car company to get it done (with perhaps a touch of help from the *Cars* movie franchise). In 2011, Frank Winspur's Moebius Models introduced the 1953 Hudson Hornet as its first model car kit (its first 1/25th-scale automotive kit of any kind was the International Lonestar Class 8 Truck, which preceded the Hudson by a year or two).

Just when longtime modelers thought they'd seen everything in 1/25th-scale kits, Moebius Models completely redefined what constitutes top-end model car offerings. Starting in 2011, it has produced a whole series of early to mid-1950s Hudsons, all with the famous Twin H Power engine. More derivatives of this kit (not shown here) include Tim Flock and Marshal Teague race cars, along with Matty Winspur's Stock class drag racer (all: Wave 4/).*

This was a kit unlike any other 1/25th-scale kit to date. The instruction/assembly manual was a sight in and of itself: printed in full color, with photos of assembled sub-components and multiple views of the completed car, along with instructional callouts, and highly detailed painting information. The kit tool was designed for additional derivatives, which have included 1952 convertible and 1954 coupe and sedan kits.

1953 Studebaker

The 1953 Studebaker Starliner hardtop is a highly regarded early 1950s automotive design, but it is seldom cited as a precursor to the muscle car movement. Nevertheless, despite the modest output of its OHV V-8, the Starliner was revolutionary in that it telegraphed the potential market appeal of a car designed for optimum proportions and visual impact, rather than practical considerations like interior space. In this way, it was a predecessor to the stylish, smaller-sized 1960s intermediates that anchored the supercar movement, as well as the entire pony car segment. For that reason, I'm including it here, even though it admittedly lies on the fringes of our subject topic.

This car was only 10 years old when it first appeared on lists of future Trophy Series kit topics at AMT. The final execution included not only a finely detailed showroom stock replica, but also a very tasteful custom version, and a wild Bonneville racer with a dual-blower 392 Hemi and components to help the builder modify the body with a chopped top.

One would be hard pressed to find a more appealing set of box art than the one that AMT debuted in 1965 for its 1953 Studebaker Starliner 3-in-1 Trophy Series kit (Wave 1/*). After at least 10 reissues, Round 2 returned to the original box art theme for this 2014 release. Note the larger box, brighter colors, and other slight tweaks of the new box art on the right.

Revell also had a showroom stock 1953 Studebaker kit under development, only to cancel the project when AMT announced its 1953 Studebaker Starliner kit. Here is Revell's actual 1/10th-scale wood master. It was to be a two-door Starlight coupe; you can clearly see the coupe's B-pillar here. AMT's kit was the Starliner hardtop. This artifact can be seen at the International Model Car Builder's Museum (themodelcarmuseum.org) located near Salt Lake City, Utah.

1955–1957 Chevrolet

AMT was first out of the gate with a full detail kit of a 1/25th-scale Tri-Five Chevy. It chose a 1957 Bel Air as the subject; this was its first Trophy Series kit of a Chevy product. Revell followed a year later with its own 1957 Bel Air kit, upping the game with the addition of working doors and trunk. All these years later, the AMT Trophy Series kit is still considered to be tied with one other kit as the best overall proportioned 1957 Chevy hardtop ever produced as a kit. Both these AMT and Revell kits have been reissued numerous times.

Both the Revell and (especially) the AMT Bel Air kits were top sellers from the word go, so more Tri-Five Chevy kits were inevitable. The next two came from Revell in 1964: a drag-themed 1955 Bel Air two-door hardtop and a custom car show–flavored 1956 two-door sedan. Per the contemporary Revell "design brief" of the day, both kits featured opening doors and trunks as well as fully detailed engine compartments and chassis assemblies. Of note, the 1956 kit featured a two-door sedan (today, called a two-door post) body style instead of the expected two-door hardtop. Both of these kits saw frequent reissues through the end of the last century.

Monogram also entered the Tri-Five kit fray in 1964 with what was, at the time, one of its finest kits ever. The 1/24th-scale

*These two were the first of seemingly countless 1/25th-scale 1957 Chevy Bel Air kits to come in future years. Tom Daniel is the artist credited with the box top image on Revell's kit. Note the detailed parts callout lists on the lower side panels of both the AMT and Revell kits (both: Wave 1/**).*

*Monogram's 1955 Chevy Bel Air box art (above) was perhaps not as stylistic as AMT's or Revell's. However, the kit's selling features were clearly explained on all box panels (Wave 1/***). The tool underwent numerous revisions in 1969 to create the Tom Daniel–designed* Bad-Man *pseudo-Gasser (Wave 1/*). It's been a best seller for Monogram ever since.*

*Revell's 1955 and 1956 Chevy kits (above) offered fully detailed showroom stock versions, plus plenty of optional "show and go" parts (both: Wave 1/**). The 1955 kit included both stock 265 and blown 409 drag racing engines; note the Winternationals drag race banner across the box top art. The 1956 kit featured a choice of plated exterior trim for the 150, 210, and Bel Air series, and a wild full-custom interior option to complement optional restyled front and rear treatments.*

1955 Chevy Bel Air could be built in showroom stock form as a hardtop or convertible or in one of several custom versions credited to Monogram consultant Darryl Starbird. The stock and custom versions of this kit were irretrievably lost when Monogram retooled the kit into the *Bad-Man* "wild, wheelin' drag machine."

AMT struck back with its second Tri-Five kit in 1965, a new 1955 Nomad kit addition for its Trophy Series catalog. In addition to the showroom stock version, the kit offered a custom version that yielded a tasteful El Camino–type car pickup, and a fuel-injected straight-axle Gasser version patterned loosely after the well-known *Wompin' Wagon* that was campaigned in the mid-1960s in the Gasser and Modified Production classes.

*The first three issues of AMT's 1955 Nomad Trophy Series kit start here in the front center with the original 1965 release, followed by the 1967 Elegance Series (left background) and 1968 Portrait Series (right background) issues (all: Wave 1/**). The Elegance kit omitted the stock and custom parts, but added a small can of AMT Pearl Lacquer to topcoat the light blue styrene, and deeply blue-tinted transparent styrene for the clear parts sprue.*

Revell's retooled 1957 Bel Air and new Nomad kits reflect late 1960s street sensibilities (both: Wave 1/). A heavily revised engine (sourced from Revell's earlier Parts Pack offering) and a raised front axle Gasser suspension were found in the updated Bel Air kit (Wave 1/*). Its 1957 Nomad kit is shown here in its second release dating from 1973.*

Monogram's new series of 1/24th-scale Tri-Five kits from the late 1970s were an excellent source of then-current aftermarket parts and accessories but compromised by unrealistic body proportions (which can even be seen in the box art built-up models seen here). The 1956 Bel Air and 1957 Nomad are shown in their original 1978 release box art, while the 1957 Bel Air is shown is the 1995 reissue (all: Wave 2/).*

Revell once again revisited the Tri-Five genre in the very late 1960s with a major redo of its original 1957 Chevy Bel Air hardtop kit, along with a newly tooled 1957 Chevy Nomad kit. The first issue box art of the Nomad famously used outtakes from the beachside *Rod and Custom* cover shoot of the Sam Hollingsworth Nomad, with the kit's chromed reverse wheels stripped in to replace the real car's Dayton-style wire wheels. Both of these kits have seen many subsequent reissues.

Skipping ahead nearly a decade, Monogram's then-new president, having previously served in the same role for AMT (and with his knowledge of the continued sales success of AMT's Tri-Five kits), directed his new product development staff to create a new series of Tri-Five kits. These kits were to offer both showroom stock and late 1970s street machine versions, along with the slightly simplified kit content and building style that Monogram had developed during the Tom Daniels–inspired Show Rod kit era. Starting in 1977, Monogram introduced 1/24th-scale kits of the 1956 Bel Air, 1957 Bel Air, and 1957 Nomad Wagon. Many modelers largely dismiss these due to accuracy and proportion errors in the bodies. These kits are still reissued from time to time; avoid them unless you are looking for a good project to allow a new modeler to gain some kit assembly experience.

AMT-Ertl surprised the modeling world in 1989 with a new 1955 Bel Air two-door ("post") sedan kit. Mostly derived from its mid-1960s Nomad Trophy Series kit, the kit included a new body, updated engine speed parts, and fresh decals. The kit was generally well received, other than the carryover Nomad hood that was slightly too small to exactly fit the new sedan body shell.

The Monogram product development team, operating under the Revell-Monogram corporate umbrella in the 1990s, more than redeemed itself by starting a series of all-new

AMT-Ertl extended the productive life of its 1955 Nomad kit tool with this kit featuring a Bel Air two-door sedan body (Wave 1/). Beyond the fresh body casting, the revised kit included a Bel-Air sedan interior, a Carter AFB 4-barrel carb with Lynx low-restriction air cleaner, and non-plated Centerline wheels. Building versions were showroom stock and mild street machine.*

This 1995 Revell/Monogram all-new tool of the 1955 Bel Air convertible was considered the best-ever 1/25th-scale kit of this vintage yet committed to scale. The first-ever 1956 Nomad kit in the popular scales was released by Revell-Monogram in 1997, using the Bel Air tooling as the basis. The 1955 Bel Air hardtop followed later; it's shown here in its 2007 Revell release (all: Wave 3/).*

Revell continues to churn out further derivatives based on its new mid-1990s Tri-Five tooling. These include this 1956 Del Ray sedan from 2001, a 1957 Bel Air sedan and Black Widow *150 series sedan (both from 2009), and most recently a 1957 Bel Air convertible introduced in 2013 (all: Wave 3/*).*

AMT-Ertl's all-new 1957 Chevy Bel Air kit series (Wave 3/) was introduced in 1998, and included many upgrades not seen in the original 1962 Trophy Series kit. The Pro-Shop kit added a photo-etched metal fret with the Bel Air rear-quarter-panel inserts, grille insert, rocker panel moldings, front-fender louver trim, windshield wipers, and Chevrolet badging, along with vinyl radiator and heater hoses and a sheet of adhesive foil trim.*

You won't find engines or detailed chassis in these 1957 Chevy Bel Air hardtop Snap-Tite kits from Revell, but these 1999 and 2004 releases (both: Wave 3/) are considered to have superb body proportions and accuracy. These kits assemble quickly and without drama, but they also respond well to minor detailing upgrades.*

1/25th-scale Tri-Five kits. First out the door were replicas of the 1955 Bel Air convertible (in both showroom stock and Indy Pace Car kits) and a 1956 Nomad. Eventually, a new 1955 Bel Air hardtop kit, based on this convertible kit tool, also joined the Revell-Monogram catalog.

Later in the decade, AMT-Ertl scheduled an all-new 1957 Bel Air hardtop kit for a 1998 release, and to be available in two versions with photo-etched parts and wiring materials added to the premium Pro Shop version. This kit reflected the advances in kit design in the 35 years since AMT's original 1957 Bel Air Trophy Series release, including an opening trunk with spare tire, engine spark plug wiring, and a fully detailed chassis with platform-style interior. Endless debates ensued as kit experts argued the plusses and minuses of these new releases versus AMT's original Trophy Series kit.

Revell and Monogram have continued to produce additional Tri-Five variants based on its new 1990s era tool, including a 1956 Del Ray sedan, and 1957 Bel Airs in two-door sedan and convertible body styles. It also produced a nice replica of the 1957 150 *Black Widow* sedan. At this point, only a 1956 Bel Air hardtop and convertible and 1955–1957 Nomads are missing from a very complete catalog of highly regarded modern-era Revell Tri-Five kits.

Finally, Revell also produced a snap-kit version of the 1957 Bel Air hardtop. This kit was sold primarily in pre-finished form, and the body in this kit is ranked at the top, side by side along with the original AMT 1957 Bel Air kit, in terms of overall accuracy and proportions. This kit would be a fun parent/child or grandparent/grandchild project for those who wish to introduce future generations to the fun of model car building and collecting!

1955–1964 Chrysler 300 Letter Series

When the 1955 Chrysler 300 debuted, it was a sensation. It was to the 1950s automotive world, in many ways, what the 1964 GTO was to the decade that followed. Not surprisingly, it followed the earlier Olds 88 formula of a top-of-the-line, most-powerful engine inserted in the body of the smaller, lighter body of the nameplate's entry-level series. In this case, however, the addition of the Imperial front grille and premium components throughout, including a real leather interior, added a sense of supreme exclusivity for anyone who had the good fortune to be able to purchase and drive the 300. Moreover, as you saw earlier with both the 88 and the Hudson Hornet, a successful competition record only added to the reputation.

Since the first Chrysler 300s debuted before the advent of the modern 1/25th-scale assembly kit, modelers went for decades without models of these influential pre–muscle car era icons. Fortunately, recent years have brought highly detailed kits of all three of the initial Chrysler 300 products. After years of customer requests, AMT-Ertl finally took the plunge and debuted a meticulously engineered 1957 Chrysler 300C kit in 1999. It soon added a Pro-Shop 300C kit with all the parts pre-painted, and overall the level of detail and execution of this painting effort was a sight to behold. However, the pre-painted body replicated 1957 Chrysler Code F Forest Green, whereas the regular production 300C was limited to just five factory colors, including the much lighter Code E Parade Green Metallic (the other 300 colors were Copper Brown Metallic, Gauguin Red, Cloud White, and Black). Moebius Models completed the early Chrysler 300 model family album with kits of the 1955 300 and 1956 300B, introduced in 2011 and 2013, respectively. The Moebius kits include comprehensive full-color assembly manuals with highly detailed photos of assembled kit components and the completed models.

A gap appears in 300 kit coverage stretching from the 1958 to 1961 model years. (JoHan produced annual kits of the 1960 and 1961 Chrysler products, but chose to base them on the top-line New Yorker series instead of the 300). JoHan moved its

The current state of the model car kit industry is well represented by these 1955 300 and 1956 300B kits (both: Wave 4/) and 1957 300C (Wave 3/*) kits from Moebius Models and AMT-Ertl, respectively. Inside the boxes are intricately detailed engines even including draft tubes and transmission dipsticks. Separately molded frames and underbody floor pans enable easily executed detail painting.*

*JoHan issued annual kits of the 1962–1964 Chrysler 300 letter series kits in both hardtop and convertible form. Shown here are the 1963 hardtop and convertible and 1964 convertible annual kits (all: Wave 1/***). The 1962 hardtop was reissued in the mid-1970s (Wave 1/**). Depending on the kit, builders found scale replicas of the single 4-barrel, dual inline 4-barrel, and/or ram induction dual 4-barrel ram letter-series 413 V-8.*

Chrysler annual kit offering to the downsized (shorter wheelbase) 300 H as part of its 1962 lineup, and produced it in both hardtop and convertible versions. These kits had the correct four-bucket-seat interior and a modestly detailed engine, along with a faintly engraved H in the rear deck alongside the 300 badging.

JoHan followed with 300 series hardtop and convertible annual kits in 1963 and 1964. JoHan did not produce a kit of the 1965 300L, but it did manufacture non-letter series 1965–1968 Chrysler 300 kits. Coverage of these kits is found in Chapter 11.

In the mid-1970s, JoHan reissued the 1962 300 as part of its USA Oldies kit series, but an inaccurate, circa 1964 300 interior tub makes this kit considerably less desirable than the original annual series release. This version is fairly easy to locate, while the original 1962–1964 annual kits are difficult to find and very expensive.

1957 Ford Custom and Fairlane 500

For a brief period in the late 1950s, Ford developed an engine family that might have presaged the muscle car genre, but the Automobile Manufacturers Association (AMA) racing ban in 1957 stopped it in its infancy. Of course, I am referencing the E-Code dual 4-barrel and the F-Code McCulloch supercharged 312 Y-Block V-8s offered in the 1957 Ford Custom and Fairlane car lines. Model builders now have all they need to replicate miniatures of both cars.

Following the overwhelming success of AMT's original 1957 Chevy Bel Air kit, AMT quickly added a companion kit of the top-of-the-line 1957 Ford Fairlane 500 to its Trophy Series premium kit catalog. Reflecting the rapidly advancing hobby, this kit added steerable wheels and opening doors to the content. A supercharger option for the kit's Y-Block engine was of a custom configuration, not representative of the real factory option. This kit has been reissued many times, but only the pre-1973 releases include all the advanced customizing parts.

For several years, there were rumors of an all-new kit topic from Revell, and it was under development for several years, but in 2012 an all-new 1957 Ford Custom two-door sedan kit finally debuted. This highly detailed kit even included scale fuel lines running from the fuel pump to the single and dual 4-barrel carb options under the hood. Several unused parts in the kit broadly hinted at a future kit with an F-Code supercharged engine. That kit did indeed follow in 2013 as a Fireball Roberts NASCAR kit. Further versions of this kit tool included a Model King private-label Police Car and Revell's Del Rio Ranch Wagon. Adult model hobbyists are still hoping for a future Ranchero kit based off the Del Rio kit tooling.

*AMT's 1957 Ford Fairlane kit was first introduced in 1963 as part of its Trophy Series (upper and lower left). The kit could be built in showroom stock, custom, and two different advanced custom versions. The 1966 Portrait Series (upper right) and the 1969 All American Show 'n' Go Series (lower right) were essentially identical to the original kit inside, except for the freshly updated decals in each reissue (all: Wave 1/**).*

Revell's all-new 1957 Ford kit series features the 116-inch Custom/Custom 300 wheelbase body and chassis (versus the 118-inch Fairlane/Fairlane 500 body and chassis in AMT's original 1957 Ford kit). By choosing various parts found in these four kits (all: Wave 4/) model builders can construct single 4-barrel Y-Block, dual 4-barrel E-Code, or McCulloch supercharged F-Code pre–muscle car era scale replicas.*

DeSoto Adventurer, Dodge D-500/Dart/440, and Plymouth Fury/Sport Fury

JoHan was the original source for annual assembly kits for most Chrysler products. Its 1959 kit lineup included the Dodge Custom Royal and Plymouth Fury, while the DeSoto Adventurer, Dodge Dart, and Plymouth Fury saw kits in 1960. The Dodge Dart and Plymouth Fury continued for 1961 and 1962. JoHan kits for 1963 replicated the midsized Dodge Polara and Plymouth Fury.

Meanwhile, Revell also produced 1/25th-scale annual kits of the 1962 Dodge Dart and Plymouth Fury; these were fairly well detailed for the time but still considered inferior to JoHan and AMT annual kits of the same period. These were reissued once, late in the 1962 calendar year, as Metalflake series products with a translucent, metallic-enhanced styrene.

Starting in the mid-1970s, JoHan reissued the hardtop versions of the 1960 DeSoto Adventurer, 1962 Dart and Fury, and 1963 Fury, as well as convertible versions of the 1962 Dart and Fury starting in the mid-1970s.

Before I move on, a bit of caution applies here. Unlike most of the highly detailed kits shown in this book, the 1959–1963 Mopar annual kits and its reissues referenced here were basic to the extreme. Some did not include engines, and the ones that did were basic in execution. Moreover, these kits generally did not replicate the performance versions of each car; it would be up to the builder to kit-bash the engines, chassis, and body trim to accurately produce a model of the applicable performance derivative of each car and model year.

Jumping several decades ahead, in 2002 AMT-Ertl introduced a new kit of the 1958 Plymouth Belvedere two-door

*JoHan definitely upped the effort for the box art of its reissued early 1960s Mopar kits. The USA Oldies kits date from 1975, while the 1963 Fury kit came later (all: Wave 1/**). Be aware that some of these reissued kits included inaccurate, later model year interior components.*

hardtop. This kit was considered fairly undesirable, in part due its generic V-8 engine (neither a correct Polysphere V-8 nor the new-for-1958 B Wedge-head V-8). Instead of the mid-line Belvedere, ideally the kit should have replicated the sporty Fury equipped with the optional 350-ci version of Chrysler's new V-8 engine family. AMT-Ertl's kit also had various body inaccuracies, the most obvious being a strange, segmented execution of the Belvedere side trim engraving versus the smooth sweep of the original car. (To the car modeling community, these mistakes were interpreted as one of the negative outcomes of

*This image reveals several early 1960s JoHan Mopar annual kits, including its 1961 Dart and 1963 Polara customizing kits (Wave 1/***). During this period, JoHan also produced some showroom-stock-only versions of its annual kits (no customizing parts plus a lower suggested list price), including this 1963 Fury convertible kit (Wave 1/**). Revell kitted several 1962 Chrysler Corporation products, including the 1962 Fury (Wave 1/**).*

There are few kits in this book that I absolutely recommend against purchasing, but this is one of them. AMT-Ertl's 2002 tooling of a 1958 Plymouth Belvedere (Wave 4/) has deformed side trim engraving and a generic engine that represents neither of the available V-8 engine families that year.*

then-owner Racing Champion's May 31, 2000, layoff of virtually all the remaining AMT-Ertl kit development staff.)

The Dodge and Plymouth performance cars' story for 1964 and beyond picks up in Chapter 7.

1960–1963 Ford Galaxie 500

Given the aforementioned mid-1957 AMA ban on manufacturer involvement in racing and the economic recession stretching into 1958, the emphasis on power lessened in the Ford product range. Not until the 1960 model year, with the FE series 352-ci 4-barrel and Starliner hardtop body style, did performance start to inch back into the lineup. This escalated with the FE 390 of 1961, and grew with the mid-year 1962 introduction of the Galaxie 500 XL series with its bucket seats and console. The concurrent introduction of a new high-performance 406 version of its FE engine family fully signaled the return of performance to Ford's product range.

AMT produced annual kits of the 1960–1962 Galaxie 500 in both hardtop and convertible forms, and a 1963 convertible. Most of these included basic engines and one-piece chassis assemblies, as did most annual kits of the time. AMT also produced a kit of the 1963½ Galaxie 500 XL fastback; that kit is covered in Chapter 11.

Many of these AMT annual kits saw reissues in the mid- to late 1960s and beyond. The 1960 Starliner hardtop was reissued as a simplified Craftsman Series kit in the mid-1960s, and the 1961 Sunliner convertible kit saw two reissues in the late 1960s. The 1961 Club Victoria (formal roof) hardtop was reissued in 1969 as part of AMT's Flower Power Series kits, and again in

Several of AMT's early 1960s Galaxie kits saw reissues, mostly later in the same decade. A more recent reissue was AMT-Ertl's Buyer's Choice rebop of the 1961 Galaxie 500 styline annual kit (Wave 1/*). There's only been one modern-era tool of early 1960s Fords, but it's a winner: AMT-Ertl's 1960 Starliner kit debuted in 2000 (Wave 4/*). The 2008 Round 2 reissue of this kit sports gorgeous, newly created box art, plus extra parts trees yielding two complete "FE" Ford engines with three different induction options.

the late 1990s as part of AMT-Ertl Buyer's Choice program. The 1962 hardtop was reissued just once, also in 1969. As were the JoHan kits previously referenced. Most of these kits are relatively basic in their execution, and anyone who wants an accurate version of the performance-themed versions of these cars will have to modify the kits to various degrees.

In the year 2000, AMT-Ertl introduced an all-new tool of the 1960 Ford Starliner. This was a highly accurate product, and the engine and chassis parts of this kit could be adapted to the AMT annual kits previously referenced for a far more accurate replica of the performance versions of the early 1960s big Fords.

AMT produced annual kits of the 1960 through 1963 Ford Galaxie 500; several are shown here (1960, 1961, 1963 kits: Wave 1/**; 1962 kit: Wave 1/). With each subsequent year, the subject of each kit became more prominent on the box end, moving from a generic image with an ink stamped "1960 Ford" (far left) to a sticker with a 1961 Galaxie profile view (middle left), a corner snipe printed image (upper mid-right), and finally to fully personalized end panel treatments (lower center right and far right).***

1961–1963 Chevy Impala/Impala SS 327/409 and Bel Air 409

After increasing emphasis on performance with the 1955–1957 model run, Chevrolet placed performance largely on hiatus for the next three years. The larger, heavier 1958 Chevy emphasized room and luxury rather than more performance, and the 1959–1960 Impalas offered stunning styling with even larger bodies. Performance as a storyline began to return with the new, lighter 1961 Impala SS and the debut of the 409 version of the W-Block V-8. More powerful 409s followed for

*Modelers looking to build performance-themed early 1960s Chevys enjoyed these 1961–1963 Impala annual kits (all: Wave 1/**). By 1963, the AMT hardtop annual kit included two versions of the 409 V-8, adhesive-backed upholstery panels, one mild custom and two "advanced custom" building versions (the latter two with then-trendy asymmetric styling), and a slew of display accessories such as chrome tools, a record player, and even a scale drive-in tray!*

1962, the fastback "bubbletop" persisted in the lighter and less expensive Bel Air series, while the Impala adopted a more formal roofline, and the revered Z-11 409 package debuted as the 1963 model year began.

AMT produced Impala hardtop and convertible annual kits during this period. (The 1961 kits wore "SMP" branding while also mentioning the AMT Corporate name and business address on the lower side panel.) The degree of detail varied, but by 1963 the kits were well developed and included 409 V-8 with lots of optional engine hop-up parts.

Among the AMT 1961–1963 annual kits, only the 1963 Impala SS hardtop has seen periodic reissues. It was originally in an unassembled promotional style release in 1967 as part of AMT's Craftsman Series. It started in the late 1980s in a mostly complete kit form, but was still missing many of the optional/customizing parts as well as the engine compartment firewall of the original 1963 annual kit release. The engine of this reissue was also less detailed than the original annual kit version (which migrated instead to the 1964 Impala kit).

AMT's 1963 Impala SS annual kit saw a renewed place in AMT/Ertl's kit rotation starting in 1987 with this Prestige Series release (bottom), followed by further releases in 1994, 1997 (shown), and 2002 (all: Wave 1/). However, serious collectors strongly prefer the original 1963 annual kit because of the crisper molding and the deletion of some of the original kit parts for the reissue.*

For years, model kit builders and collectors had pined for a 1962 Chevy Bel Air bubbletop 409 hardtop. Some advanced builders even created their own versions. Fast-forward to 1993, and AMT-Ertl finally granted our wishes with a nicely executed kit of a factory-stock 1962 Bel Air Bubbletop 409. (For more on this kit's development, see the AMT-Ertl 1966 Nova SS kit sidebar in Chapter 10). Between this kit and the Super Stock spinoffs that followed, builders could construct a highly detailed factory stock dual-quad 409, a Z-11 version with its unique intake setup and tubular exhaust headers, and a period street machine type engine with a Mickey Thompson Power Ram intake manifold and Offenhauser ribbed valve covers. An Impala SS convertible based on this same kit tooling followed four years later.

Lest anyone think that the original 409 Chevy, the one installed in the 1961½ Impala SS, has been left off the list of newly developed model kits, Lindberg introduced a full detail 1961 Impala SS409 hardtop in 1997. An inaccurate windshield sweep/cowl assembly was quickly corrected. A Super Stock version followed a year later, and then a convertible version debuted in 1999. The Super Stock version substituted a cowl-induction air cleaner, tubular headers with exhaust dumps, open rims, and period Don Nicholson livery.

Revell eventually joined the early 1960s Impala kit fray with a 2000 introduction of a 1964 Impala and a 2003 introduction of a 1963 Impala SS, both offering factory stock versions along with lowrider versions. Unlike AMT's original 1963 annual kit's

The year 1993 brought the debut of a much-wanted 1962 Chevy Bel Air 409 "Bubbletop" kit from AMT-Ertl. A series of licensed drag racing properties quickly followed, all adding the late 1962 to early 1963 Z-11 engine parts. In 1997 and again in 2000, AMT-Ertl produced another spinoff of this tooling, this time a 1962 Impala SS convertible. The "Don Nicholson" Super Stock and the convertible kits are preferred for their redone, more accurate egg crate–style front grille texture engraving (all: Wave 3/).*

Lindberg's series of 1961 Impala SS409 kits were a much-welcomed development in the hobby, as the rejuvenated Lindberg brand under the auspices of George Toteff and Craft House Corporation was turning out some of best 1/25th-scale model kits back in the 1990s. Round 2, who now owns the Lindberg tooling, developed fresh box art and a set of optional American five-spoke mags for an AMT-branded hardtop that debuted in 2016 (all: Wave 3/).*

*Counterclockwise from the upper left, annual kits of the Pontiac Bonneville from 1958 to 1960 and 1962 to 1964 are shown. As engines were added to the annual kits in the early 1960s, they typically replicated the top-line 421 in 4-barrel, tri-power, or dual-quad form (all: Wave 1/**).*

Revell's 1963 and 1964 Impala SS kits are full-detail models with slightly simplified assembly processes. Revell's 1962 Impala hardtop and Impala SS kits are highly detailed models with dual-quad 409 engines; they're slightly compromised by overly rigid wheelwell openings that don't fully capture the subtle nuances of the original car's design (all: Wave 4/).*

409 engine, this kit featured a 327 4-barrel V-8 (for those that were yet to be born back then, the 327 was a high-winding mill that racked up many street victories of its own in the early 1960s). Revell developed all-new tooling for a 1962 Impala (not SS) hardtop that debuted in 2010, with an Impala SS derivative following in 2011.

Pontiac Catalina and Ventura

From 1958 onward, Pontiac's top range Bonneville series typically offered the make's highest performance engine options available on order. Given the added length and weight of the Bonneville versus the shorter wheelbase Catalina and Ventura, not many of these luxury liners were ordered with street performance as the primary purchase criteria. Nevertheless, AMT produced annual kit replicas of the Bonneville from 1958 through 1964 (I cover the 1965 and later full-sized Pontiacs in Chapter 11).

During the last decade and a half, a new round of early 1960s big Pontiac kits have been introduced. Several of these replicate the shorter wheelbase Catalina and Ventura bodies, which, when equipped with the performance versions of the 389 or 421 engines, fall well within our pre–muscle car era operating definition.

Taking these new kits in model year order, first is the Trumpeter 1/25th-scale 1960 Pontiac, first introduced to the hobby trade in 2003. This one sticks with the longer wheelbase Bonneville configuration, and it was produced in hardtop and convertible versions. This kit has Asian kit development origins, and it builds somewhat differently as a result. The engine accuracy is very compromised, but the rest of the kit is fully presentable. Early production runs of the hardtop kit included incorrect, dull plating of the chrome tree parts. Trumpeter and its New Jersey–based importer Stevens International supplied properly plated replacements upon request, so check to see that your kit purchase has the correct parts.

In 2016, Moebius Models introduced a 1961 Pontiac Ventura hardtop kit, which is to be followed with a 1961 Catalina kit. Both these kits have excellent engines, chassis, interiors, and body castings, and Moebius's full-color assembly manuals are

The modern kit era has brought us several all-new kits of early 1960s performance Pontiacs. Trumpeter's 1960 Pontiac Bonneville is light on engine accuracy but otherwise a relatively serviceable kit (Wave 4/). The Moebius 1961 Ventura (Wave 4/*) and AMT-Ertl 1962 Catalina 421 SD (Wave 3/*) kits are highly detailed, and both sit firmly atop any ranking of 1960s big Pontiac kit accuracy.*

the best in the business. Test fitting of the windshield to the body (prior to painting and assembly operations) is recommended.

In 1998, AMT-Ertl introduced an all-new tool of the 1962 Pontiac Catalina with a SuperDuty 421 engine under the hood. Round 2 reintroduced the kit in 2009 with fresh box art and a decal sheet featuring the Arnie Beswick Super Stock drag entry.

Epilogue

Virtually all of these family sedans with performance engines continued into the mid-1960s, with a few lasting all the way through the remaining decade. Clearly, the attention of muscle car buyers was quickly migrating to the intermediate-based supercars as typified by the GTO. Large muscle car volumes dropped abruptly after 1965, even as the manufacturers tried new, more focused large performance cars including the Catalina 2+2, Ford Seven Litre and GT, and so forth. This is a story unto itself, and thus, coverage of kits of large cars with muscle car engines continues in Chapter 11.

Missing in Action

Pre–supercar era cars yet to appear in a 1/24th-1/25th–scale kit

- 1956–1958 Plymouth Fury
- 1957–1958 Dodge Coronet Two-Door Sedan with D-500/Super D-500 Engines
- 1958 Mercury Two-Door Sedan with 400-hp MEL Marauder V-8
- 1959–1961 Chrysler 300 E, F, and G
- 1963 Pontiac Catalina with 421 Super Duty Engine

Pre–supercar era cars that need a new or modern kit offering

- 1962 Dodge Dart and Plymouth Fury with Max Wedge V-8
- 1962–1964 Chrysler 300 H, J, and K
- 1962 Ford Galaxie 500 XL with 406 FE V-8
- 1963 Dodge 330/440/Polara and Plymouth Fury/Sport Fury with 426 Max Wedge V-8

Muscle Car Model Kits Scale Showroom

The following models show how several of the kits mentioned earlier in this chapter look when assembled by experienced adult model car builders. (Photography and models are by the writer unless noted otherwise.)

The 1949–1950 1950 Oldsmobile 88 is considered by many to be the first muscle car. Revell's all-new 1/25th-scale assembly kit is offered in two versions (stock or custom); this is the mild custom version.

The 1953 Studebaker Starliner proved the appeal of a car designed for eye-pleasing proportions and style rather than more practical considerations. AMT's Trophy Series kit is shown here assembled in 100 percent showroom stock form. (Builder/Photographer: Rick Hanmore)

AMT (left) and Revell (right) were the first to offer full-detail Tri-Five Chevy assembly kits. These are built both showroom stock from the kits, except for the more contemporary wheel/tire fitment.

This AMT-Ertl 1962 Bel Air BubbleTop hardtop with 409 V-8 power was built box-stock except for the contemporary American five-spokes and wide boots.

Mid-year Code LL-1 Limelight paint distinguishes this Chrysler 300 Sport two-door hardtop built from JoHan's USA Oldies series kit of the mid-1970s. (Builder: Dean Milano)

Here AMT's 1963 Impala SS annual kit has been converted to a Z-11 drag racer with the engine from AMT-Ertl's 1962 Bel Air Super Stock kits. Note the diorama backdrop and hand-painted figures. (Builder: Bill Coulter)

This 1963 Chrysler 300J was built from a restored JoHan annual kit; adding a lowered suspension and 1970s era mag wheels, it takes on an entirely different look than the showroom stock appearance.

The Supercar Is Born, Part 1

Pontiac, Oldsmobile, and Buick

Here are several kits of the Buick-Olds-Pontiac (BOP) compacts that preceded the intermediate-sized replacements that wore the same names for the 1964 model year (all: Wave 1/**). AMT offered kits of the Tempest in sedan (1961 not shown) and hardtop and convertible forms (1962 and 1963). AMT also produced Buick Special wagon kits for 1961 and 1962, while JoHan offered the Olds F-85 in 1961 wagon and 1962 Cutlass hardtop/convertible forms (the JoHan kits shown are 1970s USA Oldies reissues).

If you define the core of the American muscle car phenomenon to be the 1960s intermediate-sized supercar, then the story of the muscle car is largely the story of the Pontiac GTO.

General Motors entered the new intermediate-sized class starting with the 1964 model year. General Motors was already two years behind, as the intermediate market segment really began in the 1962 model year with the introduction of Ford Motor Company's Ford Fairlane and Mercury Meteor models. Some might suggest that the new-for-1962 downsized Dodge Dart and Plymouth Fury were also intermediates, but they were notably larger in several key dimensions than the Fairlane and Meteor, and they were marketed against the full-sized Galaxie and Impala, not as new intermediates.

Over the course of the early 1960s, the automotive market in the United States was evolving quickly, with emerging trends including highly styled two-doors, hardtops, and convertibles with bucket seats, consoles, and more powerful V-8s. Therefore, while the Ford Fairlane was an immediate success that required a market response from rival Chevrolet, what makes the GM entries of special interest is the way in which response was delivered. In the two years following the introductions of the Ford intermediates, General Motors was able to more effectively develop and "tune" its new intermediate-sized products to capitalize on these evolving trends. In doing so, General Motors enjoyed not only immediate market success for the 1964 model year, but also set the pattern for how intermediate-sized cars evolved during the following decades.

GM's response took two approaches. First was an all-new nameplate for Chevrolet, the Chevelle, chosen in part to continue the use of Chevy product names starting with the letter "c." The Chevelle was a notably more stylish car than the first Fairlanes, and the marketing very successfully capitalized on the top range Malibu and Malibu SS two-door hardtop and convertible models. For the B-O-P offerings, General Motors chose to drop its previous compact-sized Tempest, F-85, and Special models and reapply these now-established nameplates to the newly sized intermediate products. These three products also launched the format for the supercar segment starting with the Pontiac GTO, quickly followed by the 4-4-2 and Gran Sport models from the sister divisions.

GM's 1964 entry into the intermediate-sized car market was one of the most important automotive events of the 1960s. Within five years, GM's intermediates had become the style and performance leaders among GM's family cars, with the same trend starting to evolve at Ford and Chrysler. By the mid-1970s the intermediate segment entries had evolved into some of the best-selling cars in the marketplace (led at that time by the Oldsmobile Cutlass). This trend continued into subsequent decades with the Ford Taurus and Fusion, the Honda Accord, and the Toyota Camry. Intermediate-sized cars are still the best-selling passenger cars in the American market today.

But now returning to the 1964 model year, I'll bet everyone reading this book has his or her own GTO story to tell. Right now, I'm specifically talking about a "first time the GTO registered on your car guy or gal radar screen" story. This is mine.

AMT's annual kits for 1964 included the Pontiac LeMans convertible (Wave 1/), followed by the GTO hardtop (Wave 1/*****). These AMT kits are still considered the "gold standard" for 1964 Tempest/GTO body accuracy and proportions. The 3-in-1 racing version had a Rallye/Road Racing theme. That would soon change in GTO kits that followed!***

I grew up in Ann Arbor, Michigan. Despite our location less than 60 miles west of Detroit, Ann Arbor back then was not a car town (it is even less so today). As an enthusiastic pre-teen car enthusiast, I was far more likely to see a Volvo or a Saab than a GTO during the mid-1960s, reflecting the heavy local influence of the University of Michigan and the intellectual approach to car ownership of the faculty of this respected institution of higher learning.

So, imagine then one sunny fall 1964 afternoon, as our otherwise unassuming Abbot Elementary School Chorus teacher drove down Center Street into the school parking lot in her brand new 1965 Iris Mist Metallic GTO convertible. Not just that, but it was a close-ratio 4-speed manual, and Mrs. K. was not beyond driving down the street in a low gear holding the tach around 3,000 rpm or so. Oh man! If the GTO hadn't bumped into my consciousness before, it sure did that sunny afternoon in the fall of 1964! The memory still gets to me well more than 50 years later.

This was also just about the time I graduated from being an occasional model car builder to a frequent kit purchaser. Soon, I saw the new tiger-striped box with the AMT Trophy Series logo and the 1965 Goat on the end panel at the Hobby Store in Arborland, our nearby outdoor regional shopping center. I bet many of you remember that very box top yourself. That's my cue to segue into the topic of this chapter: GM's first intermediate supercars: the GTO, 442, and Gran Sport.

Pontiac GTO: The Supercar Legend

The story of the GTO's development is well known and there is no need to repeat it here. What does bear repeating is that not only was the GTO largely a groundbreaking product, it was brilliantly marketed almost from the very beginning. The combination of these two developments gave the GTO a head start in the supercar market that was not fully challenged until Plymouth's Road Runner delivered an equal dose of product uniqueness and marketing savvy five model years later. Not too surprisingly, the GTO also quickly established a leadership position in the hobby kit market that it held for years to come. The story begins in fall 1963.

1964–1965 GTO: First at Bat

The daylight hours were starting to shorten, and there was a brisk chill in the air when the AMT 1964 annual kits rolled off the line at the AMT plant located at 1225 East Maple Road in Troy, Michigan. Generally speaking, AMT would produce the pre-assembled promotional models first, as they were to be shipped primarily to car dealers to coincide with the annual new car announcements. The exterior body tools (and in many cases, the chassis and interior parts) were then repurposed as assembly kits with the addition of opening hoods and fairly simplistic engine compartments. Convertible kits were typically run first, followed by the hardtops.

All this is a way of conveying that the first 1964 Pontiac intermediate assembly kit was actually a LeMans convertible, not the GTO. The box top featured a cut-in illustration highlighting the "326 CU. IN. V-8 ENGINE." When the hardtop kits came off the line several months later, the LeMans became a GTO, the engine was now a 389 with 4-barrel and tri-power options, the hood added those two faux scoops, and the body was updated with carefully engraved GTO nomenclature. America's model car builders now had their first chance to build a scale version of Pontiac's Gran Turismo Omologato. These were well-detailed annual kits for the time, with highly accurate exteriors and moderate levels of interior and engine detail. Just one sign of the attention to detail: the GTO kit offered the builders three different styles of 4-speed transmission shift levers.

Monogram's 1/24th-scale 1964 GTO kit from the mid-1980s (Wave 2/*) has excellent detail and remains the most accessible 1964 Goat kit available to builders today. Polar Light's 1964 GTO kit (Wave 3/*) is somewhat simplified; the convertible is the only GTO kit of this body style to be produced in 1/25th scale.

While not as rare as some kits shown in this book, these two are among the most desired. AMT's 1965 GTO annual kit (Wave 1/***) and Trophy Series reissue (Wave 1/***) are both 100-percent factory stock kits. These are sought out versus later 1980s and later reissues of the kit, which contained a series of mistakes in body trim and nomenclature engraving.

These AMT 1964 GTO kits were relatively scarce to begin with, and by the 1980s they were pricey and rare collectibles. During this period, Monogram had begun to revisit the muscle car era for possible kits, and the 1964 GTO quickly rose to the top of the list. When its 1/24th-scale kit appeared in 1985, it was rendered in two-door sedan/coupe form (what today is called a post car, referring to the visible B-pillar between the driver's side window and the rear quarter-window). Instructions showed the builder how to remove the door and window frames to create a second two-door hardtop version of the kit. Set up with the iconic 389 tri-power, this was a very sharp replica kit that has been reissued several more times in the following years.

In the early 2000s, a new model company, Polar Lights (a play on the old Aurora kit name), commissioned the development of a new series of 1/25th-scale model cars. It featured snap-together assembly, along with pre-painted bodies. Among the releases was a 1964 GTO, rendered in both hardtop and convertible form. The kits were generally well done, but they never caught on strongly with the adult modeling community, perhaps due to the lower parts count and less precise engraving versus other newly tooled kits of the millennium. The hardtop was reissued in 2014, this time with an unpainted body.

By the fall of 1964, it was very evident that the GTO was becoming a huge hit in the marketplace. New vertical quad headlamps and a refined rear-end appearance made it immediately recognizable as the new 1965 version, while underhood refinements improved the performance. This was also the year that GTO marketing and merchandising fully kicked in, making the Tiger the most desirable car of all for performance-minded young adults.

AMT reacted accordingly with a 1965 GTO annual kit that mirrored the appeal of the real car. The kit started with a body that allowed the builder to construct either a factory hardtop or convertible. The custom version added a fastback hardtop that pretty accurately foreshadowed the buttress-like C-pillar of the upcoming 1966 GTO. The racing version was now drag racing themed.

All was not well, however, as AMT's new cross-town rival, MPC, soon secured the contract for upcoming 1966 GTO promotionals. This gave MPC the ability to affordably develop the car assembly kits that followed. AMT reacted quickly by re-boxing its 1965 GTO as part of its premium Trophy Series and keeping it in the lineup for several years to follow. This was the aforementioned kit with the iconic Tiger Stripe box art that seemed to jump out at you from every local hobby and discount store you visited back then. The slightly larger box now carried a suggested price of $1.70 (versus the original $1.50 price for the annual kit). Interestingly, in today's collectible market the Trophy Series reissue also sells for more than the original annual kit.

These two issues of the 1965 GTO (along with two other late 1960s reissues with different box art themes) are the only kits with the original AMT body engraving. The body tooling was fundamentally altered in 1972 as part of an AMT series of Modified Stockers; these were dirt track–style cars with huge wheel cutouts and other non-stock kit changes. For most kits of this series, this was a death-knell for future stock version reissues. In the case of the GTO, in the mid-1980s AMT-Ertl attempted to restore the tool to factory-correct 1965 GTO status. The result drew brickbats from serious modelers for poor and out-of-scale body details and engraving. Later changes attempted to correct the errors, but the result still lacks fidelity versus the original kits produced in the mid- to late 1960s. No model company has attempted a modern-day popular-scale kit of the 1965 GTO. It is a distinct market opportunity for a motivated and opportunistic scale kit producer.

MPC's 1966 GTO hardtop and convertible annual kits (both: Wave 1/), were brilliantly merchandised as kits and also showed a strong connection between the kitmaker in Mount Clemens and the Pontiac braintrust located 25 miles west-northwest in another Detroit suburb. Note the use of the GeeTO Tiger marketing theme, while the kits also promoted "detailed instructions on building an actual full-scale GTO B/Stocker."***

1966–1967 GTO: The Tiger Rules

GTO hit full stride in the American automotive marketplace in the 1966 model year. It was no longer an optional package for the LeMans; it was now a separate series within the Pontiac lineup. Accordingly, it featured greater appearance and content differentiation versus the LeMans series, and the new Coke-bottle body shape made Chrysler's equally new Coronet and Satellite immediately look a generation out of date. The Tiger merchandising approach reached its peak, and, nearly 97,000 buyers later, the final result was the best sales year ever for the GTO.

MPC took full advantage of its new GTO promo and kit franchise, as next to the Mustang this was probably the hottest annual kit franchise in the 1966 marketplace. Combined with a merchandising effort that credited Budd Anderson (the highly popular, former AMT spokesperson) as the kit consultant, the kit included parts for stock, custom, a B/Stock drag racer, and a second drag racing version. Offered as a $1.49 convertible or a $2.00 hardtop, box art for both versions promoted the "wild match car" setup featuring dramatically set-back engine and driver along with an extended air scoop for the 480-hp supercharged V-8, and new version-specific interior door/bulkhead panels and steering gear. The hardtop kit even added a Bonus "Extra Slot Racing [conversion] Pack."

MPC's 1966 GTOs were typical annual kits in that after the model year run, the "tool" that molded the models was modified and updated for the 1967 GTO changes. Thus, the 1966 GTO kits quickly became very hard to find and extremely pricey if/when located. Belatedly to the rescue, more than three decades later, the team at Revell engineered an all-new kit of the 1966 GTO hardtop that debuted in 1998. Featuring the last-ever tri-power 389 and precise underbody, and interior detail, it is in my judgment the best of all GTO kits available in the popular 1/24th and 1/25th scales.

Revell's 1966 GTO kit (Wave 3/*) was engineered and released in 1998, and it is a fine example of what I call Wave 3 of model car kit development. It has seen multiple kit versions including those shown here. (The drag racing themed kits are factory stock except for the Hurst five-spoke mags.)

As 1967 dawned, the GTO faced several new challenges: 389 and Pontiac's legendary tri-power options were gone, and the Tiger merchandising theme was history, both credited to decisions from the GM executive suite in downtown Detroit. Not only that, but the GTO's competitors were growing savvy about the development and marketing of their own supercars. Mild body changes (primarily added chrome on the lower body sides) and a new 400-ci version of Pontiac's V-8 were the main changes for 1967. Equally important, a new marketing campaign was developed: The Great One.

MPC's 1967 GTO hardtop and convertible annual kits (both: Wave 1/) are the only 1967 GTO kits with pure, pristine body forms and moldings due to later changes to the body tooling/mold. Students of commercial art will also note the first emergence of a strong diagonal split to the background of the box top and ends. It was a graphic theme that carried forward in various forms for the next four years of MPC annual kits.***

MPC's decision to replicate the* Mr. Unswitchable *GTO funny car (bottom center) required major alterations to the body sides of the 1967 GTO tool. Later when MPC decided to reissue the 1967 GTO in stock form, an effort to restore the stock wheelwell openings was not entirely successful. The resulting kits shown here (all: Wave 1/*) are considerably less desirable than the original 1967 annual kits.

MPC's 1967 GTO followed with minor changes versus the 1966 kit. The match race version was now called "funny car" and it represented the lead box art illustration on the hardtop annual kit. The body was now shown as hinged at the rear (the kit instructions noted that the builder had to omit body mounting screws at the front and leave the ones at rear loose to achieve this configuration). Budd Anderson's picture was replaced with Dean Jeffries, who was credited with the custom version of the kit. The box art further reclassified the other competition version as C/Stock versus the B/Stock-class ranking a year earlier. In a surprising omission, the MPC kit did not contain either of the 1967 production engine choices. Instead, the model builder chose between a no-longer available tri-power V-8, a non-stock dual 4-barrel setup for the 3-in-1 custom version, and the blown V-8 for the pseudo–funny car version.

Also of note, during the late 1960s and early 1970s, MPC sometimes shared tooling and kit merchandising with U.K.-based Airfix. Thus, a version of the MPC 1967 GTO kit was sold overseas with different box art under the Airfix brand. It's a real find for collectors today.

The 1966 match race/1967 funny car versions of MPC's GTO annual kits perhaps foreshadowed the end of the 1967 model year when MPC made drastic changes to the body tool in order to produce a somewhat accurate replica of Dick Jessee's *Mr. Unswitchable* GTO. Around 1984, MPC decided to reissue the 1967 GTO in stock form, but to do so it had to reverse all the changes to the body tool that made the Jessee funny car possible. The reclamation was not well done. The body had obvious flaws along the sides and, in several kit reissues, was also missing several 1967-specific interior parts. That makes the reissues, which have continued on a semi-regular basis ever since, a compromised kit series. Unless you are a very skilled model car builder, if you want to build a 1967 GTO you will really need to find the original annual kit and be prepared to pay accordingly.

1968–1969 GTO: A New Direction

After an increasingly successful run starting in 1964, Pontiac's intermediate LeMans and its derivatives took a big turn with the 1968 model year. In an era when "bigger is better" was standard operating procedure in the auto industry, Pontiac and its brethren divisions decided to split its two-door and four-door intermediates to different wheelbases. Even more surprising, the two-doors experienced a wheelbase *reduction*, from 115 to 112 inches. In retrospect, beyond all the stated reasons at the time, today one wonders whether the two-door approach was in part a reaction to the 600,000+ Mustangs sold in 1966 (when the 1968 GM intermediate program was under development). That totaled two-thirds more than the entire number of all body styles of Pontiac intermediates sold in that same year.

Speculation aside, even the most jaded Chevrolet, Ford, or Mopar fan back then would have to admit that the new, muscle-bound GTO with its color-keyed Endura front bumper was a stunning achievement. It was also a big departure from the four years of GTOs that preceded it. Model kit builders shared in the excitement with new kits from MPC replicating both the hardtop and convertible versions. MPC's annual kit box art theme continued to evolve, with an evolution of the trapezoidal background shape from the 1967 kits. None of the 1968 boxes looked better than the GTO hardtop, illustrated in bright red in 100-percent factory stock form except for the kit's optional clear hood. Both kits pushed the so-called funny car version with its Logghe-style front coil-over-shock, straight axle configuration with four-bar radius rods (today we'd call this version more accurately a Street Gasser or Street Freak). Both kits also included an optional rear spoiler that predicted the 1969 GTO Judge design. Fortunately for the showroom stock model builder, the factory stock 4-barrel engine returned, albeit with an incorrect 1967-style Ram-Air–style carb tray.

MPC's 1968 GTO kits (both: Wave 1/*) didn't set any new standards in kit design, but they contained minutely accurate bodies and the box art designs fully conveyed the excitement of the real cars. The convertible kit offered a wild bubble-top build option, and unusually showed a rear-three-quarter box top view that was, then and now, seldom utilized as a lead illustration angle in a model kit.***

MPC's 1969 GTO kits showed further evolution of the MPC annual kit graphic design. The custom bubbletop option was again featured on the convertible box top, this time in a high front-three-quarter bird's-eye view, while the hardtop illustration moved the funny car version to the box top lead in a low angle illustration that emphasized the plated straight-axle front-end option.

In 1969, Pontiac focused on fine-tuning the GTO and MPC's 1969 GTO model year updates captured these changes. Box art emphasized non-performance options such as trailer hitches and extended towing mirrors, while the convertible box side conveyed that the Judge-like spoiler was even adjustable as to what is today called the angle of attack. Under the hood, the standard 400 V-8 continued, but the 1/1-scale optional RA-III and RA-IV V-8s went missing from MPC's kit.

We've never been graced with a fully correct kit of the 1968 GTO that reflects engineering advances beyond MPC's original Wave 1 annual kit configuration. The story is more favorable for 1969, as Monogram noted that there was never an original annual kit depicting the mid-year introduction of GTO's Judge. The team zeroed in on this big opportunity in 1982, with the introduction of a 1969½ GTO Judge in hardtop form. Through the years, Revell-Monogram has taken the assignment to further refine this kit, including a more accurate air cleaner/air intake setup, and more complete/better rendered Judge graphics. Monogram also came up with a 1968 GTO Street Machine version for its 1984 kit catalog, but it was judged by the modeling community as seriously flawed, since key 1968 GTO exterior and interior elements were never changed from the original 1969 Judge kit.

1970 GTO: Reaching the Peak of the Mountain

For 1970, the GTO underwent what is called a "major freshening" in the auto industry. Almost all of the exterior sheet metal was altered in one form or another, and the Endura body-colored bumper reached perhaps its most harmonious design ever. Muscular fender blips over the front and rear recalled the 1950s Mercedes-Benz 300SL, but the overall result was as fresh and dynamic as one had come to expect from Pontiac's muscle car image leader.

MPC's 1970 GTO kit was clearly an evolution of the kit from the previous two years, as it featured largely carryover

Monogram's original 1969 GTO Judge (Wave 2/*) is a good kit that has gotten better with detail improvements compared to subsequent reissues. It's the only Judge ever produced in the popular scales. The Revell muscle release from 2009 has the most complete decal sheet and the correct air cleaner, but still retains the incorrect exhaust manifolds for the standard Ram Air III engine.

assemblies in all areas except the exterior and certain details of the interior. Build variations continued with the coil-over-shock straight front axle, now termed as the high-rise version, it's third rebranding in as many years. One new feature was a multi-piece Christmas tree, straight from your local drag strip.

Several disappointments were evident in the MPC 1970 GTO kit. First, the engine itself (a key element of the GTO's appeal then and now) continued as a carryover of a basic V-8 with parts tracing their lineage back to MPC's first GTO kit some five years earlier. Where were the soon-to-be legendary Ram Air III and Ram Air IV 400 V-8s, with their distinctive engine accouterments? How about the GTO convertible version? Finally, although it was reportedly a last minute decision at Pontiac headquarters to continue the Judge for 1970, one would have hoped for at least some of the Judge parts to make it into MPC's 1970 GTO kit. It's almost as though MPC predicted the reaction to the real car (with its rapidly sliding sales during 1970 due to a recession, gouge-worthy insurance premiums, and a general societal malaise), and scaled back its efforts as a result.

Ranting aside, the kit's updated 1970 body was still spot on. Also of note, MPC offered the 1970 GTO in a simplified, promo-type snap kit. Marketed as one of several "Fast Pack" kits for "Fast Building, Fast Racing," a new feature was "Snap-on wheels feature[ing] special engineered bearings for hot racing action." This may have been a competitive response to AMT's lineup of unassembled 1970 promos merchandised under the Motor City Stockers banner.

*MPC's 1970 GTO (Wave 1/***) was mostly a carryover of MPC's prior-year GTO kits, updated with the new exterior styling changes. The Fast Pack kit was basically an unassembled 1970 GTO promotional model marketed as though it were a larger version of Mattel's incredibly popular Hot Wheels toys.*

1971–1972 GTO: A Fast Descent

It turned out that 1971 was the last model year of the original muscle car era in which the GTO remained a separate, stand-alone production series. The redesigned front end with relocated hood air scoops improved the functionality of cars equipped with fresh air induction, and 1971 was the first year for the renowned "Honeycomb" wheel option.

Pontiac also continued the GT-37, a 1970 mid-year introduction based on the Tempest, which was yet another competitive attempt to counter the Road Runner's budget supercar appeal, and to also address the rising insurance rates being assessed on full-fledged muscle cars. With the freshened front end of the non-GTO Pontiac intermediate, this was a very attractive alternative for savvy performance enthusiasts when equipped with Pontiac's 400 V-8.

For 1972, the GTO returned to being an option rather than a series for the first time since 1965. Detail improvements included functional front fender scoops that routed hot air away from the engine compartment, and a new grille insert. The 455 HO as well as many other desirable performance and appearance options together were packaged together under the new Code WW5.

MPC's basic GTO kit carried over largely intact for these two model years as well, featuring the same options and accessories dating back to the 1968 kit, while accurately capturing the new design refinements of the real cars. Still, the top-drawer engine options remained missing from the kits, particularly the now-revered 1971 455 HO V-8 that prompted a claim in the Pontiac Performance Cars catalog that read "Installed performance of the LS5 is better than any Pontiac engine in history. Both top and bottom ends."

The MPC 1972 GTO represented the last model year for a GTO model kit (until the Polar Lights 2004 and 2005 model

*MPC's 1971 (Wave 1/***), and 1972 (Wave 1/**) annual kits were updated for the yearly changes on the real GTO, while under the revised bodies most of the rest of these kits was derived from MPC's previous GTO annual kits. By this point, MPC had moved completely away from the trapezoidal graphic background used in its prior-year annual kits.*

*The 1970 (Wave 1/**) and 1972 (Wave 1/*) GTO kits from MPC have been reissued once (the 1970) and multiple times (the 1972) during the last 30 years. They're okay replicas, but I recommend searching out the original issue annual kits if you are building a precise replica model.*

year GTO kits, which are beyond the scope of this book). Years later, MPC returned this tool to the 1970 GTO factory stock configuration. In this reissue version, the Endura front fascia was molded separately, versus being molded as part of the body in the 1970 annual kit. This reissue appeared only once, in 1987. Conversely, the 1972 GTO kit has seen multiple reissues starting in 1980 under MPC and AMT branding; the later reissues restored the stock wheels and tires that were missing from the earlier reissues.

If you consider the 1973 GTO, the 1973 Grand-Am (originally planned to be the GTO that year), or the 1974 GM "X-Body" based GTO to be legitimate late-era muscle cars, you'll be disappointed to learn that none of these have ever been offered as 1/25th-scale model kits.

Before I move on, I must mention the MPC *Monkeemobile* kit. For a full discussion of this kit and its development, I highly recommend consulting Jim Wangers's excellent book *Glory Days*. Let me say that Wangers credits MPC's president George Toteff for approaching him with the original idea for the Monkeemobile as a collaboration between Pontiac, customizer Dean Jeffries, and producers of *The Monkees* TV Show (the Monkees being arguably the hottest pop group in the land from late 1966 through early 1967). According to Wangers, the resulting MPC *Monkeemobile* kit eventually tallied more than 7 million unit sales, making it the second best-selling model car kit of all time for MPC.

Oldsmobile 442: The Thinking Man's Supercar

Oldsmobile's first intermediate muscle car followed shortly after the GTO's introduction at the 1964¼ model-year mark. It was originally available under option code B-09 and marketed as an adaptation of Oldsmobile's Police Pursuit Package. Powered by a high-performance derivative of Oldsmobile's all-new 330-ci V-8, it was a well-rounded package from the get-go. One example? The 442 included a front stabilizer bar as well as one in the rear. The latter was a key enabler of well-controlled handling and a feature that would be missing in most of the 442's competition for years to come. (Note that Oldsmobile used 4-4-2 and later on used 442 nomenclature on its cars; I'll use 442 from this point forward.)

In fact, during the entire nine-year run as a true performance car, the 442 could really be thought of as "the thinking man's supercar." While it was an exceptionally well-conceived product, its marketing support never really gained traction versus the GTO in the early years, nor versus the Mopar muscle cars as the decade ended ("Dr. Oldsmobile" notwithstanding).

1964–1965 442: Quiet Beginnings

Moving on to the world of 442 model kits, it has taken almost 40 years to fill most (but not quite all) of the gaps in the 1/25th scale history of Oldsmobile's intermediate-sized performance offerings. Even now, the first two versions (1964 and 1965) have never been graced with 1/24th- or 1/25th-scale kits.

Let's begin our coverage with AMT's 1964 Cutlass hardtop and convertible kits. While JoHan had produced Oldsmobile-branded dealer promotionals and kits for several years prior, AMT scooped up the Oldsmobile promo and kit business for 1964. AMT's 1964 Cutlass kit was a product of its high engineering standards and "with it" product planning at the time. Notice that I did not say "442" kits. Oldsmobile's prompt response to the GTO occurred after AMT's 1964 annual kits were engineered. However, given the external similarity between the Cutlass and a Cutlass with the optional 442

*AMT created an all-new annual kit for the 1964 Oldsmobile F-85 Cutlass (Wave 1/****). A highlight of the kit was the optional aftermarket Judson supercharger (it's the only kit I've ever seen with this blower setup), and the body casting itself was crisp and detailed. A hardtop kit (Wave 1/****) with the same features was also offered in addition to the convertible version kit shown here.*

package, as well as the inclusion of the new 330 4-barrel V-8 in AMT's kit (which of course formed the basis for this first-year option), a 1/25th-scale replica could be created with the added help of external 442 badging adapted from a later model year kit or the model car aftermarket and a manual transmission replacement for the Jet-Away 2-speed automatic in AMT's kit.

Meanwhile, AMT's 1965 promo contract with Oldsmobile migrated to the all-new full-sized Olds Dynamic 88 (and with it, the choice of 1965 model kit as well). AMT's 1964 Cutlass molds were never updated to the 1965 changes or to capture the second year of Oldsmobile's performance car with its new 400-ci V-8. Instead, AMT altered the body molds to run a one-time offering of an altered wheelbase, early style topless funny car kit. As of the time this book is written, the molds for the kit in this latter funny car form still exist in incomplete form. Still, it is unlikely hobbyists will ever see AMT's 1964 Cutlass kit reissued in factory stock form.

Having been engineered and first introduced in the late 1990s, the AMT-Ertl kits of the 1966 442 convertible and 442/W-30 hardtop, as well as the Lindberg kit of the 1967 Olds 442 W-30 (all: Wave 3/*) are far better detailed than most kits of muscle car kits shown elsewhere in this chapter. (Note that while the AMT-Ertl W-30 box art shows a mid-series F-85 Deluxe with the 442/W-30 option, the actual kit replicates the top-line Cutlass with the 442/W-30 option.)

1966–1967 442: Finding Its Footing

Now let's presume for a moment that you were a fan of the muscle car version of the nicely freshened Oldsmobile intermediates for the 1966 and 1967 model years. Maybe you even zeroed in on the single model year of all 442s when you could actually buy a factory-assembled L69 tri-power 442 (1966). Let's further presume you were looking to build a scale model car of the same cars. However, back then, the 442 was strangely missing from the annual kit lineups at your local hobby store. Your only alternative was to try converting the Monogram Hurst Hairy Olds drag racing exhibition car to a factory stock version. It was a formidable challenge even to the most accomplished model builders of the time.

Otherwise you would have had to wait for more than three decades to be able to do just that. It wasn't until calendar year 1997 that a factory stock 1/25th-scale replica appeared. The newly relevant Lindberg brand, being lovingly shepherded by former MPC wunderkind George Toteff, introduced an all-new kit of the 1967 Olds 442 W-30 hardtop. It was a very innovative kit, including separately molded, plated pieces of side and greenhouse trim, and engine features that had not seen replication in scale. The advances were muted by a few body errors: first, a raised rather than correctly recessed center hood area (quickly corrected by Lindberg), and an incorrect upsweep on the beltline below the rear quarter-windows (still there). Still, compared to the alternative mentioned earlier, this new kit was a revelation.

"When it rains, it pours." How many thousands of times in your life have you heard that? Well, it applies perfectly in the scale 442 kit world, as a year later in 1998, guess what? AMT-Ertl unveiled its own kit of the 1966 Olds Cutlass 442. Moreover, it wasn't just any 442, but a hardtop with the extremely rare, end of model year 442 L69 triple 2-barrel and W-30 Outside Air Induction (later called Force Air) options. It was joined a year later by a (non-W-30) 1966 Olds Cutlass 442 convertible.

These three Lindberg and AMT-Ertl 442 kits are all well-executed products, and they have recently been reissued.

1968–1969 442: The Most All-Around Capable Supercar of All?

Oldsmobile also adopted the shorter two-door wheelbase mentioned earlier for the GTO for a new 1968 lineup. It wore a highly appealing new exterior theme, inspired by the 1966 Toronado. Having remained an option package during the previous four model years, the 1968 442 graduated to become a separate, stand-alone series in Oldsmobile's intermediate car lineup. It could be argued that the new 442 was, more than ever, the supercar that had the broadest range of capabilities. Yes, the rear stabilizer bar (and the handling refinement it provided) was still standard when many competitors didn't even offer it as an option.

In the scale kit world, after the lack of any Oldsmobile 442 annual kits from 1964 to 1967, the contract for promotional vehicles (and the assembly kits that followed) returned to JoHan for the 1968 year. JoHan pulled out all the stops for its first 442 assembly kit. In addition to well-rendered stock and custom versions, JoHan added an entire Logghe funny car chassis and blower setup for the funny car version, which was the

JoHan's 1968 Olds 442 (Wave 1/**, not shown here) and 1969 442 (Wave 1/***) kits were among the best annual kits in the industry at the time of their release. Later in 1969, JoHan produced a second run of 1969 442 kits for sale under the AMT brand (Wave 1/***). All these kits are highly desirable collectibles today.***

featured illustration on the kit box top. Nobody else offered such a well-detailed Logghe chassis in any kit at the time, much less made the effort to include it in a regular 3-in-1–style annual kit. This was also the last year for JoHan's distinctive flatbox design.

The 1969 442 debuted with a return of the factory-assembled W-30 option and a new front end with the quad headlamps place together at the far ends of the grille. When this mildly updated 1969 442 debuted, JoHan's kit appeared in a new box size with dimensions similar to the AMT and MPC competition. Fortunately, all the goodies inside the 1968 box remained, but with the appropriate 1969 model year updates.

Also of note, in the late 1960s JoHan began sharing its tools with crosstown competitor AMT, resulting in a number of AMT-branded kits that were actually engineered by JoHan. Included in this arrangement were various years of Toronados, the two-seat AMX, and appropriate for our discussion here, the 1969 (as well as 1970) Olds 442 kits. In each case, to the best of my knowledge, the kit innards were the same and most likely produced in the JoHan factory; the only differences between the JoHan and AMT branded kits being the box art design and nomenclature, instruction sheet illustrations, and decal sheets.

Some two decades after the original 1969 442 annual kits hit the muscle car marketplace, AMT-Ertl sensed a market opportunity and engaged its rejuvenated car kit engineering capability to produce an all-new kit of the 1969 Olds 442 with the W-30 / Force Air option. Complete with the correct under-bumper air scoops and engine compartment ducting, this kit incorporated all the latest Wave 3 kit engineering updates, resulting in the most accurate 442 kit ever at the time of its introduction. The kit has been reissued multiple times along with a spinoff 1969 Hurst Olds kit (covered in Chapter 13).

1970–1972 442: The Ultimate Olds SuperCar

"As large a V-8 as has ever been bolted into a special performance production automobile." So proclaimed a number of print advertisements for the largely new 1970 442. You'd be crowing too if your car's standard V-8 now displaced 455 ci! Meanwhile, JoHan repeated as the "annuals" kitmaker of the 1970 442, offering a kit of the non-W-30 hardtop. The custom and funny car building versions continued as per the previous two years, and once again the 1970 kit contents appeared inside both JoHan and AMT-branded boxes

Beyond the new engine in standard and W-30/Force Air forms, for 1970 the 442 convertible departed from the two-door hardtop's curvaceous rear-quarter-panel design to adopt the more formal appearance of the new Cutlass Supreme two-door hardtop (itself a unique body style granted to Olds since they did not have a direct counterpart to the Grand Prix or newly introduced Monte Carlo personal luxury coupes). Some would argue the resulting 442 convertibles were the best combination yet of performance and luxury in the muscle car field.

The 442 continued largely unchanged for 1971, with minor front and rear-end design revisions, and engine revisions to reflect the upcoming federally mandated changeover from leaded to low-lead, and then eventually no-lead gas. Then, for 1972 the 442 returned to "option status" that year (with the 350 2-barrel as the new standard engine); fortunately, the 455 V-8 remained optional in regular and W-30 iterations.

The 1971 and 1972 442 hardtop annual kits appeared only in JoHan boxes (no AMT versions this time). Later in 1976, JoHan reissued the 1970 442 (without the funny car version) as part of its popular USA Oldies kit series. This was basically the 1972 annual kit with 1970 bumpers, grille, and

Olds 442 scale fans celebrated when the first contemporary-era kit of a 442, this newly tooled 1969 with the W-30 option, surfaced in 1988. Engineered and manufactured by AMT-Ertl, it first appeared under the MPC label (which AMT-Ertl owned at that point). It is also thought to be the last and final newly engineered kit to be introduced under MPC nomenclature. Various AMT-Ertl branded reissues followed later.

*Back in the day at your local hobby store, you might have seen 1970 Olds 442 hardtop annual kits from both AMT and JoHan (not shown; both Wave 1/***), but the contents of both kits came straight from the engineering offices of JoHan. Kits of the 1971 442 (Wave 1/****), 1972 (not shown; Wave 1/***), and reissued 1970 USA Oldies 442s (Wave 1/**) returned to exclusive JoHan branding.*

hood. Accordingly, purists will take note of an incorrect 1972 442 interior upholstery sew pattern and 1972 deck lid trim in this 1970 reissue.

To wrap up the scale coverage of 442s, I now jump all the way to calendar year 2009, when Revell debuted two all-new 1972 convertible kits. The first kit replicated the Cutlass Supreme convertible with the W-29 442 Sport and Handling Option, along with the W-30 455 V-8 option and the W-25 Force Air dual scoop hood. A second building option in the same kit was the 1972 Hurst-Olds H/O convertible. A year later, Revell unveiled a second kit billed as an Olds Cutlass Supreme Custom 2-in-1 kit. It had the standard (no scoops) hood, a full convertible up top (missing from the first kit), while retaining a 455 V-8. A third version, issued in 2015 and notable for its 1/25th-scale figure of Linda Vaughn and Indy 500 Pace Car livery also added the distinctive 1972 442 grille insert that was missing from the earlier kits.

Revell's new tool kits include the 1972 Olds 442 W-30 with the Hurst Olds option, a 455-powered Cutlass Supreme kit, and a more recent issue with the 1972 Indy Pace Car convertible markings (all: Wave 4/). This raises the possibility of an entire future family of 1970–1972 442 hardtop and convertible kits. Let Revell know if you share the dream!*

Beyond the obvious absence of any 1964–1965 442 kits, and the need for modern-era 1968, 1970, and 1971 kits, there have been no kits released with the W-31 small-block engine option of this period. The 1970-only Rallye 350 is also missing in kit form. If you consider the Colonnade-era Olds 442 to be bona-fide late-era muscle cars, there haven't been any kits of the 1973–1974 Cutlass with that 442 option either. The closest you could get were JoHan 1973 and 1974 Cutlass S promotional toys and a very basic 1975 Cutlass snap-kit.

Buick Gran Sport and GSX: Performance with a Touch of Luxury

Buick's role in the 1960s supercar wars was comparatively subdued but always in good taste, just like the classy styling employed for its best products. But when Buick's 455 engine went underhood for the 1970 model year, in conjunction with freshened styling and the Stage 1 option upgrades, the result was among the best supercars of the entire generation.

1965–1972 Gran Sports: Where Are All the Kits?

Sadly, the story in scale kits for Buick's GTO competitor is tragically brief. The initial intermediate-sized supercar from Buick, the 1965 Skylark Gran Sport, has never been reduced to 1/25th scale, not even in the mainstream (non-GS) Skylark series kit form. Fans did get a temporary reprieve, however, with the 1966 model year. For this one year only, AMT offered a 1966 Skylark Gran Sport annual kit. Underneath the hood was a scale replica of the Nailhead 400 V-8 in its last year of production. With no 1967 promo or kit on tap, the 1966 Gran Sport was reissued twice during the next several years. One version was a simplified, unassembled promotional-style Craftsman Series version targeted at the six- to nine-year-old pre-model builder and designed to be assembled without glue, in less than a half hour according to a period press release from AMT's public relations agency.

Unfortunately, this became another AMT annual kit tool that was modified in 1970 to be a part of the Late Modified kit series, meaning that the 1966 GS annual kit will likely never again be issued in factory stock form.

The only other Buick Gran Sport to reach the scale kit shelves was the 1970 GSX Stage 1, the subject of a finely detailed Monogram 1/24th-scale kit introduced in 1986. Complete in every detail except for some of the striping and

Monogram's 1970 Buick GSX (Wave 2/*) was among the finest of kits to emerge from this era of kit design. The 455 Stage 1 engine is particularly well done. Reissued several times, search out the latest version released in 2012 for the most complete decal graphics to replicate the GSX appearance in factory stock form.

Buick's 1966 Skylark Gran Sport was the only Buick intermediate to ever find itself the subject of an AMT full detail annual kit (Wave 1/*). After several late 1960s reissues, the kit was irreparably modified (some might say disfigured) into the Late Modified dirt tracker–style kit.***

blackout panels needed to replicate the intricate GSX graphic scheme, this shortfall was mostly remedied in the latest reissues of this kit.

Given the above gaps in basic model kit coverage of the 1965 to 1972 Gran Sport, this also means there is no model kit of the 1969 to 1972 Stage 1 Buicks (other than the GSX mentioned above), nor the "junior" 1967 GS-340 and 1968 to 1970 GS-350. There's little to remedy these gaps without resorting to the model car aftermarket, and even there the pickings are extremely thin. One of the premier resin casters briefly offered a 1968 GS400 trans kit, and another marketed a photo etch kit with badging to convert Monogram's GSX to the slightly more commonplace GS455 model of the 1970 model year. Both of these products are no longer produced, making them pricey collectibles of their own.

Epilogue

As influential and highly regarded as the GTO, 442, and Gran Sport are in the 1/1 scale world, their coverage in the popular scale kit world has been disjointed and incomplete. Some of the best GTO years are only available with compromised reissue kits, while other model years are missing completely unless you are willing to fork over $200 or more for an original unbuilt annual kit. The legendary RA-IV engine has never seen a credible version in scale.

As you've seen in this chapter, much the same story exists at Oldsmobile, where the first two years of 442s (as well as the 1973 and 1974 442) have never seen kit form, and fans of 1968, and 1971 versions have to spend big bucks for original annual kit releases. Worst of all, six of the eight model years of the Gran Sport (or 10 if you recognize the 1973 and 1974 GS option as a late-era muscle car) have never been the subject of a 1/24th- or 1/25th-scale factory replica model car kit.

If you are willing to consider resin trans-kits (see Chapter 15) your options are just slightly more expansive. Most of all, these omissions represent a real opportunity to the kitmakers serving the popular scale marketplace. Check out the sidebar "Missing in Action" and see if you agree with our suggestions.

Missing in Action

GTO/442/Gran Sport kits yet to appear in any 1/24th-1/25th–Scale Kit

- 1970 and 1971 GTO Judge hardtop and convertible (1970 with optional RA-IV engine, 1971 with the 455 HO engine)
- 1971 GT-37 with 400 4-barrel
- 1973 GTO or Grand Am coupe with (for extra credit) the planned (but not produced) 455 Super Duty engine
- 1964 and 1965 442
- 1968–1970 F85/Cutlass with W-31 package
- 1970 Olds Rallye 350
- 1965, 1967, 1968, 1969, 1971, and 1972 Gran Sport, including 1969–1972 Stage 1
- 1967 GS-340, 1968–1970 GS-350

GTO/442/Gran Sport kits that need a new or modern kit offering

- 1965, 1967, 1968, 1970, 1971, and 1972 GTO (1970 to include RA-IV engine; 1971 to include 455 HO engine)
- 1968 442 hardtop and convertible
- 1970–1971 442 hardtop and convertible with W-30 package

The following models show how several of the model kits mentioned earlier in this chapter look when assembled by experienced adult model car builders. Special thanks go to automotive restoration and model car expert Mike Hanson for his assistance here.

This 1970 GTO Judge is a skillful conversion of the original MPC 1970 GTO kit. It's painted in actual Code T (60) Orbit Orange lacquer, and completed with a scratch-built Judge spoiler and resin cast, trim ring-omitted Rallye II Wheels. (Builder/Photographer: Mike Hanson Photo)

Revell's 1966 GTO kit yields a precision replica, shown here with Pontiac-exclusive Code P Barrier Blue Metallic, a simulation of the rare Code 522 Red Plastic Fender Liners, and Hurst five-spoke mag wheels.

These 1970 Oldsmobile 442s are both broadly based on the JoHan annual kits, with aftermarket resin W-25 Force Air hoods and W-30 livery. The hardtop is finished in Code 55 Galeon Gold Metallic, while the convertible is based on a resin body conversion. (Builder/Photographer: Mike Hanson)

These are the only muscle era Buicks to have enjoyed kit replicas. The Code H Seafoam Green Metallic GS was built from a Modelhaus casting of the Craftsman reissue of the AMT 1966 annual kit. The Code 25 Gulfstream Blue Metallic GS Stage 1 is a modified Monogram 1970 GSX kit. (Builder/Photographer: Mike Hanson)

AMT's classic 1965 GTO annual kit/reissue is built here box stock (except for wheels/tires), and is painted in Testors Model Master Lacquer 1965 Pontiac Code P Iris Mist Metallic.

These two 1968 442s were built from AMT-Ertl's 1969 442 kit using Modelhaus's 1968 conversion parts. The factory stock 442 hardtop shows Code L Medium Teal Blue Mist Metallic, while the Hurst-Olds runs on Hurst mags. (Builder/Photographer: Mike Hanson)

Here a 1971 442 W-30 convertible conversion of the JoHan annual kit wearing Code 62 Bittersweet Metallic faces off with a 1972 442 W-30 glowing in Code 53 Saturn Gold Metallic. Note the intricate detailing of the tire sidewalls, the Olds SuperStock II wheels, and the convertible's interior. (Builder/Photographer: Mike Hanson)

Here MPC's 1970 GTO Judge stands next to Monogram's 1969½ GTO Judge, the latter painted in the Code T (72) Carousel Red introduction feature color. (Builder/Photographer: Mike Hanson)

The Supercar Is Born, Part 2

Chevelle and El Camino

"Chevelle is the Car . . . That's Made By the People . . . Who Make the Corvair and Corvette." That's the headline for a 1964 Malibu Super Sport ad in the December 1963 issue of *Hot Rod* magazine.

The midsized Chevelle was developed in response to Ford's highly successful midsized Fairlane, which debuted in 1962. However, once introduced, Chevy quickly attempted to develop a sporting image for the Chevelle, something that was largely missing from the practical approach Ford was using to sell the Fairlane.

It took a couple of years, but by 1966 the Chevelle SS began to firmly establish its reputation as a legitimate supercar. Until the Road Runner debuted in 1968, the SS396 was the most accessible and affordable supercar choice for young enthusiasts. By 1970, the Chevelle SS454 LS-6 was considered by many to be the ultimate expression of the supercar phenomenon to date. Accordingly, the SS Chevelles were consistently among the top sellers of the entire muscle car era, and today are highly desirable collectibles. (With the El Camino car-pickup being heavily based on the Chevelle wagon during this period, it too became a small but important part of the muscle car legend.)

Unlike many competing muscle cars, which were the subject of model car kits when they were new, initial full-detail kit coverage of the Chevelle SS was far from complete. It took more than 30 years, but I can now say that model kits have been produced for every key Chevelle supercar from the muscle car era.

Given the overall importance of the Chevelle SS and El Camino, I've devoted an entire chapter to model kits of just these two nameplates. One would expect that every significant Chevrolet intermediate offering of the era would have made it into the model car marketplace. However, much as you found in the preceding chapter, this is not the case. And once again, you'll find out that two of the most popular cars of this era were not kitted in fully detailed 1/25th-scale kits until more than 30 years after the original cars hit the streets. Let's take a closer look at how the Chevelle model kit offerings evolved.

1964–1965 Chevelle SS and El Camino: the Calm before the Storm?

When the 1964 Chevelle was introduced, the supercar phenomenon had yet to launch. Nevertheless, there was still plenty of excitement around the all-new midsized car from the number-one selling car brand in America at the time. Particularly in the top-line Malibu SS, America saw a car with almost all of the style of the Impala SS, in a slightly smaller and less expensive form, with an all-new shape and style. What was not to like? When first introduced, the 283 V-8 was the largest choice, soon augmented by the 327 V-8 in two versions at mid-year.

AMT knew the new Malibu was going to be big, so it took a rather unique approach with its 1/25th-scale replica kits. Instead of doing the expected, which would have been a full detail kit of the Malibu SS two-door hardtop, AMT instead issued this body style in an unassembled, promo-style Craftsman Series kit, with simplified construction and no engine. If you wanted more detail, you bought the companion full detail Chevelle four-door wagon kit. Wait, did I just say *wagon?* Yes, in one of the few instances where the wagon body-style ended up in an annual kit box, AMT's Chevelle wagon incorporated the more typical 3-in-1 annual kit features.

Yet another companion kit was the introduction of AMT's new Chevelle-based El Camino. Both this and the wagon kit featured a fully detailed Chevy Six under the hood. An optional small-block V-8 was only provided in a non-stock hot

*AMT produced 1964 and 1965 snap kits of the Chevelle SS hardtop, along with full detail kits of the Chevelle wagon and El Camino. Shown are the AMT annual kits of the 1964 Craftsman Series hardtop (Wave 1/ *** if unassembled), the 1965 Wagon (Wave 1/**) annual kit, plus the El Camino in 1964 (Wave 1/***) and 1965 (Wave 1/*).*

Debuting under Revell nomenclature was this 1965 Chevelle Z-16 (Wave 3/). It has seen at least three reissues since the 1996 debut with the box art shown here. The highly detailed kit includes underhood details such as molded heater hoses and an air cleaner decal.*

rodded form that was missing several factory stock components (among them, a water pump and air cleaner).

Fresh off a highly successful introductory year, the Chevelle and El Camino received minor revisions for their sophomore year in the American marketplace. The two big changes were a longer and more shapely front-end design, and the mid-year arrival of the big-block Z-16 hardtop, which included of course the first intermediate-sized application of Chevy's new "Mark IV" 396 V-8.

All three of the AMT annual kits were updated to include the fresh front-end treatment for the 1965 Chevelle. The Malibu SS continued in the simplified Jr. Trophy Craftsman Series form. The 1965 wagon and El Camino now had the missing stock parts for the (presumably) 327 small-block V-8, along with a hot-rodded dual-quad and headers setup; the six-banger engine was gone. Also missing was a replica of the 350 hp L79 version of the 327 that sort of carried the supercar banner for the Malibu, that is, until the Z-16 debuted at mid-year (more of which in a moment).

AMT never updated its annual kit tooling to the 1966 Chevelle design, so the 1965 wagon was reissued several times in the late 1960s and early 1970s, once in the late 1980s, and again several times in recent years. The 1965 version of the El Camino kit has enjoyed more than 10 reissues through the years, with varying themes including a 1965-era Camper pickup box for several of the versions.

Other than all those AMT 1965 Wagon and El Camino reissues, modelers waited until 1996 for fresh first-generation Chevelle styrene, this time courtesy of Revell-Monogram. An all-new tool debuted replicating the rare and highly desirable 1965½ Chevelle SS Z-16. This made it the first-ever fully detailed kit of the 1964–1965 Chevelle two-door hardtop body style.

1966–1967 Chevelle SS396 and El Camino: The Cavalry Arrives

For 1966, the Chevelle SS became the SS396. Introduced in 325 and 360 hp versions, a third 375-hp version of the 396 big-block was added late in the year. The SS396 enjoyed immediate success, finishing the model year second only in sales volume to Pontiac's GTO among the supercar entries that year. Yet in one of those inexplicable omissions of the model kit world, when the 1966 model year began no 1/25th-scale annual kits were to be found of the new Chevelle.

For nearly two decades, if you wanted to build a factory stock 1966 Chevelle SS396 model, your only choice was to try to convert these non-stock late 1970s kits from Monogram (Wave 2/). Only the most talented model builders could pull off a project of this scope.*

Revell's 1966 El Camino and wagon kits (both: Wave 3/*) share much of the mechanicals underneath the body, just as with the full-sized counterparts. The wagon kit doesn't offer a completely factory stock version, but swapping the hood, wheels, and tires from the El Camino kit (and possibly a 327 small-block from the parts box) would allow the modeler to build his own showroom replica.

Back in the day, many experienced model builders quickly learned to avoid kits with the Lindberg name. All that changed in the mid-1990s when new owners introduced a series of top-notch 1/25th-scale assembly kits. Lindberg's 1966 Chevelle (Wave 3/*) offering filled a key void in the SS396 kit world, and it easily ranks among the best Chevelle kits shown in the chapter.

While the 1966 and 1967 Chevelles were omitted from the annual kits lineup, a 1/1-scale car as popular as this was a prime subject for additional kits in the following years. In the late 1970s, a newly revived and relevant Monogram (after years under control of toymaker Mattel) introduced the first-ever popular-scale 1966 Malibu kits. As was its marketing angle at the time, however, the two kits were produced only in street-machine themed versions. Seemingly right off the pages of *Car Craft* magazine, they included non-stock features such as one-piece, forward tilting front end, a tubular style front frame clip with a Gasser-style straight axle, dual 4-barrels atop a high-rise–style intake, and a racing-style rear differential/suspension assembly. The kit was well detailed, but as was the case with a number of other Monogram kits introduced during this period, the body itself had proportion errors.

It took another 20 years until Lindberg surprised everyone by introducing an outstanding new 1966 Chevelle SS396 hardtop kit. With box art depicting the real car resplendent in Marina Blue metallic with the simulated five-spoke mag wheel covers and red line tires, inside was an exquisitely detailed replica (right down to decaled ornamentation for the steering wheel). Lindberg even included air cleaner decals depicting all three versions of the 396 engines that year! In fact, this 1998 kit introduction was perhaps the high point of the entire 1990s Lindberg product development effort.

Also in 1998, Revell-Monogram got around to filling a very important gap in the scale El Camino catalog. Its new 1966 El Camino kit replicated a real car, or rather pickup, which had been factory ordered with the 396 V-8 along with bucket seats and console, which was the closest one could get to an SS396 version using the factory order form that year.

Finally, rounding out our kit coverage of 1966 Chevelles, in 2003 Revell-Monogram announced a 1966 Chevelle four-door wagon based on its 1966 El Camino kit tooling, marking the third time (after AMT's 1964 and 1965 annual kits) a kit manufacturer has made a wagon body style available in a Chevelle-based kit. This kit represents a slightly modified street machine–style car with a non-stock SS-style hood and big-block 396 V-8.

Chevy updated the Chevelle SS396 and El Camino for 1967 with modest changes. Most obvious were the new "tilt ahead" front end replacing the wrap-around grille of the previous year. This time the wraparound treatment migrated to the rear, with new vertical-style taillamps.

What also continued from 1966 in the world of scale models was the omission of any 1/25th-scale annual kits representing the 1967 Chevelle and El Camino.

The long wait for a 1967 SS396 kit was worth it, for when both Revell and AMT-Ertl introduced new kits (both: Wave 3/*) in 1989 and 1990 respectively, they were far more accurate and detailed than would have been the case with annual kits engineered in the 1960s.

It took all the way to 1989, at which point *both* AMT-Ertl and Revell-Monogram announced their intent to produce *all-new* stock-bodied 1967 Chevelle SS396 models. Modelers went 22 years without, and then within a 12-month period *both* of the major domestic kit manufacturers introduced brand-new beautifully detailed kits of a car never before available in 1/25th scale. Model car scribes and builders argued about which kit was better, but the general vibe was more of a tie for first place, with each kit excelling in areas that the other kit did not.

1968–1969 Chevelle SS396 and El Camino SS396: Riding the Wave

The 1968 Chevelle was by far the most changed since its introduction five years earlier. It also adopted the split wheelbase approach discussed in Chapter 4, and combined it with very fresh design language that still proudly denoted "Chevrolet" to the now growing and loyal owner body. The same 396 engine options as 1967 continued, as did the SS396 nomenclature.

AMT finally added the Chevelle back to its annual kit lineup with a 1968 Chevelle SS396 hardtop, wearing drag-race based *Chevam* box art. The 3-in-1 approach again applied, but instead of stock/custom/racing, the three versions were *street*/custom/racing, which meant that the engine no longer contained stock induction and exhaust parts, instead substituting Hilborn fuel injection and headers in place of the respective factory/showroom components. This kit continued with updates in 1969. The custom versions by this point no longer were identified with a 1/1-scale customizer. Instead now designed by AMT's art department personnel, these custom parts yielded a car design any late 1960s 1/1-scale car stylist would have been proud to call his own.

By this point, AMT's box art approach was commercial art at its finest. Its art department first developed an umbrella graphic layout for the entire 1968 annual kit lineup, and then it created unique box art for each individual kit subject. Its 1968 SS396 kit (Wave 1/) captured the excitement of the supercar movement with this drag racing–themed execution. Note the Dodge Scat Pack–style bumblebee stripes.***

Three decades later in 1998, AMT-Ertl introduced an all-new tool of the 1968 El Camino SS396. Representing the scale version of the only year when the El Camino offered a standalone SS396 series (it became a freestanding option the following year), this was an intricately detailed kit. I consider it among the best of AMT-Ertl's Wave 3 offerings engineered by long-time AMT engineer John Mueller and his team. In 2017, Round 2 reissued this kit with a Soap Box Derby racer and box art derived from AMT's original 1969 (not 1968) El Camino kit that also featured a Soap Box Derby.

The 1969 model year again brought design refinements to the Chevelle, and I recall thinking at the time that unlike many second-year design updates, this one actually improved on rather than diluted the previous year's design. The SS396 returned to an option status and was now orderable on the lower series DeLuxe 300 coupe and hardtop for the first time (a response to the success of the previous year's Plymouth Road Runner?). This would also be the last year that the 396 V-8 was top dog in the Chevelle lineup (other than limited COPO/private branded production runs).

AMT's 1969 Chevelle kit was likewise a refinement of the previous year's model. The "Street" in place of "Factory Stock" engine compartment approach also carried over. Beyond this hardtop kit though, AMT had two more 1969 Chevy supercar kit surprises up its sleeve.

To further develop its 1969 annual kit lineup, AMT surprised hobbyists with an El Camino annual kit equipped with the SS396 package. This was a much-loved and rare kit that mirrored the 3-in-1 build options of the Chevelle kit that year.

An important gap in the El Camino kit lineup was plugged when AMT-Ertl unveiled this 1968 El Camino SS396. The most recent kit reissue added a 1/25th-scale Soap Box Derby racer kit premium originally patterned after the winning racer from the real 1969 Chevy Soap Box Derby World Championship (both: Wave 3/*).

*Depicted here are the top, end, and both side panels of AMT's 1969 SS396 hardtop annual kit (Wave 1/**). Different illustrations depict the factory stock (light blue), custom (copper bronze) and drag (yellow/green) options for the 3-in-1 kit, along with the kit components that made 1960s annual kits such enjoyable projects (then) and collectibles (today).*

*AMT's 1969 convertible SS396 kit (Wave 1/**) was a late bloomer, first breaking ground as part of AMT's 1978 Countdown Series kit lineup. Note that the only reissue of the kit revisits the 1969 AMT annual kit box art theme and graphics, yet with a fresh interpretation.*

It was reissued midway through the same year in a Soap Box Derby version that added a scale replica of the gravity racer that won the Chevy-sponsored national competition that year. While the AMT 1969 Chevelle hardtop kit has been reissued multiple times, the AMT 1969 El Camino kits were produced only during that one year.

Nearly 10 years later, AMT completed its 1969 SS396 surprises by offering its first-ever Chevelle convertible kit, based on the original 1969 convertible promotionals body tooling married with the detailed chassis and interior from the aforementioned hardtop assembly kit. This kit was merchandised as part of AMT's Countdown Series; it was a major feature of its 1978 sales catalog. The 1969 hardtop kit was also reissued as part of the Countdown Series catalog. Recently, Round 2 dusted off the convertible tool for a 2013 reissue that features new box art that is inspired by the original AMT 1969 annual kit box design.

Completing our coverage of the 1969 SS396 kit lineup, the original hardtop annual kit has been reissued multiple times during the following decades. Both this hardtop and the convertible kits continued one error from the original annual kit release that has never been corrected; they retained the engraving of the 1968-only SS396 lower body side moldings.

1970 Chevelle SS396/SS454: The Pinnacle of Supercar-dom?

Even those people who are not really Chevy fans would have to admit that the maturity, muscle, and content of the redesigned 1970 Chevelle SS was a high point

*AMT's 1969 El Camino (Wave 1/****) marked the return of this body style to its annual kit lineup for the first time since 1965. The Derby Champions kit (Wave 1/*****) box art featured 1969 Soap Box Derby World Champion Branch "Twig" Lew and a scale copy of his racer inside the kit.*

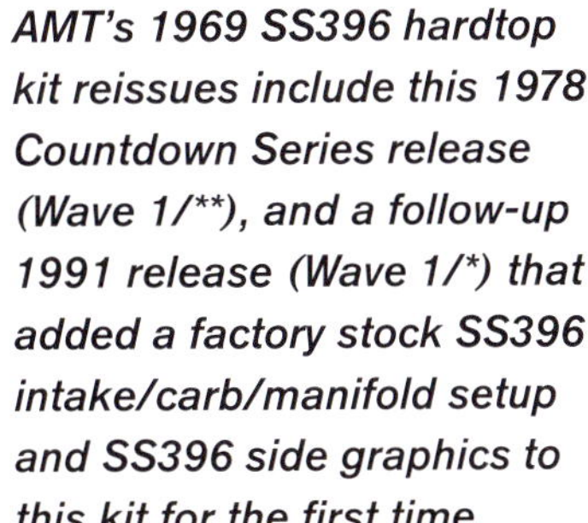

*AMT's 1969 SS396 hardtop kit reissues include this 1978 Countdown Series release (Wave 1/**), and a follow-up 1991 release (Wave 1/*) that added a factory stock SS396 intake/carb/manifold setup and SS396 side graphics to this kit for the first time.*

*AMT's 1970 SS396 annual kit (Wave 1/***) featured factory stock, strip, and "show" versions. The depiction of the Chevelle's new side panel flares was not entirely accurate, though. Fortunately, the stock induction system returned to the kit after being missing from the 1968–1969 kits. The Motor City Stocker version (Wave 1/**) shared the annual kit's exterior and interior, but omitted the engine and substituted a simplified chassis.*

The popularity and significance of the 1970 SS454 has justified several newer-tooled kits from Monogram (Wave 2/) and Revell (Wave 4/*), along with an updated version of the original AMT 1970 annual kit (Wave 1/**). The Revell kit has the most accurate body shape, but omits the engine and full chassis detail of the other two kits, and it substitutes toy-like stickers in place of a waterslide decal sheet.*

in the world of mainstream performance cars. It was a pinnacle that was not fully surpassed until the second decade of the next century. The major freshening adopted body color sheet metal around quad headlamps, and superb design studio modeling of side panel bulges extending from the front and rear wheel openings. A new optional hood with a center bulge culminating in a working cowl-induction fresh air setup was optional for the SS396 and the new SS454 versions. Best of all, an LS-6 version of the 454 carried a 450-hp rating; it was the highest gross horsepower factory rating of the entire muscle car era. The El Camino shared the engine updates but instead of those masterful new side flares, it continued all the 1968–1969 sheet metal in all areas except for a modest tweak of the front fenders to meet the new 1970 Chevelle grille and hood (and the 1970 Monte Carlo bumper).

New AMT body castings were developed to replicate the freshened 1970 Chevelle SS454 body design, but the kit otherwise remained essentially the same as before. For 1970, this body style came in both full detail and a Motor City Stocker Series version that returned to the simplified assembly approach of the Craftsman Series 1964 and 1965 Malibu kits. The 1970 full detail kit was graced with compelling box art that featured a blown SS454 seemingly jumping off the box top, accompanied by a digger rail pilot in a full racing mask on the left and a checkered pattern at the right. While AMT produced a convertible version in promo form, it never migrated to kit form in 1970. Although AMT announced plans for a 1970 El Camino SS kit, it was never actually produced.

Monogram developed a 1/24th-scale 1970 Chevelle SS454 kit that was first introduced in 1980. This kit replicated a factory stock SS454 body, but, as with several Monogram kits developed during this era, the body was somewhat inaccurate in its proportions and surface development.

In 1994, AMT returned its 1972 SS454 annual kit tooling to the 1970 form. New for this reissue were a factory stock cowl-induction air cleaner and pan and an LS-6 air cleaner decal. The previous optional engine versions were replaced by a 1990s-style aftermarket port-injection setup. The earlier side panel flare inaccuracies were still there, however.

Revell (which was at this point actually the Monogram product development team in Morton Grove, Illinois) was back at it in the year 2000 with yet another newly tooled 1970 Chevelle SS454, this time in a 1/25th-scale simplified-assembly, prepainted SnapTite kit that some Chevelle experts believe to be the most accurately scaled 1970 Chevelle body yet.

1971–1972 Chevelle SS454: Fading Fast?

Relatively minor 1971 front-end design changes yielded a major change in appearance for the Chevelle SS454. I was never

*Hobbyists enjoyed 1971 and 1972 annual kits from both AMT and MPC. Drag racing was the featured box art theme from both the 1971 AMT kit on the left (Wave 1/**) and the 1972 MPC kit on the right (Wave 1/**). Unfortunately, neither of these kits fully captured all the front-end changes of the real cars.*

a fan of the move from quad headlamps to dual headlamps for 1971, although in retrospect this was good design evolution strategy as it created a design linkage to the next-generation Colonnade-era Chevrolet (that was originally planned for introduction in 1972 rather than 1973). The SS replaced the SS396, now orderable with the 350 small-block; the SS454 continued with reduced horsepower. The new 15 x 7-inch factory five-spoke wheel design developed for the 1970½ Z-28 was one of the coolest factory mag-type wheel designs ever. It became a factory option for the Chevelle this year.

The 1972 update was modest. The wraparound turn signals at front evolved from a split to a single-lamp configuration, and the grille trim now continued outward to include the headlamps.

Both the AMT and MPC 1972 SS454 kits have seen reissues (all: Wave 1/). Shown are the 1972 and 2002 reissues of the AMT kit, along with the 1980 and 1983 reissues of the MPC kit. Each reissue includes slightly different content in terms of engine options, wheels and tires, and decals.*

For 1971 and 1972, the manufacturer promotionals contract moved from AMT to MPC. In the past, this typically meant that the annual kit source would have moved to MPC. In this case, it did, but AMT also continued with yearly updates to its Chevelle annual kit, meaning that the scale enthusiast could choose between both AMT and MPC versions of the 1971 and 1972 Chevelle SS454. The new MPC kit was developed in line with its kit theme for the year. It featured "mild" (stock) and "wild" (with huge spoof body parts patterned after its Zingers kits). It also included an optional high-rise dual-quad induction manifold and tubular headers for the engine. The MPC kit carried over for 1972 with continued availability of several spoof parts and the same engine options. AMT's updated kits carried over the choice of three engine versions (stock, Hilborn-style fuel injection, and 6-71 blower) and multiple wheel and tire options, along with the 1971 and 1972 sheet metal updates.

The 1972 versions of both the AMT and MPC kits have been reissued multiple times. AMT's reissues started with the "Red Alert" version, which continued the 1972 kit content (and building options) along with a new decal sheet featuring the livery of Bob Hamilton's 1/1-scale drag car. MPC's kit saw a non-stock street funny mid-year kit version, and a kit called the *SSlasher* introduced in 1980 repeated the 1972 kit content except for the omission of factory stock wheels, tires, and spoof parts.

Epilogue

Looking back at the history of Chevelle SS and El Camino kits, some observations are appropriate. It has taken decades upon decades, but finally *virtually* all the offerings of the immensely popular 1964 to 1972 Chevelle were produced in 1/25th scale! In addition, several major gaps in the El Camino lineup have been filled as well. However, the lack of assembly type kits of the 1964 and 1965 (small-block) Malibu SS hardtop

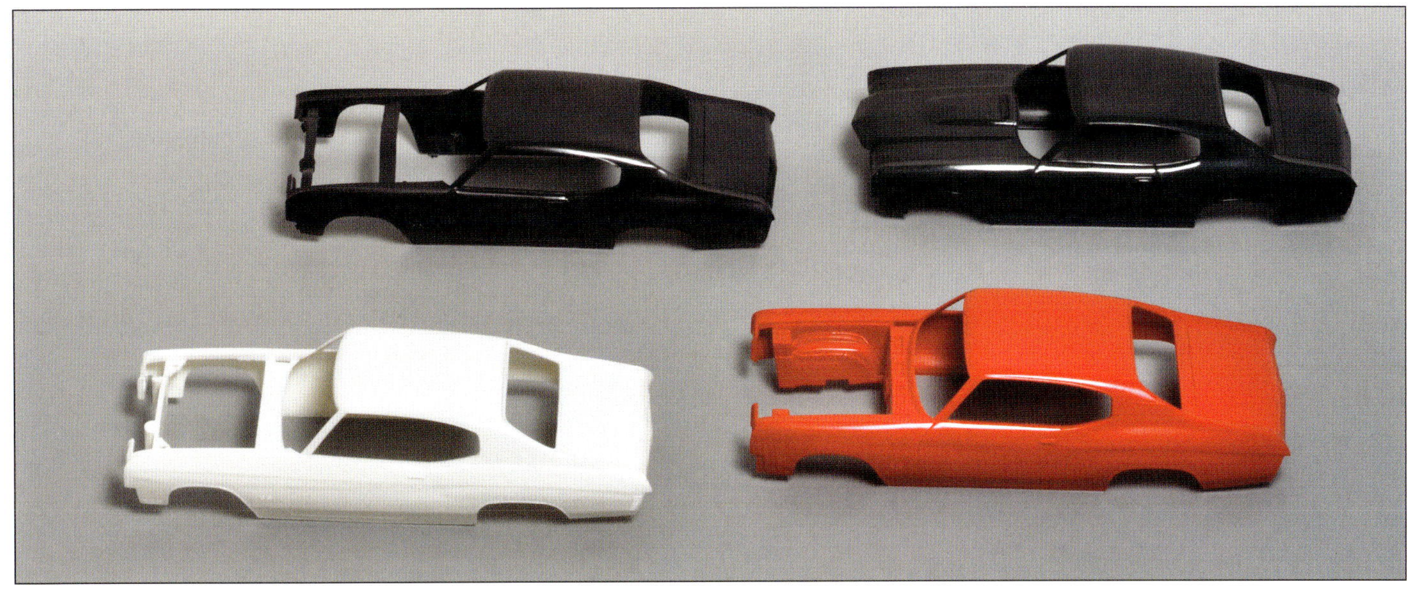

Clockwise from the upper left are MPC's 1/25th 1972 SS454, Revell's 1/25th 1970 SS454, Monogram's 1/24th-scale 1970 SS454, and AMT's 1/25th 1970 SS454. Revell's kit is the closest to the real car, but its snap-tite kit format omits the engine and chassis components typically found in a full assembly kit.

or convertible is an obvious omission in the kit world. The lack of kits of 1967 and 1970 to 1972 El Caminos also represents a business opportunity for the kit industry. For those that consider the 454-powered versions for the post-1972 Colonnade Chevelles to be part of the muscle car era, no stock kits of the 1973 or 1974 Malibu (as the successor to the Chevelle was called) have ever been offered, though this later body style did find applications in some AMT and MPC NASCAR kits.

An equally important observation is that though modelers and collectors have enjoyed an unusually broad choice of 1970 to 1972 Chevelle SS kits through the years, all of these kits have issues for the scale enthusiast. Starting with the 1970 to 1972 AMT kits, a close inspection of the side panels shows that the flares extend from the wheel openings and are reasonably accurate at the top, but then abruptly fade out. They are almost like the blisters in a Mercedes-Benz 300SL Gull-Wing coupe, which is completely wrong versus the 1/1-scale car where the flares subtly fade down the side panels. The MPC kit is better with the flares, but has misshapen front fender turn signals (the part that extends into the fender) yielding an unrealistic appearance.

The Monogram 1/24th-scale 1970 SS454 kit has the most problematic body, with a linear development of the front end that does not look realistic. As a general rule, more recently developed model kits often have bodies that are less realistic than the original annual kits, but in this case, most experts agree that the most lifelike kit body for the 1970 to 1972 Chevelle resides in the "Wheels of Fire" snap-tite kit introduced by Revell in 2000. However, this kit, because of the design approach, does not include an engine or detailed chassis.

Finally, it kind of stretches the credibility of the scale kit industry that a fully detailed and completely accurate, modern-era tooling kit of one of the most influential of all supercars, the 1970 Chevelle SS454 LS-6, hasn't been seen yet. Revell, to their credit, has justintroduced an excellent, all-new 1968 Chevelle SS 396 kit.

Missing in Action

Chevelle and El Camino yet to appear in a 1/24-1/25th–scale kit

- 1967 El Camino with 396 V-8
- 1970 SS454 convertible with LS6 454 V-8
- 1970 El Camino with LS6 454 V-8
- 1971–1972 El Camino with LS5 454 V-8

Chevelle and El Caminos that need a new or modern kit offering

- 1964 Super Sport hardtop or convertible
- 1965 Super Sport hardtop or convertible with L79 327 V-8
- 1969 El Camino with SS396 option
- 1970 SS454 hardtop with LS6 454 V-8
- 1971–1972 SS454 hardtop with LS5 454 V-8

Muscle Car Model Kits Scale Showroom

The following models show how several of the model kits mentioned earlier in this chapter look when assembled by experienced adult model car builders. (Photography and models are by the writer unless noted otherwise.)

Here AMT's 1969 Chevelle SS396 kit has been converted to the Malibu series hardtop (including eliminating the raised hood and converting the bucket seats to a front bench-seat interior). Note the added vinyl top and aftermarket photo-etched grille. (Builder: Lyle Willits)

This 1967 SS396 hardtop was based on the Revell kit and wears Code LL Tahoe Turquoise; it's a replica of the builder's real car. The 1969 Code 52 Garnet Red convertible is based on AMT's Countdown Series kit release from the late 1970s. (Builder/Photographer: Mike Hanson)

While it's not the most detailed kit of 1970 Chevelle SS454, Revell's snap-tite model has the most accurate body and proportions of all of them. It is molded in styrene colored to match Code 48 Forest Green Metallic.

Here a factory-fresh 1969 Chevelle SS396 convertible compares to a Yenko-converted 1969 Chevelle hardtop, painted in Code 76 Daytona Yellow. (Builder/Photographer: Mike Hanson)

Dearborn Responds

Ford and Mercury Performance Intermediates

New product innovation has always been a risky game in the automotive industry. Get it right and you win big. Really, really big. Get it wrong and the automotive and business media will never, ever forget it.

Automotive historians still cite the Edsel as a product innovation that failed, but the real story of Ford Motor Company in the late 1950s to late 1960s is that it had a whole series of other, highly successful product innovations, and very few that failed. This is especially true when comparing Ford to its competition during this period.

What were some of those Ford successes? The Mustang ('nuff said about that one). The four-passenger Thunderbird, which single-handedly created the personal luxury segment (Riviera, Toronado, Eldorado, et al). There was new idea after new idea on the full-sized Ford range (the longer wheelbased top-line Fairlane 500 in 1957, the Thunderbird-roofed Galaxie 500 in 1959, and the luxurious LTD in 1965). Then there's the compact Falcon, which far outsold the complex Corvair and the unusually styled Chrysler Valiant. And how about the 1960s and 1970s Ford Econoline, which was the most innovative and functional interpretation of the compact pickup/van through each succeeding generation, ultimately leading to Ford's dominant position in the commercial van business during the last three decades. Each of these product innovations forced competitive responses, generated untold profits for the company, and enhanced Ford's "Better Ideas" market positioning in the 1960s and 1970s.

Fairlane GT/Torino Sport/Torino Cobra/Gran Torino Sports: Ford's Midsized Muscle

There's one more Ford innovation I failed to mention, and it's one that helped lead directly to the entire supercar movement. In 1962, Ford introduced the new-sized Fairlane.

Dimensioned approximately equidistant between the compact Falcon and full-sized Galaxie, the Fairlane (and its Mercury sister, the Meteor) were unmatched in the marketplace for two full years before General Motors responded with its all-new intermediate-sized Chevelle, LeMans, F-85, and Special. We know where those led, right? Some might say that the downsized Plymouth Fury and Dodge Dart for 1962 were competitors for the new Fairlane, but these Mopar twins were marketed as full-sized cars (not intermediates) and they were larger in key dimensions. Likewise, those suggesting that the Rambler Classic was an intermediate should compare key dimensions to the Fairlane. The Classic was 7 inches shorter with a 7-inch shorter wheelbase to start; the wheelbase was even shorter than the compact Falcon.

During 1962 and 1963, the new Fairlane sold in large numbers and built a strong sales tailwind before the Chevelle finally surpassed it several years later. Later, the 1972 Ford intermediate entry buried the Chevelle with a nearly 100,000-unit sales victory that model year. Sounds like just one more winning Ford product innovation.

While the Fairlane was a winner in the sales charts, and to

The extensive annual kit coverage of 1960s and early 1970s Ford Motor Company's intermediate products is conveyed by this photo of AMT and MPC offerings back then. Later additions from JoHan, Monogram, and Revell added to the breadth of kit choices for Ford and Mercury modelers.

some degree a winner on the racetracks as well, it was somewhat less successful as a winner on the Woodward Avenues of America. It certainly started out on the right track, with the addition of a two-door hardtop in 1963 and the introduction of the Hi-Po 289-ci, 271-hp small-block V-8 in 1963½. For 1964, it looked pretty good too, at least at the drag strips around the country, considering the limited-run Thunderbolt 427 factory racers.

As you know all too well, Pontiac changed the rules of the game in 1964 with the GTO, and the very limited runs of 1966 and 1967 427 Fairlanes just didn't have much of a visible impact in the local street wars. Arguably it wasn't really until the 1968½ introduction of the 428 Cobra Jet that the Fairlane asserted the same street performance potential in the supercar world that the mainstream Fairlane had already achieved in the overall intermediate marketplace.

A quick scan of the annual kits offered during the 1960s would show that the Ford brand had more complete uninterrupted model kit coverage of almost all of its varied product lines than any other brand including Chevrolet. This certainly held true for the Ford's intermediates. While there were gaps in annual kit coverage of almost all of the other supercars of the era (the GTO and Charger excepted), every single model year of Ford's intermediate carline occupied the kit display shelves of hobby and department stores back then. More recent kit introductions have furthered that coverage. But the story of kits of the Mercury Comet/Cyclone/Montego GT is somewhat less complete, as you shall see.

The first three years of the Fairlane are covered by these AMT kits: a 1962 Fairlane two-door sedan (top), a 1963 Fairlane 500 hardtop, and a 1964 Fairlane hardtop (all: Wave 1/**). The 1964 kit added building options of a non-stock dual-quad 427 FE Wedge engine option, and a Barracuda-like glass fastback roof.

1963–1965 Fairlane: The First Intermediate, but Not the First Supercar

Ford's intermediate Fairlane debuted for the 1962 model year, but the idea of street performance didn't really materialize until the spring of 1963 when the Fairlane hosted the debut of Ford's now legendary, high-winding K-Code small-block V-8.

The 1964 Fairlane provided a major update to the exterior sheet metal, including a plated, angled pseudo air intake on the rear-quarters beneath the quarter-windows. But while the 389-ci engine resided in the GTO at the Pontiac showroom of your local auto row, the Fairlane engine compartment and front-suspension design restricted the engine offerings to small-block V-8s. Even though the extremely limited-run 427-powered 1964 Thunderbolt carried Fairlane's honor to the dragstrip, there was no commensurate showroom product.

For 1965, the Fairlane received new exterior sheet metal for the second year in a row, but the design was complex and did little to appeal to most of the youth-minded buyers on the prowl for new cars that year. In addition, the engine compartment restrictions continued another model year.

AMT annual kits were offered for all four years of the first-generation Fairlane, and a much later addition from Revell filled an important gap. The growing influence of drag racing in the car culture is very evident in the evolution of box art in this four-year period.

While the 1962 to 1964 Fairlane annual kits were produced only for a few months during their current model year, the 1965 annual kit was later re-boxed and reissued in 1969. This tool was later irreparably altered into a Modified Stocker race car.

During the 1960s annual kit era, the 1964 Thunderbolt was one of the most interesting Fairlanes for model kit builders,

AMT's 1965 Fairlane annual kit (Wave 1/) was quite a value at a $1.50 retail price. It included two complete engines: a factory stock 289, and an optional 427 Wedge that carried over from the 1964 annual kit. The dual-scoop hood included underhood ducting, an unusual kit detail back then. A 1969 reissue in a bigger box (Wave 1/***) now retailed for $2.00.***

Revell's Thunderbolt kits were well-detailed representations of the real semi-factory drag racers, including an excellent 427 Wedge engine. A more recent issue (left) added some (but not all) of the parts needed to recreate a showroom stock Fairlane sedan.

yet it remained unavailable at the local hobby store. It wasn't until the early 1990s that the team at Revell decided to engineer a Thunderbolt-specific kit. Originally released in both Russ Davis Ford and Tasca Ford liveries, this kit has been reissued multiple times, including a recent version that added some non-Thunderbolt parts. This kit is rumored to have not sold all that well for Revell, but it certainly completes scale kit coverage of the most important Fairlanes.

The box art of AMT's 1966 (Wave 1/***) and 1967 (Wave 1/****) Fairlane GT annual kits showed the continued emphasis on drag-related accessories. The illustrations were intended to be a 1966 B/FX class competitor (Boss) and a 1967 A/XS entry (Desperado). The 1966 kit has never been reissued; the 1967 kit saw one reissue late in the year as part of a Color Me Series kit.

1966–1967 Fairlane GT and GT-A: How to Cook a Tiger?

One of the more memorable print ads of the 1966 model year showed the all-new Fairlane with a striped tiger tail being chomped by the hood of the Fairlane's engine compartment. Titled "How to Cook a Tiger," it wasn't subtle. Most car magazines of the era suggested that the GTO got the better of the new Fairlane rather than the other way around. Regardless, it certainly telegraphed Ford's ambition for its all-new intermediate entry.

The second-generation Fairlane was new from the ground up, sporting a vertical, Pontiac-like side sculpture kick-up ahead of the rear wheelwells, and a new chassis design that provided the engine compartment space for Ford's 390 FE V-8. There was also new nomenclature for a performance sub-series, the GT (or when equipped with Ford's SelectShift Automatic), the GT-A.

While there was some disappointment with the street performance of the 390 V-8 rated at 335 hp, a limited run of 427-powered Fairlane 500s produced for NHRA regulation upheld Ford's honor at the dragstrip. Both the 390 and limited production 427 returned for 1967 in a mildly updated Fairlane wearing a new front end and more extensive side ornamentation.

AMT again covered the 1966 and 1967 Fairlanes in the 3-in-1 annual kit catalogs. The underbody detail of these kits tended toward the simplified side, but the body contours were flawlessly produced in 1/25th scale in the 1966 kit. The 1967 kit, however, had a body that reportedly omitted the lower body crease that was present on the real car.

Moving on to the early 1990s, AMT-Ertl had enjoyed considerable success with its recent muscle car kit intros. (Among them a 1966 L-79 Nova SS, a 1968 Road Runner, and an 1969 Olds 442, all covered elsewhere in this book.) With annual kits of the 1966 Fairlane having become pricey and rare collectibles, the 1966 GT/GT-A was committed to new 1/25th-scale tooling

AMT-Ertl's early 1990s kits of the Fairlane GT/GT-A and Fairlane 427 (both: Wave 3/*) featured strikingly similar box art layouts. Look closely enough, and you'll see that the GT/GT-A boxtop buildup may have been based on the original 1966 AMT annual kit, while the 427 kit shows the actual greenhouse window errors of this modern kit series.

as a 1992 calendar year addition to AMT-Ertl's muscle car product catalog.

Like many Wave 3 kits, the underbody/interior/engine detailing was superb. In fact, the FE engine in this kit and its derivatives is among the best ever in this scale. But the body sculpture appeared slightly off, later traced by kit experts to too-small windshield and backlight openings caused by top window headers that were located too low on the "greenhouse." This kit was quickly followed in 1993 by a second version replicating the 427-powered 1966 Fairlane 500.

Monogram's 1/24th-scale 1969 Torino Talledega (Wave 3/*) was an all-new, from the ground up effort yielding a very authentic showroom stock replica. A reissue included a cardboard Diner diorama (Wave 3/*). AMT/Ertl's 1/25th-scale 1969 Talledega (Wave 1/*) was a less successful update of its original Torino annual kit, with an unrealistic add-on clip that glued to the stock front-end assembly.

1968–1969: A Magic Formula Cooks Up a Winner

The 1968 model year once again brought all-new sheet metal to the Fairlane. An additional fastback body style debuted, perhaps the most appealing execution of the entire genre of 1960s sloping rear rooflines. The new top-line Fairlane, with its return to horizontal quad headlamps and an overall handsome style, was called the Torino. The sport derivative now became the Torino GT.

Then at mid-year, Ford finally asserted the street authority to match its domination of the racetracks of the world with the introduction of the 428 FE Cobra Jet. Massively underrated at 335 gross horsepower (more likely a net hp figure parading as gross hp), the Torino was now equipped to go head-to-head with GM's and Mopar's most competitive supercars (except, perhaps, Chrysler's 426 Hemi if properly tuned).

The 1969 Torino GT sported a minor freshening with two new grilles replacing the 1968 design and three vertical hash marks on the C-pillar versus five on the year-earlier 1968 fastback, which was now called SportsRoof. The side stripes inspired by the Le Mans–winning Ford Mk IV gained a new layout as well, and the 428 Cobra Jet enjoyed better availability. A new Torino Cobra budget supercar version approximated a Ford response to Plymouth's Road Runner. Finally, a new 351 Windsor V-8 also debuted.

AMT's 1968 Torino GT kit (Wave 1/*) promoted street and drag versions, while its 1969 Torino GT annual kit (Wave 1/***) promoted stock, custom, drag, and NASCAR options. That NASCAR version was uncommonly complete, with a full roll cage, reinforced driver's seat, separate floorboard driveshaft tunnel, and differential oil cooler. The 1990 reissue of this tool (Wave 1/*; lower left) has minor tweaks to represent the Torino Cobra versus the original GT annual kit release.***

AMT's annual kit lineup followed Ford's lead, with annual kits of the 1968 Torino GT and the 1969 Torino. A kit of the 1968 Torino GT Indy Pace Car convertible augmented these, as did a notchback version of the 1969 Torino Cobra. Both were introduced at mid-year to give AMT a second crack at filling the retail distribution network with more kits. (The 1969 notchback kit was actually the 1968 convertible body carried over with a separate roof section; the convertible boot also remained in the kit.) Later, the fastback version of this tool was substantially altered to produce a Modified Stocker racing kit in 1972; in 1990 it was modified to a showroom stock version of a 1969 Torino Cobra.

One can't leave the 1969 model year

One can't leave the 1969 model year without mentioning the Torino Talladega. This snub-nosed racing homologation special debuted late in the model year, well after AMT had moved on to developing the 1970 annual kits. Accordingly, it's not surprising that there was no annual kit of this car at the time. By 1990, this omission became a business opportunity for the kitmakers, and Monogram stepped up with an all-new kit of a factory stock Talledega.

AMT-Ertl also decided it would be a good time to get its share of the Talladega kit sales potential, so it whipped up a not-very-well-done conversion for its 1969 Torino Cobra kit, which was also introduced in 1990. Unless you are a hard-core Ford kit collector, leave the AMT-Ertl version on the shelf and find one of the Revell/Monogram reissues.

1970–1971: All New, and under the Hood Too

As good as the 1968–1969 Torino was, the 1970 version was even more impressive. Yet another all-new body shell featured fresh styling, while the top-line Torino Brougham and GT could be ordered with a hidden headlamp grille treatment. Two killer new engines, the 335 series 351 Cleveland and the 385 series 429 Cobra Jet joined in, replacing the previous 428 Cobra Jet and (in some applications) the still-new 351 Windsor. Super Cobra Jet/Drag Pack and Ram Air upgrades brought some highly desirable kits to the street (and drag strips). Perhaps the only retrograde setup was the return to a more traditional mainstream instrument panel design versus the performance-influenced 1968–1969 execution. The 1971 Torino GT and Torino Cobra had minor detail and powertrain revisions but otherwise carried over intact.

AMT continued with full-detail annual kits of both the 1970 and 1971 Torino Cobra. The 1970 version also received the Motor City Stocker treatment via an unassembled promo-style kit. The 1971 kit was the last Fairlane/Torino to see a newly tooled kit from AMT, ending a 10-year streak of model maker consistency unrivaled by any other supercar-era nameplate. These last two model years of AMT kits also reflected the quickly changing product development landscape at the automakers, as the only powertrain included in these kits was the Boss 429 engine that was originally planned for Torino/Cobra series production, but later cancelled at the last moment by Ford Division.

Toward the end of the 1990s, the Revell-Monogram team debuted a new kit brand, Monogram Pro Modeler. Several highly detailed aircraft and car model kits eventually became available in this premium kit format. One of these was a 1970 Torino GT. A Revell-branded kit of the Torino Cobra followed. The GT kit featured the hidden headlamp grille and the integral hood scoop treatment, while the Cobra version included the exposed-headlamp grille, and the Shaker air intake/hood scoop treatment.

Most important, both kits included fully authentic 429 Cobra Jet engines, the first truly correct replicas of the 385-series engines (excepting, of course, the Boss 429) to ever appear in kit form. The GT is among the first 1/25th-scale kits to include

*This is the full detail version of AMT's 1970 Torino Cobra annual kit (Wave 1/***). While the only engine was the Boss 429 (cancelled for 1/1-scale series production after the kit was designed), it included well-developed factory stock and NASCAR racing versions. The racing interior was even more accurate than the previous AMT 1969 annual kit, and there were additional NASCAR chassis parts, too.*

These are the most detailed Ford supercar-era kits to ever see a hobby shop shelf and a kit collector's closet. The original Pro Modeler Torino GT and Revell Torino Cobra (both: Wave 3/) were introduced to the kit trade in 2000 and 2001. The Revell-branded Torino GT (Wave 3/*) is the one you want; it has important corrections that make a great kit even better.*

kit series were incorrect low-back bucket seatbacks and inaccurate shaping in the lower rear-quarter-panel areas. To Revell's everlasting appreciation among scale Ford fans, both of these inaccuracies have been corrected in the latest 2014 reissue of the Torino GT kit.

1972: The End Is Near

Many muscle car fans consider 1971 to be the end of the Ford supercar story, but hold on just a minute. A truly all-new Gran Torino debuted for 1972, and it was the most changed car in the entire history of Ford's intermediate offerings. With a body on frame design (just like GM's intermediates since 1964) replacing the previous unit body, it was a heavier car, designed for style and comfort. Facing off against GM's very long-in-the-tooth 1972 model year competitors, the new midsized Ford was a smash hit, selling nearly 500,000 units (an all-time Ford intermediate record) in a relatively subdued sales year for the auto industry.

The styling of the new car was highly engaging, perhaps the best ever for a Ford intermediate. The SportsRoof version was the pick of the very desirable litter. Most of the powertrain offerings that year were emasculated by the new emissions requirements and low-lead fuel capability, but there remained one version for the supercar fan to search out: the Gran Torino Sport with the Rallye Equipment Group and the 351 Cleveland 4-barrel V-8.

In the model car world, JoHan would replace AMT as the Ford intermediates' kitmaker, but it only offered a fully detailed stock-bodied 1972 Gran Torino body/grille/taillamp assembly in a NASCAR-style kit. It was released with AMT as well as JoHan branding. Later a JoHan unassembled promo, stock kit version was produced. To date, no one has stepped up with a full detail kit of the 1972 Gran Torino.

This JoHan kit is the one to find if you plan to build a showroom stock 1972 Gran Torino. As it is essentially an unassembled promotional, unfortunately it is missing an engine and detailed chassis.

The JoHan and AMT branded NASCAR-style kits on the left (both: Wave 1/**) include a fully factory correct, 1972 Gran Torino exterior casting complete with body side and greenhouse moldings, nameplates, as well as stock grilles and taillamps. By contrast, the MPC 1972 Gran Torino kit at right and the recent Model King reissue below (both: Wave 2/*) are fully correct NASCAR kits with (non-stock) streamlined body and grille components.

While the Gran Torino Sport and Rallye Equipment Group continued for 1973, the heavy-handed implementation of the new federal 5-mph bumper standard was so unattractive that I can't honestly call that even a borderline supercar. The reign of the Fairlane/Torino/Gran Torino as a car of interest to muscle car fans had finally ended.

As noted in Chapter 5, several supercar versions of Chevy's El Camino were honored with model car kits. For fans of Ford's car-pickup, replicas of the 1957 (Revell), 1959 (PMC), 1960 and 1961 (AMT), and 1965 (Trumpeter) have been produced. However, not even a single kit of any Ranchero from the supercar era has reached kit form.

Comet GT and GT-A/Cyclone/Montego GT: Mercury's Midsized Muscle

So far, I've only touched on Ford's intermediate offerings. During these same years, Mercury was also offering some of the industry's most compelling supercar offerings. Unlike the constant kit coverage that the Ford brand enjoyed, the Mercury kit range has been far more subdued.

1962–1963 Meteor: The Faintest Inklings of Performance

To set the stage for Mercury's intermediate range, I actually need to step back to 1960½ when the Comet debuted as a larger compact based on Ford Falcon mechanicals. While the Comet was sold from Mercury dealerships, it was actually designed to be the compact offering for the Edsel franchise. Conversely, Mercury's first smaller car offering was originally planned to be

AMT's annual kit lineups included the 1962 Mercury Meteor two-door sedan and the 1963 Meteor two-door hardtop (both: Wave 1/**). Having been derived from AMT's dealership promotionals tooling, these kits featured precise exterior accuracy combined with somewhat simplified interiors, engines, and chassis.

the intermediate-sized 1962 Meteor, a sister to the equally new 1962 Fairlane.

When the Comet transferred to the Mercury brand, the intermediate-sized Meteor did not represent enough of a step up from the premium compact Comet (which by 1962 was already a highly successful product) to be successfully sold side by side in the Mercury showroom. Therefore, while the intermediate Fairlane was a large hit right out of the gate, the intermediate Meteor languished in the market almost from the word go.

Nevertheless, the first inkling of a performance execution of small Mercury came with the mid-1963 addition of the now-famous 289-ci 271 hp V-8 to the new Meteor S-33 hardtop. AMT was the purveyor of 3-in-1 annual kits for both the 1962 and 1963 Mercury Meteor.

When the 1964 Mercury lineup debuted, the Meteor was gone, superseded by a slightly larger but still compact-class Mercury Comet. The 1965 Comet was the best interpretation yet for Mercury's small car, but it was evolving ever closer to an intermediate-sized car rather than a compact. (The Mercury Comet is covered in detail in Chapter 10).

AMT's annual kit of the 1966 Cyclone GT (Wave 1/***) was a superbly turned-out replica of the real car. By this time, the optional custom and drag versions of AMT's 3-in-1 annual kits included a number of engine, interior, chassis, and exterior parts to differentiate these building versions from the showroom stock offering.

1966–1967 Cyclone GT and GT-A: Premium Muscle under Development

Mercury followed Ford's lead with all-new bodies for the 1966 Comet and its Cyclone supercar derivative. Mercury's smaller car was now a fully fledged intermediate instead of the previous sizing that bridged the gap between compact and intermediate market segments. The styling shared front doors and the greenhouse with the Fairlane, but otherwise incorporated its own sinewy rear-quarter-panel execution and a distinctive front theme featuring dual horizontal grille openings (and matching dual hood scoops for the Cyclone). The 1967 update featured the normal year-to-year variations. Cyclone powertrain availability for both years matched the Fairlane GT/GT-A.

AMT returned with annual kits of the 1966 and 1967 Cyclone. Drag racing once again figured prominently in the kit content, with fully developed competition-themed offerings among the 3-in-1 kit building variations. After the 1967 annual kit run, the body tooling was heavily modified to resemble a

Comparing this 1993 kit introduction from AMT-Ertl (Wave 3/*) with the original 1960s AMT Comet kits, the new kit has far more detail in the engine, interior, and chassis areas, but lacks some of the crispness and fine detailing of the exterior components in the original annual kits.

kit run, the body tooling was heavily modified to resemble a shortened-wheelbase A/FX-style drag racer. This explains why builders never saw a reissue of either the 1966 or 1967 Cyclone annual kits.

In the mid-1990s AMT-Ertl developed a third version of its new 1966 Fairlane GT/GTA and Fairlane 500 427 tooling, replicating the 1967 Cyclone. This new kit shared the excellent underbody content of its sister kits, but again the body was flawed, this time by side to side variations in the complex contours of the Cyclone rear quarter-panels. Specifically, there was an added (and incorrect) ridge engraved along the upper beltline reveal of the passenger's side. The greenhouse/upper windshield and backlight header issues of the Fairlane kits were mostly, though not completely resolved. These relatively minor issues only slightly detract from an otherwise enjoyable building experience.

1968–1969 Cyclone: Present and Accounted For, Except Where Are the Kits?

Mercury once again benefitted from the aggressive 1968 Fairlane/Torino product program, sharing the swoopy fastback profile and the new mid-year Cobra Jet powertrain introduction. The upper series Mercury intermediates wore Montego MX nomenclature, while the Cyclone branding remained for the sports series. As attractive as the Fairlane/Torino was, many enthusiasts thought the Cyclone was an even more compelling design achievement, and it enjoyed considerable success as a NASCAR racer as well.

Minor changes for 1969 were the addition of the Cyclone CJ, Mercury's response to the Road Runner budget supercar. At mid-year came several special editions wearing Spoiler identification, of which one was a Mercury fraternal twin to the limited production Torino Talledega.

Amazingly, no 1/24th-1/25th–scale kits have ever been made of the showroom stock 1968–1969 Cyclone. This omission represents a huge hole in the world of model muscle kits; it's one that will, I hope, be rectified in future years.

1970–1971 Cyclone, Cyclone GT, and Cyclone Spoiler: Streep Scene

For makers of supercars, the 1970 model year represented a culmination of what was learned during the previous six model years. Mercury's response was among the most aggressive that took place that year.

All-new bodies delivered more Mercury differentiation than ever versus the Ford Torino. This new sheet metal even included different front doors this time. Three distinct product offerings, the budget Cyclone, upscale Cyclone GT, and the Cyclone Spoiler (essentially, Mercury's response to the GTO Judge) were powered by the new 385 Series 429 Cobra Jet and Super Cobra Jet V-8s. Hidden headlamps alongside a "gunsight" center grille insert topped the GT and Spoiler models. Unlike the Torino, the Montego and Cyclone featured a single two-door hardtop roofline that was slightly more practical, though nearly as visually distinctive as the Torino's fastback SportsRoof. Finally, an umbrella marketing/merchandising theme played off a contraction of the words *street* and *strip*: Mercury's Streep Scene. On paper, Mercury's 1970 supercar lineup looked like a winner, but the rapid disintegration of the muscle car marketplace that year had other plans.

Sensing the commercial potential of this killer 1970 product line, MPC stepped up to break the long string of previous AMT-based Mercury Comet/Cyclone kits with its own 1/25th-scale annual kits of the 1970 and 1971 Cyclone Spoiler. Just as with the AMT-based Torino kits those years, these MPC Cyclone kits featured the Boss 429 engine underhood. This reflected Mercury's very late decision to cancel this powertrain offering, which occurred well after the tooling for the new kits was reaching completion.

After the 1971 annual kit run, MPC's Cyclone body was modified in a number of ways to produce a NASCAR-themed kit, and that version has seen sporadic reissues in later years. It would be difficult to convert back to a factory stock replica, once again highlighting a market opportunity for an all-new Cyclone kit to enter the market. We'd love to see Revell take this on as a spinoff of its already-existing Pro Modeler Torino tooling.

For the first time, annual kits of Mercury's midsized 1970 (Wave 1/*) and 1971 (Wave 1/***) Cyclone came from MPC instead of AMT. These two kits were essentially identical to each other except for the box art, decal sheets, and the 1971 kit's omission of a small fret of thermoplastic parts for the racing version. Only the 1970 version had the factory "Spoiler" side graphics on the decal sheet.***

I haven't shown NASCAR-only kits in this book, but in this case, the Model King private label reissue of the MPC Cyclone NASCAR kit added a large decal that included factory-stock 1970 and 1971 Spoiler side graphic stripes in both white and black. These could be a key for someone trying to complete a showroom Cyclone Spoiler replica, particularly the 1971 version.

1972: A Fresh Direction

The all-new Mercury Montego was a huge step away from the supercar influenced 1970–1971 product program, but it was also perfectly timed for an automotive marketplace moving away in droves from performance cars. Yet, if you looked beyond the handsome new body, particularly the return of a fastback-roofed two-door option that added tasteful simulated vertical louvers on the rear quarter-panels, there was a pretty attractive option for the few supercar buyers that remained.

It was called the Montego GT, equipped with the 351 Cobra Jet engine and Cyclone Performance Package. Perfectly bridging the gap between pure muscle cars and the evolving market trend to luxury intermediates, such a car in 1972 Mercury Code 2B Bright Red was a real looker and well-rounded performer. Sadly, a year later most of this good was overwhelmingly negated by the 1973 Montego's blocky 5-mph bumper solution.

Equally sad is that there has never been a 1/25th-scale kit of the 1972 Mercury Montego GT.

Epilogue

Thanks to AMT's close relationship with Ford and Mercury during the 1960s, almost all the key Ford supercars, and some of the Mercury offerings as well, have found their way into 1/24th-1/25th–scale kits at some point. Still, key gaps including performance versions of the Ranchero, the 1968–1969 Cyclone, and the 1972 Torino GT/Montego GT are future opportunities for ambitious current and future model car kitmakers.

Missing in Action

Rancheros and Montegos yet to appear in a 1/24-1/25th–scale kit

- 1968–1969 Cyclone and 1969 CJ/Spoiler/Spoiler II
- 1969–1971 Torino GT convertible with 428 Cobra Jet Ram Air V-8
- 1967–1971 Ranchero GT
- 1972 Montego GT Fastback with 351 Cobra Jet V-8 and Cyclone Performance Package

Fairlanes, Torinos, and Cyclones that need a new or modern kit offering

- 1967 Fairlane GT/GTA
- 1968 Torino GT fastback and convertible with 428 Cobra Jet Ram Air V-8
- 1971 Torino Cobra
- 1970–1971 Cyclone, Cyclone GT, and Spoiler with 429 Super Cobra Jet V-8
- 1972 Gran Torino Sport SportsRoof with 351 4V and Rallye Equipment Group

and models are by the writer unless noted otherwise.)

This dual-quad FE 427–powered Fairlane was built from a Holthaus resin copy of the body from AMT's 1967 annual kit. This super-detailed model even includes scale drag strip timing slips in the glove box! (Builder: Nick Zuk)

Early Ford intermediates were attractive cars (and fast too, if powered by the K-Code 289 V-8), but they did not have an aggressive muscle car appearance. These are AMT's 1962 and 1965 Fairlane 500s. (Builder: Dean Milano)

AMT's 1970 Torino Cobra annual kit was the basis of this model, but the builder modified it to replicate top Torino GT trim level. It wears 1970 Ford Code F Medium Blue Metallic. (Builder: Larry Zobeck)

Revell's 1964 Thunderbolt kit was used to build a 1990s-style street machine (note the paint colors and wheels) conversion of a Fairlane 500 hardtop.

This photo clearly shows the stunning evolution of Mercury's intermediate-sized products throughout a seven-year period. These models were built from the AMT 1963 Meteor and MPC 1970 Cyclone Spoiler annual kits. (Builder: Dean Milano)

It's All about the Packaging

Chapter 7

Chrysler and AMC Supercar Intermediates

"Just what is a GTX, anyway? I'll begin by telling you what it isn't, namely another run of the mill supercar, or by any other name, an intermediate with a big engine." Take that, GTO! This excerpt from a 1967 Plymouth GTX two-page magazine advertising spread nicely sums up Mother Mopar's philosophy for engineering its entries during the muscle car era.

However, our friends at Chrysler Corporation were about to learn a lesson. It wasn't just the *equipment* that it packaged in the muscle cars, but also the *way* the equipment was *packaged* (or *merchandised*) in the marketplace. The GTO's standard equipment list was sometimes missing a few of the essentials for a truly complete, well-rounded muscle car. Nevertheless, the merchandising approach and resulting sales for the GTO left Chrysler's early supercar entries behind.

That is, until Chrysler finally figured out that the broader definition of "packaging" meant not only fully equipped cars but also truly adventurous styling (hello, 1968 Charger). It also included innovative merchandising strategies such as the Warner Brothers Road Runner tie-in for its new budget supercar, the Scat Pack and Rapid Transit System families, the Six Pak 440 6-barrel, Air Grabber and Shaker hood intakes, High Impact paint colors, and more.

In retrospect, the story of the Mopar B-Body in the supercar era started slowly, but you could probably argue that these cars moved to the top of the pack during the very end of the 1960s through the early 1970s. Fortunately for model car builders and kit collectors, the very rich history of Dodge and Plymouth during this period is reflected in the many model kits available for collecting and building.

One final note: With Chrysler's acquisition of AMC-Jeep in the late 1980s, it has become customary to include AMC muscle era cars under the Chrysler banner. I will do that here for the model kit coverage as well.

1964: Can You Say "Max Wedge"?

We'll start our coverage of Mopar's muscle car model kits with the 1964 B-Body entries, as this was the first year in which you could actually buy a well-detailed model kit of the Plymouth Fury and Dodge Polara. (While JoHan and Revell both offered 1962 Fury and Dart B-Body kits, and JoHan marketed 1963 kits of the same cars, these were not the high-performance Max Wedge versions, and were very basic in kit content. You can see more on them in Chapter 3).

For 1964, Dodge and Plymouth continued their march back toward more mainstream and appealing styling. Accordingly, JoHan's 1963 model year B-Body exterior and interior molds were updated to the design of the 1964 Mopar B-Bodies, and were offered in both two-door hardtop and convertible versions. But the real highlight was the highly detailed 426 Max Wedge engine now under the hood of these new kits, replacing a very basic and generic Mopar big-block engine in the preceding 1962 and 1963 "annual" kits. The now-familiar Max Wedge cross ram intake with dual 4-barrels offered the builder a choice of plated air cleaners or the factory-style open air-intake ducts. Likewise, builders could choose between the factory installed "up and over" exhaust manifolds or plated headers with individual tubes. The finishing touch? The factory-correct valve cover graphics on the kits' decal sheets!

The chassis, carried over as a simplified casting shared with the promotional toys from the JoHan catalog, still comprised a single part

Just as Chrysler Corporation learned to merchandise its intermediate-sized muscle cars more effectively during the late 1960s and early 1970s, kit-maker MPC also refined its box art and kit contents strategy during those years. Here, the complete catalog of MPC Dodge Charger annual kits for the muscle car years.

*JoHan's 1964 Fury and Polara kits (Wave 1/****) brought a new level of realism to factory stock 1/25th-scale replica kits. Of note is that JoHan included the bucket seat/console setups of the 1/1-top range Sport Fury and Polara 500, even though the exteriors replicated the mainstream Fury and Polara models. Both hardtop and convertible kits were offered.*

*JoHan's 1964 Fury and Polara kits were reissued multiple times during the next three decades (Wave 2/**), but never in a completely factory stock form. First, they were updated with 426 Hemi engines, and then released with a Logghe-style funny car chassis added (center), and then finally in just the NASCAR (Fury) and Super Stock (Polara) versions shown here. Stock exterior trim was unrealistically altered, plus the molding quality suffered as the molds aged.*

except for the ride adjustment "lowering blocks." These JoHan kits also included extra parts for Super Stock Drag, Custom, and Late Model Stock Racer building versions.

At the end of the 1964 model year, Dodge's 1965 promotional toys contract went to a new, third Detroit-based model company by the name of MPC, while the Plymouth 1965 promos contract stayed with JoHan but graduated to the all-new full-sized C-Body Sport Fury. The result was that the JoHan 1964 Plymouth and Dodge B-Body tools were retained and modified, rather than updated, for the 1965 models, and they've seen as many as six subsequent releases during the following decades. None of these versions, however, allowed the building of a factory stock model.

Some three decades later, a newly invigorated Lindberg Models surprised the model car hobby with a series of all new, very well detailed 1/25th-scale model kits. Behind these new models was the skill and merchandising talent of one George Toteff, a key AMT executive during the formative years of that company, who left its employ in 1964 and set up rival model maker MPC in the northeastern Detroit suburbs. Among his first Lindberg offerings were 1964-vintage Plymouth and Dodge B-Body kits, proving that Mr. Toteff could still box miniature automotive magic. While various drag racing versions launched first, the most relevant kits here are the Plymouth Belvedere (mid-series)

The late 1990s saw all-new factory-stock kits of the 1964 Plymouth Belvedere and the Dodge 330 (both: Wave 3/). These Lindberg kits replicated different series/trim levels than the original Johan 1964 kits, and they included new engine options: the most highly detailed Slant Six found in a model kit, and a stalwart 383 4-barrel. Recent reissues are shown at the bottom.*

two-door hardtop and Dodge 330 (low series) two-door sedan (post) kits. While these kits built only a single, factory stock replica (unlike the four building options in the original JoHan kits), the level of interior and chassis detail far exceeded any Mopar kit originally tooled in the 1960s.

1965: The Hemi, and the Intermediate Cars

Fans of the 1965 intermediate-sized Chrysler B-Bodies encountered a much different model-building situation depending on their brand loyalty. A spectacular kit of the Dodge Coronet 500 debuted under the AMT label, but it was not actually an AMT kit. Fans of the Belvedere would have to wait an entire half-century later to build a 1/25th-scale replica of their favorite Mopar B-Body.

When George Toteff established his new company MPC, an agreement was negotiated wherein AMT would get first "dibs" on the first production run of five new kits engineered and manufactured by MPC. Among these kits was the 1965 Dodge Coronet 500. Any modeler who was familiar with AMT kits immediately noticed the unusual box art theme, and buyers of the kit couldn't miss the simplistic line-drawing assembly sheet (compared to those "work of art" instruction sheets originating from AMT's Art Department).

Model manufacturer origins aside, the kit inside the box built (mostly) factory stock, drag, and custom versions. The kit was also among the first to include a 1/25th-scale second-generation Mopar Hemi engine. That engine (the only choice in the kit) appeared to replicate Mopar's A864 Hemi with its offset dual 4-barrel intake, while the individual tube headers were obviously non-stock. Beyond the Super Stock drag version, parts for a match race–style 6-71 blower were also in the box.

*This AMT 1965 Dodge Coronet 500 (Wave 1/*****) stands among the most desirable of all Mopar muscle kits. When first introduced, many modelers couldn't understand why the kit included a single exhaust and muffler option to go with the standard dual exhaust setup, but now it is recognized that some features of this kit came straight from the WO51/A990 Coronet factory drag racing parts bin.*

Polar Lights's new 1965 Dodge Coronet 500 kits (Wave 3/) came with pre-painted bodies that were showcased in a clear box art window. The somewhat simplistic kit design and a few questionable body details limited their appeal for serious adult model builders and collectors.*

Red and White Ramchargers livery dominated the decal sheet.

In the early 2000s, Polar Lights engineered an all-new kit of the 1965 Coronet 500, and merchandised it in both hardtop and convertible versions. These kits were actually fully detailed even though they featured mostly snap-together assembly, and featured the factory optional 365 hp 426 Street Wedge engine. The body itself failed to capture the gently sweeping front-to-rear body swage line (instead, it sagged across the middle of the body), and the result has never appeared exactly right to my eye.

For all those 1965 Plymouth B-Body fans, it took exactly 50 years, but finally in 2015 Moebius Models introduced a factory-stock 1965 Satellite two-door hardtop, followed a year later by a mostly stock 1965 Belvedere two-door (post) sedan, set up as a current street warrior. The Satellite kit includes the 365-hp 426 Street Wedge, while the Belvedere features a non-stock, 1964-ish 426 Max Wedge engine. I expect to see more mid-1960s B-Bodies from Moebius that are derived from the basics of this kit tool.

Moebius's new 1965 Satellite and Belvedere kits (Wave 4/) reflect the latest thinking in kit design and detail; they build into excellent scale replicas. The innovative thinking behind these kits extends to the highly informative, full-color assembly instruction sheets.*

1966–1967: Power to the People

A landmark year in the history of Mopar B-Bodies was, of course, 1966. Beyond the introduction of the famous 426 Street Hemi, Dodge added the Charger to its lineup at the 1966-¼ model year. MPC's Coronet 500 tool (the one that was sold under the AMT label for 1965 but manufactured by MPC) returned for 1966, this time with MPC branding. In place of the Coronet body and interior was the stunning new fastback Charger exterior and its four-bucket-seat interior. Some of the WO51 parts were gone too, but the A990-style A864 Hemi engine persisted in place of what should have been the dual inline carb/intake Street Hemi setup. MPC then updated the Charger to the 1967 version with the same minor exterior and interior changes found on the 1/1-scale versions.

In what is clearly the all-time most troublesome omission in kit coverage of the entire Mopar B-Body era, to date there never has been a kit of the 1966 Plymouth Belvedere/Satellite or the 1966 Dodge Coronet. This gap remains a real business opportunity for the model companies targeting today's adult model car builder and collector.

In the mid-1990s, Revell/Monogram engineered a new Mopar B-Body tool that yielded the 1967 GTX, R/T, and (later on) Charger models shown here (Wave 3/). Baby boomer modelers who intimately remember the original cars have criticized some of the body details of the GTX and R/T kits, along with the omission of the Dana rear axle that should have accompanied the 4-speed/Hemi powertrains depicted in all three kits.*

Moving onward, 1967 was another watershed year in the development of the Mopar B-Body muscle car legacy. Finally, both Plymouth and Dodge brought to market new cars that packaged a more appealing exterior and interior appearance along with carryover high-performance chassis parts while adding a new engine derivative (the 440 Commando/Magnum) and catchy "GTX" and "R/T" nomenclature. The crisp Satellite and Coronet bodies looked a little boxy next to the swoopy GTO, but word on the street became "watch out" as Mopar's very capable factory muscle cars finally began to develop some credibility with the then–young adult car-buying market. Other than the MPC 1967 Charger kit, model car enthusiasts drew a blank on annual kits of the 1967 GTX and R/T, and would do so for nearly 30 years.

*MPC's 1966 and 1967 Charger annual kits (Wave 1/**** and Wave 1/***, respectively) featured the 426 Hemi and reflected the expected level of kit detail inside and under the hood. The 1967 version has been reissued multiple times, though never again in the entirely factory stock configuration of the original 1967 annual kit shown here.*

Finally, as part of its drive to expand its muscle car kit catalog, Revell-Monogram introduced factory stock replica kits of the Plymouth GTX in 1994 and the Dodge Coronet R/T in 1997. This time the 426 Street Hemi appeared in correct dual inline intake/carb configuration along with the cast factory stock exhaust manifolds. Revell added a third 1967 model year Mopar in 2000, a highly accurate 426 Charger kit. These three models have what is probably the most accurate 426 Street Hemi ever placed in a 1/25th-scale kit.

1968–1969: Finally, It All Comes Together

By the 1968 model year, Chrysler Corporation brought to market the results of hard-learned lessons of the previous four model years, particularly Pontiac's phenomenal marketing behind the GTO. The boys from Hamtramck were ready to get even in the muscle car marketplace, and get even they did!

*MPC's new 1968 Charger kit (Wave 1/***) was a smash hit in the hobby kit market, just like the real car was in the automotive marketplace that year. Note the evolution of MPC's box art theme that started in 1967 with the diagonally split background and the dynamic angle of the lead image that appeared to be jumping off the box top.*

*The 1968 Coronet R/T (Wave 1/****) depicted here was a combination of several merchandising themes. Note the standard R/T wheel covers and redline tires juxtaposed against a drag racing-themed bodyside livery and non-stock clear hood scoop covering a Hilborn-style fuel-injection system. The U-Haul-It trailer looked just like the 1/1-scale U-Haul trailers seen at the corner gas station back then.*

The stunning new Charger abandoned its fastback guise and replaced it with the freshly original "double diamond" body form, then added a deeply recessed rear window and a deeply inset wide front grille. It was a stunning surprise, best summed up by a great copy line from the 1968 Dodge muscle car brochure that said, "You wouldn't change a line of it even if you could."

The Dodge promotionals toy contract stayed with MPC for 1968, so the all-new Charger model kit once again appeared under the MPC name. It featured the 426 Street Hemi, along with the usual stock, custom, and race car building versions. (This basic tool would go on, in slightly altered from, to eventually become one of the very top selling model car kits of all time; more on that later.)

Nearly as shocking as the Charger was the shapely new 1968 Coronet, particularly so the R/T version with its "bumble-bee" rear stripe. Equally surprising was that MPC developed a new kit of the R/T, the first Coronet to appear in kit form since the AMT (really MPC) 1965 Coronet 500 kit. Under the scale hood resided a newly tooled 440 Magnum V-8. MPC was becoming a master of merchandising by this point, often adding extra parts and features to increase the appeal of its kits. This time, it was a "U-Haul-It" utility trailer that would reappear later in another MPC Mopar kit. At mid-year, MPC offered a special Coronet R/T convertible kit wearing Super Bee box top nomenclature, but as you know, Dodge's actual mid-year introduction of the real Super Bee was based on the lower-series Coronet 440, and there was no Super Bee convertible offered.

This brings me to the 1968 Plymouth GTX and Road Runner, wearing a shapely new body of its own. You now know that the Road Runner was a relatively late development in the 1968 Plymouth product development cycle, and neither it nor the GTX ever made it to a scale kit that year, continuing the famine of Plymouth B-Body annual kits that started 1965. Builders had to wait all the way to the late 1980s to see a 1968 Road Runner kit, the product of an AMT model product renaissance resulting

The 1/25th-scale kit coverage of the 1968 B-Body lineup was finally completed when AMT-Ertl added a 1968 Road Runner to its kit lineup in 1989 (Wave 3/). The original release is shown at the top left, while the latest Round 2 reissue at the right carries all-new box art cleverly designed to appear to be part of the original AMT 1968 annual kit lineup.*

These two views of the MPC 1969 Charger (Wave 1/**) show MPC's typical kit accessories, as when these kits were first built, most modelers constructed the models in non-stock forms. Build options such as the exhaust dumps, rear window louvers, clear hood with an opening for the "stacks," and a custom grille with operating hidden headlamps were important sales tools.

AMT-Ertl developed these tool extensions based on its 1968 Road Runner kit pictured earlier. The 1969 GTX convertible (Wave 3/*) debuted in 1990 and the hardtop (Wave 3/*) followed in 1993. These were well-detailed kits; with the convertible running a 426 Hemi and the hardtop featuring the 440 4-barrel.

from the acquisition of the AMT name and assets by the Ertl die-cast farm tractor toy empire. Like many other Wave 3 models, the new kit had outstanding interior, engine, and chassis detail, but the body proportions appeared just a little off from certain angles.

Moving on to the 1969 model year, MPC captured all the relatively minor updates of the 1/1-scale Dodge Charger and Coronet R/T. Once again, a Coronet R/T convertible kit was offered at midyear, hiding in factory stock form inside a box promoting the mildly customized *Mission Impossible* TV theme car.

Over at JoHan, which had exclusively featured kits of the new C-Body Plymouth Fury for 1965 through 1968 (see Chapter 11), the Plymouth Division promotional toys contract for 1969 switched over to the midsized Plymouth lineup. Finally, kits of the Plymouth B-Body (and not just one, but both the Road Runner and GTX) found their way to the hobby shop shelves! True to JoHan's heritage, the bodies on both these kits were spot-on, and though the chassis lacked the detail of more recent kits, many Mopar purists prefer these instead of the AMT-Ertl kits also discussed here. The Road Runner version was reissued multiple times during the next two decades, although the later reissues suffered as the JoHan tools grew old and lacked adequate preventive maintenance. Meanwhile, the aforementioned AMT-Ertl Plymouth B-Body tool from the late 1980s was soon expanded to include both a 1969 GTX hardtop and convertible kit.

Continuing with the 1969 model year Mopars, in the late 1990s, Revell-Monogram launched a new series of premium aircraft and car kits under the Pro Modeler trade name. These kits featured new levels of detail (such as the structural car body framing between the interior and luggage compartments), instruction sheets with actual photography of the model under assembly, and a level of extra parts unseen in newly developed kits during the previous two decades.

Part of the Pro Modeler car catalog was an all-new 1969 Charger R/T kit. Shortly after it appeared on the market, widely heard

JoHan's new 1969 Road Runner kit (Wave 1/**) featured box art pulled straight from Plymouth's advertising and merchandising materials (collectors of vintage model cars and box art often encounter handwritten box top messages such as that seen here). The reissues (below and right) retained the original release's Petty NASCAR version parts and the custom version inspired by the Chuck Miller-built Probe show car. Of course, Richard Petty actually drove a Ford Torino during the 1969 NASCAR season.

Revell's original Pro Modeler 1969 Charger R/T (Wave 3/) shown in its 1997 release here, has seen multiple reissues since. It was eventually modified into the 1968 version (Wave 3/*) also shown here. These kits combine accurate body proportions with outstanding underbody, engine compartment, and interior detail.*

comments questioned the accuracy of the body shape. To Revell-Monogram's credit, it quickly decided that the body had to be corrected and that the decal sheet needed corrections as well. Buyers of the initial release were soon provided with replacements for both parts. The kit is considered to be one of the best detailed of all the 1968–1970 Mopar B-Body kits out there. It also fathered several 1968 Charger R/T kit versions in later years.

1970: Biding Time or Not?

By the 1970 model year, reportedly one out of every five Dodge cars sold was a member of the Dodge Scat Pack, which that year included the Dart Swinger 340, Charger/Challenger/Coronet R/T's, the Super Bee, and the Challenger T/A. Nevertheless, the Mopar B-Bodies were in their third year and starting to look a little dated (a consequence of Chrysler's late decision to postpone its next-generation B-Body range to the 1971 model year). You'd never know it from the scale kit offerings from MPC (Dodge Charger R/T, plus for the first time, the Coronet Super Bee) and JoHan (GTX and Road Runner).

As part of Monogram's new focus on developing muscle era kits, Monogram introduced a somewhat simplified 1/24th-scale 1970 GTX kit in 1986. This kit tool later spawned a 1970 Road Runner kit, first appearing in 2000.

A few years later, AMT-Ertl took the body and interior from the 1970 Coronet Super Bee annual kit and combined it with the engine and chassis from its late 1980s tooled 1968–1969 Plymouth B-Body kits. This was a challenging approach, as it combined kit engineering Wave 1 body and interior components with Wave 3 engine and chassis parts. Builders were instructed to make their own modifications to parts in order for everything to fit together.

As this book is being written, Revell has just introduced an all-new kit of the factory stock 1970 Charger R/T kit. While

*MPC's 1970 Charger (Wave 1/****) box art lost none of the excitement of previous annual kit releases, but showed an evolution of its annual box art graphic layout. The triangular background split was now implied with the background, while the positioning of the car jumping off the box was more prominent than ever.*

*JoHan's 1970 Road Runner (Wave 1/****) featured box art derived from Plymouth's Rapid Transit System marketing efforts. Like the JoHan's 1969 Road Runner kit, this one featured NASCAR-themed and "Probe"-themed custom versions, but unlike the 1969 kit, the 1970 kit was never reissued, making it a highly valued collectible today.*

Monogram's 1970 Plymouth GTX (Wave 2/**) box top depicted a period-correct street machine version, but the kit also included parts for a factory-stock GTX as seen in the cut-in image at the lower right. This tool eventually evolved into a 1970 Road Runner kit (Wave 2/*). Monogram's Wave 2 muscle car kits were produced in 1/24th scale, yielding a fractionally larger replica versus the more popular 1/25th scale.

this kit is produced from all-new tooling, builders will see a clear design lineage with the earlier Pro Modeler 1969 Charger kit. An all-new kit of the 1970 Charger (along with a new 1968 Coronet R/T kit) has been at the top of Mopar modelers' wish lists for several years, so this new introduction should be very well received.

1969½–1970½: The Specials

As the 1960s muscle car hit its peak, mid-model year introductions reflecting the latest advancements became common at the local Mopar dealerships. First out of the gate was the Charger 500, with a flush mounted rear window, streamlined moldings at the A-pillar, and a flush grille derived from the 1968 Coronet, all in the interest of achieving a more streamlined appearance for the race car versions that competed at high-speed NASCAR racetracks. Surprisingly, only one kit of the Charger 500 has ever been available. This kit was derived from the original MPC 1968–1970 Charger tool, along with its later modifications, first as the race track version of the Daytona and then as the Dukes of Hazzard kit, which retained the retooled flush rear window. This Charger 500 kit, introduced by AMT-Ertl in 1987 but merchandised under the MPC brand, is a passable replica but lacks the detail of modern tooled kits.

A couple of months later, Mopar rocked the streets of America with its factory code A12 Road Runner and Super Bee specials running beefed-up 440 Wedges with a three–2-barrel

AMT-Ertl's 1970 Coronet Super Bee (Waves 1 and 3/*) is shown here in its 1993 release, along with the most recent version at the bottom (this version features box art inspired by the original 1970 annual kit release). Note that these kits feature the optional code N96 factory "Ramcharger" dual fresh air scoop hoods, versus the "pitchfork" faux hood scoop included in the original MPC 1970 Super Bee annual kit.

The 1980s brought us replicas of the Dodge Super Bee Six Pack (Wave 2/*) and the Charger 500 (Wave 1/*). The original releases are shown on top with examples of some of the reissues of these kits on the bottom.

carb setup, a radical lift-off fiberglass hood, and 15-inch blackwall tires on steel wheels with no hub caps. No kit of the Road Runner 440 6-barrel version has been produced, although the Super Bee Six Pack was the subject of a 1/24th-scale Monogram kit tooled in 1983. The kit contains an accurate engine, graphics, and ornamentation offset by a fairly basic chassis and suspension detail. Unlike some other Monogram kits developed during this Wave 2 era of model car kit engineering, the body proportions here are spot-on.

At the very end of the 1969 model year, Dodge introduced the Charger Daytona. It took the Charger 500 body and added a wedge-shaped front end to the upcoming 1970 Charger front fenders and hood, along with fender-top vents and a wild rear spoiler designed to clear an opened trunk.

JoHan's SuperBird kit (Wave 1/**) was introduced soon after the run of regular 1970 Road Runner and GTX kits had concluded. The original kit release is on top, while the 1979 reissue is at lower right. In 1987, Monogram introduced its 1/24th-scale SuperBird (Wave 2/*) with a more accurate body portrayal of the real car.

Meanwhile in the 1/25th-scale world, at the end of the 1970 model kit run, MPC modified its Charger tool to replicate the racetrack version of the Daytona, but the kit did not readily produce a replica of the street car. AMT-Ertl later developed a half-hearted showroom stock Daytona kit in 1990, which was basically the aforementioned Charger 500 kit with a new and poorly fitting front cap. (This kit is best avoided by all but the most avid kit collector.)

This shows one of the worst, as well as probably the single best, examples of late 1960s B-Body model car kits. The parts in AMT-Ertl Daytona Charger (Wave 1/*) on top were incapable of delivering a model with an appearance even close to that of the box art illustration. Conversely, the Revell-Monogram Pro Modeler Daytona is a superb example of the model-making art.

Modelers had to wait until 1998 to get a fully accurate version of the factory-produced street Daytona. Revell-Monogram came to the rescue with a derivative of its recently introduced Pro Modeler Charger R/T kit. This one was spot-on in all details, and is probably the single very best kit replica ever produced of the 1968–1970 Charger generation.

The last of the B-Body specials debuted late in the fall of 1969, when Plymouth introduced its version of the Daytona. Based on the 1970 Road Runner with a modified 1970 Dodge Super Bee front clip and different versions of a streamlined wedge front cap and sky-high rear spoiler, the SuperBird was completed with a modified rear window and slight tulip panel changes (partially hidden under a standard vinyl top). JoHan was first to the market with a scale SuperBird, modifying its 1970 Road Runner/GTX body tool to replicate the SuperBird changes, and achieving a mostly correct overall shape but omitting the finer details of the factory modification (including the vinyl roof engraving and tulip panel mods). In 1987, Monogram developed a SuperBird derivative of its earlier 1/24th-scale 1970 GTX kit, which included the correct tulip panel/vinyl roof details.

1970: Meanwhile, across Town at AMC . . .

The factory team at American Motors played a small but important role in the muscle car wars just before and after the turn of the decade. (You'll find more extensive coverage of AMC's muscle cars in Chapters 9, 10, 12, and 13.) The 1970

JoHan's AMC Machine kit was reissued in later years in box art that appears here (Wave 1/**). The original annual kit version (Wave 1/) featured a wild, Plymouth-like cartoonish image on the box top (reprised here on the box art of the side panel), and it included additional funny car and Super Stock drag racing versions (versus the factory stock-only parts in the reissue version shown here).***

MPC's 1971 Road Runner (Wave 1/) and GTX (Wave 1/****) kits shared most of their contents. The GTX kit included the standard hood (versus the Air Grabber hood in the Road Runner) and GTX factory graphics. The phantom SuperBird version on the left shows unmistakable similarities to photos of factory aero studies for a second-generation SuperBird that never actually entered production.***

AMC Rebel lineup featured what was perhaps the purest competitive copy of the Road Runner's roots yet. American Motors called it the Machine. It was a budget muscle car that had nearly everything the original 1968 Road Runner had, other than the wily cartoon character and the "beep-beep" horn.

From its years as the Rambler Classic to the then-current AMC Rebel nomenclature, JoHan included AMC's intermediate-class offering in its annual model kit lineup. It was pretty easy for JoHan to update the 1969 Rebel hardtop kit to replicate the new 1970 Machine. Unfortunately, the kit carried over some major inaccuracies in the engine compartment (JoHan made minor changes to the previous-generation V-8 in its AMC kits rather than replacing it with an accurate replica of the new 360/390/401 engine family), and as the kit was later reissued, quality lapses such as misaligned silk screening on the decal sheet made it difficult to build an accurate scale replica.

1971 and 1972: The Best of Times, the Worst of Times

When the all-new 1971 Dodge and Plymouth intermediates were under development in 1968 and 1969, Chrysler's product planners expected the muscle car marketplace to continue the explosive growth it was showing during the 1969 model year. Accordingly, the 1971 B-Body program was expansive in its ambition and delivery. Sadly, as you know, the muscle car market turned downward in 1970, and pretty much collapsed as the 1971 model year began.

The model car industry mirrored the 1/1-scale industry plans, and it shared the expectations of continued success with muscle car kit topics. Accordingly, MPC made sure to continue

MPC pulled out all the stops for its 1971 Charger R/T kit (Wave 1/). Beyond the unusual vertical orientation of the box top imagery (right), here I'm illustrating both the side panels and box end. Bodies were molded in two different shades of styrene that loosely replicated the factory code V2 Hemi Orange and L5 Butterscotch High Impact colors, with an added non-stock translucent black fade applied along the fender tops and belt line.***

its Dodge product line, and it also outbid JoHan for the rights to the Plymouth promotional toys and the model kits derived from them. The subsequent kits that MPC developed were innovative and accurate replicas of the real cars.

For 1971, MPC developed a kit tool that supported marketing of both a Road Runner kit, and a seldom-seen GTX kit as well. The Road Runner kit included an optional building version that you now know was derived from plans for a factory

Monogram's 1971 Satellite kit (Wave 2/*) was a Road Runner in all but the name on the box top and the lack of Road Runner nomenclature engraved on the body and graphics printed on the decal sheet, probably due to licensing issues. There were no nomenclature omissions in the follow-up GTX kit (Wave 2/*), which delivers an excellent scale replica. The MPC Road Runner kit (Wave 1/**) was a one-time only reissue of the original 1971 annual kit.

MPC's annual kits featured a new box art layout with red and blue colors and a racing stripe graphic along the right edge of the box top. The Road Runner kit included a version inspired by the 1971 Rapid Transit Caravan show car designed by Harry Bradley and built by Chuck Miller. The Charger replicated the 1971 Charger graphics from one of the Rod Shop drag team entries. Both kits include the 440-6-barrel engine option that was cancelled after just a few 1972 cars with this engine escaped from the factory.

1971 SuperBird. An equally new Charger R/T kit even included the 1969 GTO Judge-like rear spoiler that was developed and included in the long-lead press announcement materials for the 1971 Charger, but cancelled before reaching the production line.

It was not a marketplace success for a number of reasons, most of which were beyond the control of the carmaker, but many consider the 1971 Mopar B-Body lineup to be the company's high point of the entire decade. The model companies apparently agreed, as by 1985 Monogram had already developed an all-new, somewhat simplified 1/24th-scale 1971 Plymouth Satellite kit. This tool was updated and improved in 1995, resulting in an excellent replica of the 1971 GTX marketed under the Revell label. In 1987, AMT-Ertl unearthed the 1971–1972 Road Runner body dies for a single kit reissue (Wave 1/**) that also included the SuperBird parts from the original annual kit release.

Just past the turn of the century, AMT-Ertl debuted an all-new 1971 Charger R/T kit. Despite some issues (the incorrect bench seat, decal accuracy problems, and wheel placement in the front fender opening), this is the best-detailed replica yet of the 1971 to 1974 Mopar B-Bodies. It can also be used (with modifications) to improve the accuracy and detail of any 1/25th-scale 1971 to 1974 Mopar B-Body model car project.

Back in the 1/1-scale world, the industry-wide poor sales of muscle cars in 1971 prompted a drastic simplification of the 1972 factory B-Body lineup, with the GTX, R/T, and SuperBee series temporarily consigned to history. MPC offered a slightly updated Road Runner kit along with a defanged Charger in a new Rallye guise.

AMT-Ertl's 1971 Charger R/T (Wave 3/*) includes the optional code J78/J81 spoilers (top center). The Street Machine version on the lower left built a non-stock replica, but it included the factory optional code N96 Ramcharger hood scoop/fresh air package and famous Bazooka exhaust tips. The most recent R/T reissue (lower right) is preferred for its decal sheet with corrected R/T graphics. (These kits all use the standard R/T front grille, versus the original MPC annual kit with the optional, Charger SE-type hidden headlamp grille.)

1973–1974: Picking Up the Pieces

It seemed that Chrysler's 1973 competitors were competing to produce the most ugly front and rear ends in response to the new federal 5-mph front and 2½-mph rear bumper impact standards. Chrysler developed a comparatively handsome

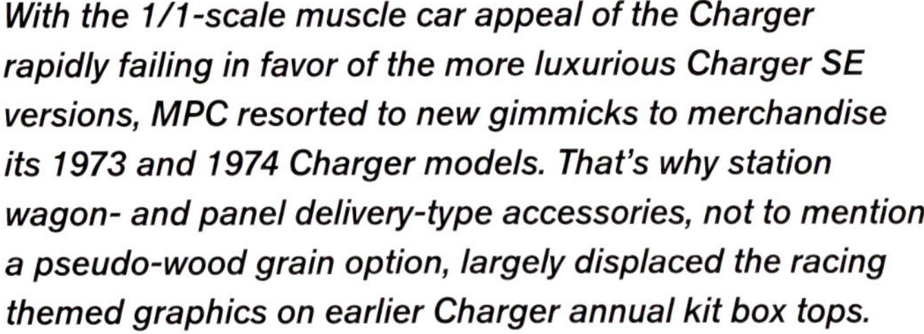

With the 1/1-scale muscle car appeal of the Charger rapidly failing in favor of the more luxurious Charger SE versions, MPC resorted to new gimmicks to merchandise its 1973 and 1974 Charger models. That's why station wagon- and panel delivery-type accessories, not to mention a pseudo-wood grain option, largely displaced the racing themed graphics on earlier Charger annual kit box tops.

MPC's Road Runner kits were updated to the major revisions to the 1973 and 1974 Plymouth B-Bodies (Wave 1/**). Fans of the final second-generation Road Runner should search out this recent metal box kit version of the Road Runner on the right. It's the most factory-correct version of this kit. The Dukes of Hazzard version is a close second best, only omitting the factory Road Runner "bird" graphics from the decal sheet.

alternative that involved rubber blocks. These were further improved with the optional chrome surrounds, which were offered on all models. Chrysler also refused to abandon the muscle car marketplace. Plymouth invested in a major body freshening for 1973 that was better received in the marketplace than the 1971–1972 styling, and it continued the Road Runner with fresh graphics and a new dual exhaust version of the 318 2-barrel, with a resulting substantial sales increase. MPC's kit reflected the body updates and continued with a 440 4-barrel engine, but omitted the new graphics on the decal sheet. Dodge's changes to Charger Rallye were less obvious but also incorporated in the MPC kit tool.

For model year 1974, both cars remained essentially the same except for the longer rear bumper impact pads, and far more important, the introduction of the new emissions-compliant code E58 360 Wedge, which was a benchmark performance engine that was sadly omitted from MPC's 1974 Mopar B-Body kit lineup. Late in the same decade, MPC reissued both the 1974 Road Runner and Charger, but in a modified form. I cannot recommend these street machine forms to serious muscle car fans. The Road Runner kit has seen continued reissues (several with major chassis and interior inaccuracies). The one to search out is also the most recent (as this book goes to print). It is a version in a metal box that includes the factory Road Runner graphics in all 1974 available colors, a restoration of the original annual kit's correct dual exhaust system, Rallye Instrument Cluster, and engine air cleaner decals for the (1973) 340 and (1974) 360, 400, and 440 engines.

1966 Marlin and 1974 Matador X

Though the AMC "Machine" was the only truly bona fide supercar from AMC, I feel obligated to reference two other AMC cars that, had things worked out differently, might have made the list. The first is the fastback Marlin. Had it been built on the compact American platform, such as the original Tarpon concept, and had it been combined with the 390 V-8 that found a home in the 1969½ SC/Rambler, the Marlin would have been a junior supercar aggressor. Even the final, intermediate-sized Marlin fastback body that reached production, had it been combined with the 390 V-8 that broke cover in 1968½, would have surely rated mention in any discussion of 1960s supercars.

Another near miss was AMC's radical new 1974 Matador coupe. At a time when everyone else's intermediates were carryovers of the previous years' designs, the Matador was the only truly fresh choice for the intermediate coupe buyer. The sporty model was called the Matador X, and among the available engines was the 401 4-barrel that also saw use in the Javelin AMX. According to the book *AMC Muscle Cars* by Larry G. Mitchell, this combo was a legitimate 15-second quarter-miler. Among sources the author cites for this claim was a test in *Super Stock and Drag Illustrated* of a bone stock 1974 Matador X 401

*Models of AMC near-muscle cars are rare. JoHan's original annual kit of the 1966 Marlin was reissued around 1975 as part of JoHan's USA Oldies series (Wave 1/**); the kit engine replicates AMC's first-generation V-8 that was still in use for this model year. AMT's all-new 1975 Matador X (Wave 1/**) was a well-designed kit with an accurate 360 V-8 underhood. It appears also to closely replicate the 1974 Matador X, and since the 360 and 401 V-8s appear essentially the same in external appearance, this kit could be used to build the 1974 Matador X 401 referenced in the text.*

yielding a best quarter-mile time of 15.38 seconds at just under 95 mph. That meets my self-imposed muscle car definition. However, with less than 1,000 units built and no real promotion, this was an unsung supercar that few even knew existed.

JoHan, Rambler's 1960s kitmaker, and AMT, which played the same role in the mid-1970s, produced kits of the Marlin and the Matador X, respectively. These are both excellent kits that are worthy of being searched out by fans of these designs.

The *General Lee* and Charger III Concept

While the following is not directly related to the factory stock B-Body offerings, I can't conclude our discussion of Mopar B-Body kits without mentioning the *Dukes of Hazzard General Lee* Charger kit. When that television program first hit the airwaves, MPC unearthed its 1968–1970 Charger kit tool, which had most recently sold as a semi-accurate, non-stock replica of the Bobby Isaac #81 and Richard Brooks #22 NASCAR race cars. MPC pursued a partially successful attempt to restore the tool to the 1969 model year design, but it left elements of the 1970 freshening and the Daytona race car version that were wrong for the real *General Lee*. Modelers back then didn't care about these inaccuracies; the new Dukes kit went on to be one of the very best selling MPC model kits of all time. Round 2 has followed on with an all-new snap-together kit of the *General Lee*, reflecting its continued popularity well into the new millennium.

An all-time best seller, with millions of kits sold? Who would have guessed that MPC's 1968–1970 Charger kit tool would eventually achieve such success? The General Lee *kit was derived from the Daytona race car kit of the lower left (Wave 1/***) and was released in the original box art shown above (Wave 1/*), with many reissues following. An all-new* General Lee *tool kit with snap-style assembly debuted in 2014 (lower right).*

*MPC's Charger III kit (Wave 1/****) was an excellent kit that featured many operating features. Under the front tilting hood/upper fenders unit was a 426 Hemi, while the roof canopy/door unit tilted rearward to reveal a tilting steering wheel/instrument cluster. The body was reused for a later MPC funny car kit, but the kit has never been reissued in its original form.*

Worthy of note as well is the Charger III, a concept vehicle from the Dodge Styling Studios that broke cover in 1968. A radical design in the same genre as the Corvette Mako Shark II and AeroVette, this sleek two-seater was notable for its lack of a back window and a seating configuration that lifted to meet the driver and passenger. There were never kits of Dodge's Charger I and Charger II concept cars, but the Charger III did briefly see kit form courtesy of MPC.

Missing in Action

Mopar B-Bodies yet to appear in a 1/24-1/25th–scale kit

- 1966 Coronet (hardtop and/or convertible)
- 1966 Satellite or Belvedere (hardtop and/or convertible)
- 1968 GTX (hardtop and/or convertible)
- 1968½ Super Bee (two-door coupe or hardtop)
- 1969½ Road Runner A12 440 6-barrel

Mopar B-Bodies that need a new or modern kit offering

- 1968, 1969, and 1970 Coronet R/T (hardtop and/or convertible)
- 1971 and 1972 Road Runner
- 1972, 1973, and 1974 Charger Rallye
- 1970 AMC Machine (with the correct 390 V-8)

Muscle Car Model Kits Scale Showroom

The following models show how several of the model kits mentioned earlier in this chapter look when assembled by experienced adult model car builders. (Photography and models are by the writer unless noted otherwise.)

The Code AA-1 Silver Metallic 1966 Charger and MM-1 Turbine Bronze Metallic 1967 Plymouth GTX are both based on Revell-Monogram's 1990s kit introductions. (Builder/Photographer: Mike Hanson)

This T5 Bronze Fire Metallic 1969 Plymouth GTX was built straight from the kit box and is the actual model car that AMT-Ertl photographed for the box art of its 2003 kit reissue. (Builder: Steve Goldman)

This project combines the MPC 1969 Coronet R/T body and interior with the much better detailed chassis and engine from the AMT-Ertl 1969 Plymouth GTX kit. (Builder: Mike Kollver)

These 1968 Charger R/T and 1969 Daytona Chargers were built from Revell kits. While it is hard to pick out in this photo, the precise engine detail in the underhood compartment is a combination of kit engineering and builder detailing skills. (Builder: Tim Harber)

The Code Y1 Top Banana 1970 Super Bee is AMT-Ertl's hybrid kit introduction from 1993, while the 1969½ Super Bee Six Pack is based on the 1983 Monogram kit and wears mid-year F6 Bright Green Metallic and a builder-added vinyl roof.

Moebius Models recently introduced an all-new kit of the 1965 Satellite hardtop in 2015. This model was built straight from the box and painted to match Plymouth Code L Dark Turquoise Metallic. (Builder: David Dale/Photographer: Paul Miles)

MPC's 1970 Charger R/T annual kit is assembled here with a number of builder-added improvements. The factory white with black interior is the perfect contrast to the Code J5 Sublime paint. (Builder: Mike Kollver)

Two Road Runners based on the MPC annual kits: the Code J6 Sassy Grass Green 1971 model features the optional N96 Air Grabber hood and a builder-added factory V4 Canopy Vinyl Roof; the 1972 model presents the standard Road Runner hood and mid-year J3 Meadow Green paint.

The Code T5 Copper Metallic 1969 R/T is from Revell, but with a builder upgrade to R/T SE specs. The Y9 Dark Gold Metallic 1971 R/T is based on the AMT-Ertl kit, with an added vinyl roof and a conversion to the factory-correct bucket-seat interior.

JoHan's 1970 Rebel, the Machine, shows builder-added details like opening doors and trunk, an intricately detailed engine compartment, and code P-79 Bittersweet Orange Metallic paint. (Builder: Tony Franklin)

The Pony Car Brigade, Part 1

Mustang and Camaro

When new product innovation succeeds against all odds, the result can be a spectacular, enduring success. Need proof? Can you say "Mustang"?

As the former co-leader of a new product innovation effort during the last part of my career in the automobile industry, I can assure you that the many challenges and risks associated with truly new automotive ideas often seem insurmountable to the teams that develop them, and to the corporations that must fund and ultimately deliver them.

As a result, more than a few great concepts never see the light of day. Further discussion of this topic is well beyond the boundaries of this book, but for those that are interested, I can recommend two books: *Mustang: The Complete History of America's Pioneer Pony Car* by Gary Witzenburg and *Mustang Genesis* by Robert Fria.

Not by coincidence do these books deal with the development of the Ford Mustang. While there were numerous obstacles, doubts, and challenges that were encountered during the development of the Mustang, it was a great idea that enjoyed unparalleled initial success. Even more important, it eventually created an entirely new market segment, one that is still relevant and vibrant today. Half a century later, the Mustang is still overall the top seller in its class in America. Moreover, as this book is being written, Mustang has just become the top-selling car of its type in the entire world.

Moving now to the larger world of muscle cars in total, if you had to single out just two cars that first created, and then nurtured the entire muscle car phenomenon, they would be the GTO (which personified the supercar genre), and the Mustang. While the GTO's influence was immediate and hard-hitting, the Mustang's role in the muscle car world took a few years to fully blossom. Then, as the intermediate-sized supercar faded completely from public acceptance in the early to mid-1970s, it was the end-of-decade Fox-bodied Mustang and its successors that ensured that the muscle car remained a viable product segment for five decades now.

Equally important is the story of the Mustang's longest running nemesis and sparring partner on the drag strip and racetrack, the Camaro. While the Camaro came to market two and a half years after the Mustang and has not been available for all of the 50+ years of the Mustang, its role was and remains vital to the development of the muscle car.

I'll cover the first-generation Mustang kits here initially, and then follow with the first and early second-generation Camaro kits. The rest of the pony car combatants (Barracuda, Cougar, Firebird, Javelin, and Challenger) will be covered in Chapter 9.

Mustangs and Camaros were perhaps the most-kitted of all muscle car–era vehicles, particularly during the original 1960s to 1970s era of annual kit introductions each year. Here are examples of each model year of Mustang and Camaro, all being annual kits from AMT, MPC, and Revell.

Mustang: The Original, and the Definitive Pony Car

When the first-generation Mustang was introduced in spring 1964, it was a national spectacle. Here was a new, modestly priced compact-sized car that prioritized sporty proportions and styling over the practical considerations of people-space and luggage capacity. The car-obsessed American public had never seen anything like it. Mustang made the covers of the top newsweeklies and the introduction coincided perfectly with the New York World's Fair, where 27 million people saw it over the next few months. Mustang quickly became an American sensation.

1964½–1966: Creating a Stampede

A model kit of the Mustang was a sure thing, and it debuted under the the auspices of the boys in Troy (Michigan), AMT. The kit allowed the builder to construct both a hardtop and convertible Mustang from the same kit, and it followed the usual AMT 3-in-1 marketing format. The observant collector will note that most AMT annual kits from this era put the custom or race versions in the lead box top and/or end cap position, with an illustration of the factory stock version relegated to a secondary position on one of the box sides. Not so this time. Instead, a showroom fresh two-door hardtop in gold with a black vinyl top, along with an inset of the now-famous Mustang corral grille badge, graced the box top of this inaugural kit.

For 1965, Ford added a third Mustang body style, the Fastback 2+2. According to the production date printed on the backside of the Mustang 2+2 specific decal sheet, AMT's kit of this new body style went down the AMT assembly line in February 1965. This time the showroom stock 2+2 was featured on the endcap illustration, while the top illustration was somewhat reminiscent of the first Shelby GT 350 R. The kit's custom version was said to be an "authentic replica of the Ford Custom Car Caravan's exciting Mustang Fastback, Customized by George Barris."

The modest revisions of the 1966 Mustang carried over to two follow-up AMT kits replicating the hardtop/convertible and the 2+2, which were little changed from the earlier debut kit forms. A new competitor, at least on the hobby shelves, emerged when

AMT's first Mustang 2+2 fastback kit (Wave 1/) had a box-top subtitle proclaiming "With Shelby American Mustang GT Features." However, the kit had the same 260-style Ford V-8 and one-piece chassis with engraved single exhaust detail that was found in AMT's earlier hardtop/convertible Mustang kit.***

MPC also introduced its version of the 1966 Mustang 2+2 fastback. With a bird's-eye rear-three-quarter view looking at a race car with an offset racing strip and a spare tire and wheel peeking through the rear fastback window, the compelling box top also promoted MPC's new relationship with kit designer/marketer Budd Anderson, who had moved on from AMT to IMC and now to MPC.

Meanwhile, AMT's 1966 Mustang hardtop/convertible kit has been reissued with a singular hardtop body (probably derived from the original AMT promotional tooling). At least 10 reissues of this kit have occurred, with the most recent version under Round 2 ownership including box art inspired by AMT's original 1966 annual kit lineup graphics layout. By contrast, AMT's 1966 2+2 Fastback kit has never been reissued. As noted in Chapter 2, parts of this kit tool were irrevocably altered to create several other kits. This makes AMT's 1966 2+2 kit one

The first-ever 1/25th-scale pony car kit was this Mustang from AMT (Wave 1/*) that could be built as either a hardtop or convertible. The kit included two custom versions, one influenced by the "Mustang II" concept vehicle that was first shown the previous fall, plus showroom stock and mild drag racing versions.***

AMT's 1966 Mustang Fast-Back (note the revised spelling) annual kit (Wave 1/*) was revised to include the GT package grille with fog lamps, and the Interior Décor Group option (better known as the pony interior, with its stampede of Mustang horses embossed on the upper seatback upholstery). Note the box art illustration featuring Tasca Ford livery.***

*AMT's 1966 Mustang annual kit was buildable as a convertible or hardtop, but it has never been reissued in that form (not shown, Wave 1/**). A hardtop-only kit followed, shown here in the 1977, 1980, 1989, 2001, and 2012 releases (Wave 1/*). The box in the foreground is the 2012 Round 2 release, with fresh artwork composed to match the original 1966 annual kit campaign.*

of the most valuable of all collectible original issue Mustang model kits.

In 1985, Monogram tooled up an all-new 1/24th-scale kit of the 1965 Mustang 2+2 Fastback. Like most of Monogram's kits from this era, the kit content was somewhat simplified but, with detailed component painting and careful assembly, the resulting model was very presentable. Monogram reused the basic engine and underbody tooling along with a new convertible body shell for a 1964½ Indy Pace Car kit first introduced in

Monogram's 1/24th-scale Mustang 2+2 (Wave 2/) was introduced more than 30 years ago but has a contemporary kit vibe. The Indy Pace Car kit (Wave 2/*) includes both an up top and convertible boot, and full Indy 500 Pace Car livery. These are the only 1964½ to 1966 Mustang convertible and 2+2 kits that can be purchased today without paying collector prices.*

1995. (This tooling was also used for several Shelby GT350 kits, which, like all the Shelby Mustang kits, are covered in Chapter 13).

1967–1968: New Oats for the Pony

After two and a half years of having the sports compact marketplace mostly to itself, the Mustang now faced new competitive threats with the Camaro and Cougar introductions for the 1967 model year, and, shortly thereafter, the Firebird. Accordingly, the 1967 Mustang was thoroughly revamped in all regards, delivering a more expressive product that continued to lead sales in this now highly competitive market environment. Some in the automotive design and enthusiast community, this writer included, view the 1967 Mustang as the ultimate expression and interpretation of the original Mustang concept.

AMT's only 1967 Mustang annual kit featured the GT Fastback with the Interior Decor Group, but it was far more complete in its scope and development than AMT's previous Mustang kits. The previous one-piece chassis pan was replaced with a fully detailed chassis with separate, highly detailed front and rear suspension components, even allowing the builder to position the front wheel and tire assemblies as though the car was turning right or left. The now-separately molded, new dual

*AMT's 1967 Mustang kit (Wave 1/***) was all new and featured a highly detailed chassis that allowed the builder to position the front tires in a right or left turn. A 1966 Mustang drag car campaigned by Trudell Ford, a local Detroit dealership back then, inspired the box art this time. MPC's kit featured four building versions: stock, custom, drag, and a grand-touring Mustang designed by Budd Anderson.*

exhaust system included a transverse rear muffler assembly. Under the hood was a new 390 FE Ford V-8, augmented by a replica of Ford's SOHC 427 drag engine for the kit's racing version. A very tasty customized option that was credited to AMT consultant Gene Winfield included a sculpted rear panel with a second set of stock Mustang lights. It yielded 12 individual Mustang taillamps in total.

MPC also featured the 1967 Mustang GT Fastback with (Pony) Interior Decor Group. The showroom stock engine was the 289 V-8, while the drag version featured the 427 engine. This kit also included a separate exhaust system (versus the two-dimensional, molded-in exhaust systems still found in many late 1960s annual kits). Budd Anderson was again prominently noted on the box top and side panel.

In the early 1990s, AMT-Ertl's product team went about engineering modern assembly kits of some of the great muscle car topics of the 1960s. Part of this effort was an all-new tool of the 1967 Mustang GT. As the tooling was to later be used for a 1967 Shelby GT-350 kit, the GT featured the Hi-Po 289/271-hp small-block V-8. The kit had excellent engine, chassis, and interior detailing, but was somewhat compromised by an incomplete execution of some of the exterior body trim. (A model car aftermarket company, Replicas and Miniatures of Maryland, includes corrected front and rear fasciae for this kit as part of its product offerings).

The Mustang for 1968 showed detail refinements inside and out. The big news, of course, was the spring arrival of the Cobra Jet 428 engine. For the first time, the regular production Mustang was a front-line performance contender at the drag strips and on the streets of American cities. (AMT and MPC tooled their 1968 annual kits during the summer of 1967, so they did not include this mid-year 428 engine introduction.)

*The spectacular box top illustration on AMT's 1968 Mustang GT kit (Wave 1/***) carried the signature of AMT artist Don Greer. The kit carried over a well-executed optional SOHC 427 V-8 from the 1967 release. By contrast, the optional engine in MPC's 1968 Mustang kit (Wave 1/**) was a 427 Wedge, and the box included two illustrations featuring the Logghe funny car–style tubular front suspension option.*

AMT-Ertl developed this all-new 1967 Mustang GT kit (Wave 3/) and first brought it to the market in 1994. Most performance Mustangs in 1967 were ordered with the 390 FE, but this kit included what is probably the best replica of the 271-hp 289 K-Code V-8 ever produced in 1/25th scale.*

This is a relatively recent kit entry from Revell (Wave 4/), but the kit is not taken seriously by kit experts because the body tool proportions and accuracy are thought to be compromised (for instance, the lack of depth in the side contouring). The underbody detail is also simplified in some areas when compared to most modern kits. Some early releases of this kit also included incorrect 1967 interior pieces.*

MPC's 1968 kit was pretty much the 1967 content with added parts to provide a Gasser-type straight axle front suspension option. AMT's kit was also a nearly complete carryover of the excellent 1967 annual kit. After the regular annual kit run, AMT's tool was converted to replicate the 1968 Shelby GT-500.

During the early 2000s, kitmaker Revell was also producing a line of 1/25th-scale die-cast metal replicas. Included among these was a 1968 Mustang Cobra Jet 428. Revell later introduced a styrene assembly kit using this same die-cast tool. The detail of this kit was somewhat simplified versus contemporary model kits, and the body contours were compromised by the tooling adaptations needed for the original die-cast production run.

AMT's 1969 Mustang annual kit (Wave 1/*) is still the only fully accurate, properly scaled body of the first-ever Mach 1; regrettably it has never been reissued. MPC's 1969 Mustang annual kit (Wave 1/**) actually replicated the GT option but was merchandised as a Mach 1. The MPC box art illustration was inspired by a Super Stock class race car campaigned by Paul Harvey Ford in Indianapolis.***

1969–1970: Building "Muscle Car Cred"

By the time the 1969 model year rolled around, pony cars were evolving toward the supercars with their high-powered big-block V-8s. The 1969 Mustang reflected this trend in spades. For the first time, the performance versions of Mustang seemed to be dictating the product development brief. The Mustang now had its hooves in both the pony car and muscle car camps. It was wider in width and track, more aggressive in body proportions, and featured a new performance-themed series called the Mach 1. A new engine, the midsized 351 Windsor, was introduced and made standard on the Mach 1. A second new series called the Grande was a luxury-themed version of the Mustang, exclusive to the hardtop body style. At mid-year, new Boss 302 and Boss 429 derivatives furthered the performance cause. The Mustang GT option remained in place for all three body styles, but the Mach 1/Boss 302/Boss 429 products were only offered in the Fastback (SportsRoof) body style.

AMT and MPC, of course, offered their annual kit releases of the 1969 Mustang Fastback, with AMT's kit replicating the new Mach 1, and MPC's featuring the GT package. AMT's original annual kit is the only one (then or now) with an accurately scaled body combined with a fully correct, accurately proportioned 1969 Mustang grille and headlamp area. Under the box lid, builders found a non-stock dual-quad FE engine with a Shelby-style dual car air cleaner that was totally incorrect, of course, for the optional, Shaker-style hood scoop found on the real Mach 1. The one-piece promo-style chassis looked to be reborn from the 1964½–1966 kit, and it was a big step backward from the AMT's detailed 1967–1968 Mustang kit chassis (which itself continued in production as an updated AMT 1968 Shelby GT 500 kit). In spite of these underbody mistakes, the AMT 1969 Mach 1 remains a highly coveted model kit collectible.

MPC's 1969 Mustang kit also featured the top-line (at the beginning of the model year) FE-based Cobra Jet 428 engine. MPC's body was strangely undersized for a 1/25th-scale model. This shortcoming was offset to a degree by MPC's decision to replicate the GT option in its last year in the marketplace, instead of the new Mach 1. It also included a much more accurate replica of the 428 Cobra Jet engine, even including engraved block serial numbers and an emissions air pump and the associated plumbing.

Nevertheless, there was another chapter to the 1969 Mustang annual kit story. Down at the local hobby store, a well-respected kit brand introduced its first annual kit offering since its ill-fated run of the 1962 Chrysler family kits. Yes, Revell was re-entering the annual kit business, and it chose the 1969 Mustang GT hardtop and convertible as the basis for its new assembly kit.

The kit was developed during a period when some Revell kits were pretty mediocre efforts, but this one included a correct 428 Ram Air/Shaker assembly and a multi-piece chassis/suspension that shamed the facing AMT kit that year. One drawback was the inverted rear-quarter-panel air scoop seen only on the Mustang hardtop and convertible that year. It was not accurately reproduced on the kit's bodyside. This kit was not a big seller back in the day, was never reissued, and is not well known now. If assembled with care, the result is a presentable replica of the Mustang in two body styles that had not been seen in 1/25th-scale assembly kits since the end of the 1966 annual kit run.

In the 1990s, Revell-Monogram added a new 1969 Mach 1 Cobra Jet 428 kit based on the earlier development work that

*Revell's 1969 Cobra Jet hardtop/convertible kit (Wave 1/***) was a sleeper when introduced that year; no one knew quite what to make of Revell's return to the annual kit business. This was a well-detailed kit, with advanced features like a separate plated windshield frame that would not be commonly seen until the advent of modern-era tooling in the 1990s. Revell's more recent Mach 1 kit (Wave 2/*) features a modern kit design approach and a highly detailed 428 Cobra Jet engine, but it suffers from a distorted front-end appearance.*

*Revell's 1970 Mustang Grande kit box art perfectly captured the zeitgeist around the turn of the decade (Wave 1/***). Inside was a coupon for a $33\frac{1}{3}$ rpm 7-inch record on which Pete Brock and drag racer Skip Hess "talk over the best of the breed: the Ford Mustang." MPC's 1970 Mustang kit (Wave 1/**) box art depicted a Boss 302, but the small-block Ford engine inside was still the same as its 1966 kit.*

Monogram used for its 1970 Boss 429 kit introduced more than 10 years earlier. This kit has excellent engine and underbody detail but is highly compromised by a front clip that fails to capture the graceful lines of the full-sized 1969 Mustang dual-quad headlamp and grille design.

While many Mustang collectors and fans consider the 1969 Boss 302 and Boss 429 to be among the most desirable first-generation Mustangs, no 1/24th- or 1/25th-scale assembly kits of these two iconic pony/muscle cars have ever been produced to date. However, Revell plans to produce a new 1969 Boss 302 kit that will be converted from its existing 1969 Mustang Mach 1 kit in early 2018.

The Mustang for 1970 continued the Mach 1, Boss 302 and Boss 429 sub-series, but the GT option was missing when the car line debuted in September 1969. A new midsized 335 series 351 Cleveland V-8 was introduced.

For their 1970 annual kit offerings, AMT, MPC, and Revell appropriately updated their annual kit toolings. The Revell kit replicated the new Grande Series offering, with an added non-Shaker air cleaner option. While the Grande-style roof was engraved properly, the builder had to mold it to the lower body structure for an accurate finished appearance. AMT again chose the Mach 1 for its kit, while MPC went with a base (non-Mach 1) fastback.

While MPC's 1970 Mustang kit box art implied that the builder would find a complete Boss 302 inside, only an outdated 289 V-8 and the carryover 428 Cobra Jet were in the kit box. (This lack of underhood updates was growing increasingly common in 1/25th-scale annual kits around the turn of the decade).

If you look closely at the AMT Mustang's rear quarter-panel (just below the quarter-windows), you'll see an incorrect treatment of the blanked-over simulated air scoop from 1969. Whether this was just a tooling error or an actual early production design for the real car is unknown. Meanwhile, none of the model kit-makers included Mustang's new 351 Cleveland engine in their kits (AMT at least included a Boss 429 V-8 in its kit). There have been no reissues of any of the 1970 Mustang annual kits.

Monogram's Boss 429 kit (Wave 2/) spawned a whole series of spinoff 1970 Mustang kits during the next 25 years (all: Wave 2/*). If you're looking for the most accurate Boss 302, 351 Cleveland, or Boss 429 engines rendered in the popular scales, these are the kits you'll need to search out.*

An all-new 1970 Mustang kit was introduced to the marketplace 12 years later. This wasn't just a 1970 Mustang, but probably the most outrageous single Mustang product of the entire 1964½ to 1973 generation. Unlike the original 1970 annual kits described above, this one was correct to a T. Yes, the team in Morton Grove, Illinois, brought to market a highly authentic 1/24th-scale replica of the 1970 Boss 429 Mustang. It was arguably the most authentic, detailed showroom stock Mustang ever at the time of its introduction. It also signaled the emergence of the adult modeler expectations in kit development topics and detail.

Monogram later used much of this kit tooling for an equally accurate replica of the 1970 Boss 302. In just the last decade, it introduced a third derivative, a 1970 Mustang Mach 1 powered by the first-ever, mostly showroom stock 351 Cleveland engine to appear in a 1/24th- or 1/25th-scale model kit.

The biggest change yet for the Mustang was captured in these 1971 and 1972 kits from MPC and AMT (all: Wave 1/**). Note the similarity in box art composition from these competitors. Both 1971 kits feature front driver's side elevations, while the 1972 kits show bird's-eye front-three-quarter passenger-side depictions, with the cars seemingly driving off the box top.

1971–1973: Wrong for Its Time, but the Ultimate Expression of the Original Pony Car/Muscle Car?

This brings me to the last of the first-generation Mustangs, the 1971–1973 iteration. It was the most changed Mustang yet. Longer, wider, and heavier, the Mustang was evolving in exactly the wrong direction for the societal changes occurring at the time. While the market was now looking for a solution more in line with the original 1964–1966 Mustang and the new German import called the Mercury Capri, the radical (for its time) 1971 Mustang was designed based on where the market was headed from an earlier 1968–1969 perspective. It featured a fastback body with a near-horizontal rear window treatment, and a new generation of 385 series 429 Cobra Jet and Super Cobra Jet engines to replace the previous FE based 428. In a last-minute decision, the Boss 302 was replaced by the Boss 351, and the nearly hand-built Boss 429 was discontinued.

While it may have missed the market at the time, some Mustang aficionados, this writer included, believe that the 1971 Mustang has been given a bum rap by the automotive enthusiast world. Its design was stunning at the time, and seems equally provocative (in a good way) today. The Boss 351 is now respected by the hard-core enthusiast community for the stunning all-around performer it actually turned out to be. And with the 429 Cobra Jet gone for the 1972 model year, the 351 Cobra Jet and HO engines were star performers in their own right in a new world of reduced compression/low-lead/no-lead fuels and emissions controls.

AMT and MPC both produced kits of the 1971–1973 Mustangs. AMT replicated the Mach 1 with its lower body blackout treatment but with a generic V-8 engine block; it used either regular cylinder heads and valve covers, or undersized Boss 429 cylinder heads and valve covers. Neither of these was an accurate replica of the new factory stock 429 Cobra Jet in the

AMT-Ertl took the original MPC 1973 Mustang tool and attempted to rebox it as a 1971 Boss 351 (Wave 1/*). There were three engine options in the kit, but none accurately replicated the distinctive appearance of the 1/1-scale 351 Cleveland engine. The front-end appearance was not properly backdated to the 1971 configuration, and the kit's Sport wheel covers were not a factory option for the Boss 351. So model car builders and collectors are still waiting for an accurate Boss 351 kit.

The Most Important Muscle Car Kit of All Time?

Yes, this is one of, if not *the* most important of all muscle car model kit introductions. I'm talking about Monogram's 1982 introduction of its 1/24th-scale 1970 Boss 429 kit.

Up until this point, most muscle car model kits did not fully and accurately reproduce the exact details of the showroom originals. Typical omissions included the lack of showroom stock exterior livery and badging. More errors were prevalent in the engine compartment, including incorrect air cleaner assemblies, omitted fan belt accessories, generic rather than correct intake and exhaust manifolds, and so forth. Sometimes, even the engines were entirely wrong (such as AMT's and MPC's failure to update their Mustang kit engines to the new 335 series 351 Cleveland and 385 series 429 Ford V-8s). To the young kit builders of the 1960s, these were not major sins. As the decade turned from the 1970s to 1980s, adult model builders were becoming more prominent and more outspoken about these minor to major inaccuracies.

Enter Monogram Models. Two key managers there, Roger Harney and Bob Johnson, had just finished a kit series involving curbside (no engines) 1/24th-scale kits of European cars including Porsche, Ferrari, BMW, and Mercedes-Benz, as well as the Ford Europe Capri and the Japanese Datsun 260Z. These products sold very well, generating funds for more new Monogram kits to be developed. Equally important, they secured valuable shelf display space for follow-up Monogram products at the major retailers of the era (such as K-Mart).

After much discussion about what those follow-up products might be, Harney and Johnson agreed to do a series of fully detailed muscle car kits. By the early 1980s, some 1960s and early 1970s muscle cars were once again becoming objects of lust, and Harney and Johnson reasoned that if they produced kits that appealed to adults who loved muscle cars, they would benefit from those sales in addition to the younger kit buyers who snapped up virtually any new model products that hit store shelves. In considering this project, Monogram quickly realized that it had a real strategic advantage over AMT, MPC, and Revell in that it could start from scratch with these new kits, rather than being limited to adapting an existing kit tool to deliver the new kit.

The first three kits in the series were the 1970 Boss 429, the 1971 Hemi-Cuda, and the 1970 Chevelle SS454. The Boss was assigned to Monogram kit development engineer Dave Jones. Just before the "measuring session" of the real 1/1-scale Boss 429 took place, the car's owner took Mr. Jones for a quick ride. *Really quick,* as Bob Johnson relates the story. When they returned, the smiles said it all. That enthusiasm clearly carried through to the resulting kit.

The 1970 Boss 429 kit was introduced in 1982, and this kit set a very high standard for future muscle car and pony car model kits. Every correct detail was there, inside, outside, under the hood, and under the body. Really, only the tires were not factory correct but, back then, most restorations ran contemporary rubber rather than original tires (and reproduction tires weren't available then, anyway). The kit construction was simplified slightly, consistent with Monogram's kit design approach at the time. The front-end appearance was ever so slightly off, but that didn't really matter. This kit was seen as a strong acknowledgment that the adult kit builders' expectations were going to be met. Model manufacturers now realized that they had to reach for a higher standard when designing new model kit introductions.

Monogram's new kits were a tremendous market success and other muscle car kits followed: the Dodge Super Bee Six Pack and Challenger T/A, a GTX, a Judge GTO, a GSX Stage 1, and the aforementioned 1964½–1966 Mustangs. Seeing this success, the other kitmakers jumped in with new, freshly engineered, and fully authentic muscle car kits of their own. Was Monogram's Boss 429 the most important muscle car kit of all time? Maybe it was.

Monogram's 1970 Boss 429 kit set the standard for all muscle car model kits to follow. It also signaled the completion of Monogram's journey to return to its early 1960s reputation for scale model car kit accuracy and quality.

real car. MPC produced a kit that incorrectly repeated the prior-year kit's engines: a 289 that was falsely promoted as a Boss 302 on the 1971 kit box art, equally falsely referred to as a 351 Cobra Jet on the 1972 box side, and also labeled as a 428 Cobra Jet. Accurate replicas of the 351 Cleveland and 429 Cobra Jet engines were nowhere to be found.

Years later, MPC (under the ownership of AMT-Ertl by that point) attempted to backdate its Mustang tooling to replicate the 1971 Boss 351 in kit form for the first time. This was an indifferent and inaccurate effort, and was roundly criticized by the adult modeling community (and rightly so) at the time. Both the AMT and MPC 1973 Mustang kits have been reissued multiple times during the following decades.

Mustang Concepts in 1/25th Scale

Before I leave the subject of Mustangs from the muscle car era, I want to mention Mustang concept vehicles. First, as students of the Mustang's initial development know, the first use of the name Mustang was on a two-seat mid-engine sports car concept that debuted at the 1962 U.S. Grand Prix at Watkins Glen. This concept was, sadly, never the subject of a 1/25th-scale kit.

The next Mustang concept, known as the Mustang II, was unveiled at the 1963 U.S. Grand Prix at Watkins Glen. It was based on an early Mustang production sheet metal buck, with mildly exaggerated front- and rear-end treatments and a chopped top along with a steeper windshield angle. It was also the subject of a model car kit, produced by a Detroit-based automotive supplier named Industro-Motive Corporation, or IMC. The kit featured box art that appeared to be inspired by the Ford Press Release photo of the original mid-engine Mustang 1 (as it's now called) concept sitting on a banked race track turn. The kit was designed by model car celebrity Budd Anderson, who had just left AMT in hopes of creating new model car kits that were more in line with kit builder expectations as he understood them.

Another Mustang Concept called the Mach 1 was first unveiled in 1966. This concept hinted at the more extreme fastback roof of the production 1967–1968 design, and also introduced the series nomenclature that would eventually be used for the performance version of the 1969 Mustang. AMT introduced a kit of this concept in late 1967 (the box art graphic layout was consistent with AMT's 1968 annual kits), and is believed to have used the interior/engine/chassis tooling from the AMT 1965–1966 Mustang 2+2 kit along with an all-new body tool. This kit was reissued at least three times, as the Hi-Per Autolite Special in 1968, the SuperStang (with added parts for a supercharged version) in 1969, and the Iron Horse in 1974.

The Mach 1 concept was freshened for the 1968 Auto Show circuit featuring a new front end with aerodynamic glassed-in headlamps. Yet another Mustang concept was the Milano, a 1970 auto show feature with a side character line that appeared to be lifted directly from Dodge's just debuted 1970 Challenger. These latter two concepts have not appeared in 1/24th- or 1/25th-scale assembly kit form.

IMC's rendition of the Mustang II concept vehicle first appeared in the box at the far left (Wave 1/). The box art was updated to a corporate-wide IMC graphic format in 1966 (top right), along with some minor tweaks to the kit contents (Wave 1/**). The tooling resurfaced under the Lindberg brand in the early 1990s (Wave 1/*).***

AMT's replica of the Mustang Mach 1 show car (Wave 1/**) reflects the first of the two versions, which was the one that made the show circuit in 1966. Note how the box art matches the graphic format of AMT's 1968 annual kits. Shown beside it is one of the three modified kit reissues, a drag strip/street machine that could also be built in a topless roadster version (Wave 1/**).

Camaro: The Other Partner in the Pony Car Duel

It's a pretty safe bet that the Camaro would not have existed if the Mustang had not come first. Camaro fans might also argue (with some justification) that the Mustang would not *still* exist today if not for the Camaro.

Either way, Mustang versus Camaro has been a fight for the ages. Ask any car magazine editor or publisher, and if they're candid, they'll often confide that the best way to pump newsstand sales is to put a Mustang or Camaro (or a Corvette or Ferrari or Porsche) on the cover of the next issue, preferably painted in red (or yellow). You'll note, by the way, the price difference between the Mustang/Camaro and those other newsstand attention grabbers.

Automotive historians suggest that, at first, General Motors did not plan to counter the Mustang. When the Mustang was introduced in April 1964, the Corvair was just months away from an all-new top to bottom rebirth, and was expected to sell very well. However, after the Mustang piled up an unprecedented 100,000 sales during the first four months on the market, General Motors reportedly began to reconsider its options. The plan became to use the underpinnings of the new 1968 Chevy II/Nova program as the basis for its own pony car entry, which was developed under the Panther project name.

*AMT's mid- to late 1960s box top illustrations were always a timely look at the latest street and drag trends. Here, Chevy's brand-new Camaro (Wave 1/***) was depicted in a nose-high Gasser/A-FX–style stance. The side panels showed a fastback conversion credited to the Alexander Brothers, and an optional, rare, and highly desirable Man-A-Fre intake setup.*

1967–1968: Origins of a Future Legend

When the Camaro finally debuted two and a half years after the Mustang broke cover, it was a well thought out program with a broad range of appearance and power offerings. The design language was pure GM mid-1960s Coke-bottle–style combined with some of the Mustang's long hood/short deck proportions, and the new Camaro added at least one major appearance option not available on the Mustang: the RS with its hideaway headlamps. An SS option group gave buyers still more to consider. Mid-year brought an option package under order code Z-28 that homologated a new 302-ci version of Chevy's small-block V-8 for the new Trans-Am racing series. Perhaps the Camaro's biggest shortcoming was the single-leaf rear suspension (derived from the Chevy II program), which severely compromised traction on cars equipped with muscle powertrains.

The Camaro was an immediate success, though Ford noted that four months after the Camaro was placed on sale, the Mustang was still outselling the Camaro *and* all the other pony car competitors *combined*. That, too, changed when Camaro became Mustang's most virulent competitor for sales and performance leadership in the following years.

The first Camaro model car kit came from AMT, and it was an annual kit of the 1967 Camaro SS350 hardtop in typical showroom stock/custom/drag strip 3-in-1 form. A few months later, a convertible kit with Indy Pace Car decals appeared.

Look closely at the end panel of AMT's 1968 Camaro kit (Wave 1/) and you'll see the words "for 1968" instead of the simple "1968" on most of AMT's other 1968 annual kits. This kit was a guess (and not a good one) at the real car. For that, you had to search out the MPC kit (Wave 1/***). The optional Gasser/A-FX–style version was illustrated on the side panel with a large "Yenko Super Camaro" logo on the door.*

The 1968 Z-28 kit (Wave 2/*) on top dates from the period when AMT was owned by Lesney-Matchbox. The body was accurate, while the underhood depiction and chassis was somewhat simplified. The kit tool was amended in 1998 to offer a 1967 Z-28 (Wave 2/*). Revell's 1967 Camaro SS (Wave 4/*) was introduced in 2014 and features the big-block 396 underhood.

The 1968 Camaro included a new grille for non-RS versions, and the front-door vent windows were dropped. The Z-28 added exterior badging. AMT and MPC also brought out annual kits in 1968. However, only MPC's kit was correct for a showroom stock SS396 Camaro, as AMT's model was the carryover 1967 kit modified to reflect an uneducated guess as to what the 1968 Camaro would be (thus, the explanation for the wishy-washy "For 1968," versus declarative "1968" nomenclature on the box art). This was the result of AMT losing the 1968 promotional toys contract for several Chevrolet products to MPC. Also of note, no kit version of the Z-28 was to be found in the annual kits lineup.

When Lesney bought the AMT assets in 1978, many modelers wondered whether they would ever see any more kits of cars that would interest domestic modelers. The answer came several years later when AMT-Lesney introduced an all-new kit of the 1968 Z-28. Not only was this the first accurate showroom stock Z-28 in 1/25th-scale kit form, it was a serviceable effort that suggested more to come from this now foreign-owned enterprise. In the 1990s, AMT-Ertl introduced a derivative of this kit replicating the 1967 Z-28.

Recently Revell tooled up an all-new 1967 Camaro SS396 kit, which is the most accurate kit of all when it comes to the first two years of Camaros. It was compromised only by too-small wheels diameter, and the omission of two prominent horizontal bars in the base (i.e., non-RS) exposed headlamp grille.

1969: The Most Iconic of All Camaros?

Many Camaro fans consider the 1969 version to be the single most iconic of all the years this product has been produced. A fairly major freshening replaced most of the prior-year sheet metal, while new colors such as Daytona Yellow and Hugger Orange, along with color keyed hound's-tooth upholsteries to match, brightened up the visual impact. The Z-28 became the conceptual image leader for the brand and a very successful seller to boot, while the ZL-1 and various COPO (Central Office Production Order) versions are the subject of legends both then and now.

AMT and MPC offered 1969 Camaro hardtop annual kits, and for this year AMT's kit was now factory-correct. AMT added a convertible kit with Indy Pace Car Livery later in the year. This kit featured a unique and very striking box art layout with a photo of the actual car (instead of an illustration). MPC's kit promoted a straight-axle Gasser front end, along with a hypothetical turbine engine (also shared with MPC's 1969 Firebird kit). MPC's kit had a correct Camaro instrument panel, but the interior bucket was incorrectly sourced from its Firebird kit. Once again, there were no annual kits of the Z-28.

In the 1980s, AMT-Ertl attempted to restore their 1969 MPC Camaro tool to stock status, after it had been earlier heavily modified into a Camaro Super Stocker Series oval dirt track racer. The effort came off poorly; kit builders were suit-

MPC's 1969 Camaro kit featured a turbine funny car version on the box top and side panel (Wave 1/). The turbine engine, air intake ducting, and exhaust ducts appeared to be lifted straight from JoHan's Chrysler Turbine Car kit! The same Logghe Stamping Company–style straight axle front axle and suspension found in other 1968 and 1969 MPC kits was here as well.***

Revell's original 1969 Camaro Z-28 kit (center) was an outstanding replica, except for the extra "RS" grille badging. That was quickly fixed on subsequent production runs like the one on the lower left. All the other kits shown here are descendants of this original kit tooling, with features like 396/427 engines, chambered exhaust systems and (where applicable) decals to replicate the optional hound's-tooth interior upholstery! (All kits: Wave 3/*.)

ably disappointed. It also still had an incorrect Firebird interior. Another version of this tool with a convertible body and some seat and console changes debuted later. (Monogram had also introduced a 1/24th-scale 1969 Z-28 Street Machine in the late 1970s, but the body was misshapen in a number of ways and attempting a conversion of this kit to a factory stock status was beyond all but the very most talented model builders). As of the late 1980s, the only real option for the serious 1969 Camaro model builder was to locate, and pay big bucks for, either the original AMT or MPC 1969 Camaro kit. Model builders and collectors looking for a factory stock 1969 Z-28 remained flat out of luck.

All this changed when Revell decided to produce a 1/12th-scale kit of the 1969 Z-28. This kit was immaculately designed and produced, and, more important for the mainstream 1/24th- or 1/25th-scale market, it made it relatively easy for Revell to produce a 1/25th-scale spinoff series of 1969 Camaros. The explanation for the incredibly accurate body in these new Revell Camaro kits? In an interview for this book, former Monogram/Revell executive Bob Johnson reports that Chuck Jordan, the vice president of design for General Motors, provided a set of 1/10th-scale scans of the real car to Revell. (Chuck was well known in the kit collector world back then, being frequently seen at toy shows, particularly if they featured Ferrari models.)

If you're a fan of 1969 Camaros, these kits are to be avoided. The MPC reissues on the left (Wave 1/*) unsuccessfully attempted to restore the stock body, and the version on top even has incorrect Pontiac OHC Six and 400 V-8 engines! The Monogram kits on the right (Wave 2/*) faithfully represent late 1970s street machines, but the 1969 Camaro bodies have major accuracy issues.

Revell's first 1/25th-scale offering was a Yenko Camaro (covered in Chapter 13), followed quickly by a terrific factory stock 1969 Z-28 kit. The body proportions were perfect and the kit contents spot-on, even to the GM Parts Counter dual-quad cross ram intake/carbs, period tubular headers, and the factory chambered dual exhaust!

Revell's basic 1969 Camaro tooling has spawned a whole series of kit spinoffs, including a convertible SS396, Indy Pace Car, ZL-1, and several tuner offerings (again, covered in Chapter 13). It has sold countless kits to adult modelers and collectors, and proves the value of creating kit tooling correctly from the start. It becomes a consistent stream of revenue for its maker for decades to come.

1970½–1974: Redefining the Pony Car/Muscle Car Genre

While many consider the 1969 Camaro to be the ultimate Camaro, my vote squarely lands on the 1970½ and 1971 versions. Perhaps the most radical departure from any original pony car product to date (I'm excepting the Mustang II era from this discussion), the 1970½ Camaro and its Firebird cousin literally rewrote the book on what it took to be a leading edge

With the second-generation Camaro came all-new kits from AMT (left) and MPC (center and right). Both AMT and MPC featured the SS396 rather than the Z-28. The AMT kit was sold through 1971 but was really accurate for 1970 only. MPC switched from the base (full bumper) front end to the split-bumper RS version for its 1971 kit (all: Wave 1/**).

pony car/muscle car. True 2+2 sports car proportions combined with styling that combined both traditional Chevy and foreign/exotic design cues, along with an all-new chassis that made the most of the low center of gravity, plus a new LT-1 based Z-28, suddenly made every other pony car appear instantly outdated. Minor updates greeted the 1971 version, most notably replacing the low-back buckets and headrests with the combined high-back buckets from the new 1971 Vega product line.

AMT and MPC once again developed new annual kits to replicate the second-generation Camaro. These kits both replicated the big-block SS396 rather than the Z-28 that was the image leader for the full-sized Camaro. AMT's 1970½ annual kit was introduced in February of that year and sold all the way through 1971. This kit featured the base and SS front end with the end-to-end blade bumper, and also included an engraved vinyl roof. MPC's kit was introduced two months later in April 1970, and also included the standard base Camaro and SS grille/bumper/turn signal layout. MPC did update its kit for 1971, revising it to the split-bumper RS front-end design. MPC's added "Wild Put On" parts were just as tasteless then as now.

After continuing to update annual kits to reflect the major freshenings of the second-generation Camaro throughout its lifespan (MPC did all the annual updates through 1981, while AMT gave up after the 1977 model year), in the late 1980s AMT-Ertl attempted to backdate the original AMT tool to replicate a 1970½ Z-28. Camaro enthusiasts were quick to cite major inaccuracies in the backdating effort, and the tool quickly (and apparently permanently) went out of production in that guise.

For a truly accurate early second-generation Camaro model kit, modelers waited all the way until 2001 for an all-new, modern generation tool to be produced of the 1970½ Z-28. Developed during the late AMT/Ertl era, but most likely rushed to market to meet a big box retailer deadline before final fine-tuning could be completed, the kit has been criticized by some. With minor and easy to accomplish kit builder corrections, it is now by far the premier choice for a second-generation Camaro Z-28 kit.

The 1972 Camaro once again featured minor changes, but was greatly affected in the marketplace by both the general move away from pony cars as well as a protracted strike at the sole assembly site. A modestly revised 1973 Camaro followed this near-death experience; it met the new front bumper impact standards with a very handsome treatment. In addition, a Z-28 version, while not quite as powerful as the previous model year

In 1989, AMT-Ertl attempted to backdate its Camaro annual kit, last seen in the 1977 version, to the 1970½ model year and convert it to Z-28 status (Wave 1/*). Second-generation Camaro fans were not impressed with the retooled front end or the incorrect use of a single engine block casting to represent both small and big-block Chevy engines.

In 2001, AMT-Ertl more than made up for its previous second-generation Z-28 kit misses with this all-new 1970½ kit tool (Wave 3/*). The kit was reissued in 2007 under the Model King private label brand, along with a much-improved decal sheet that makes this the kit to search out.

iterations, was still among the premier marketplace performers that year. The 396 (really 402) big-block was dropped that year and a new Type LT series replaced the SS version.

While critics argue about the success of the new bumpers and front and rear treatments of the 1974 Camaro, it was clearly eye-catching. Moreover, the Z-28 (minus those "airport landing strip" hood stripes, please) remained a star performer in the context of 1974 competition.

AMT and MPC dutifully followed the 1972–1974 product changes and produced annual kits of each of these Camaros. Of note is that for 1973, MPC finally modified its tool into the Z-28 version, while AMT's 1973 Camaro kit was marketed as an SS350 even though the Type LT replaced that model on the real car.

Epilogue

As a career marketing professional with experience in both the real automotive marketplace and the scale model kit business, a number of interesting observations strike me about the Mustang and Camaro.

First, this is perhaps the longest running and most focused of any domestic auto industry rivalry during the last 50 years. The only other one that comes to mind as being comparable is that of the Ford F-Series and Chevy C-Series pickups, but the difference there is that Ford has beat Chevy for each of the last 40 years as of the date this book was prepared. The Camaro has been more successful in chalking up several sales victories over the Mustang, not in total, but at least during several periods over its lifetime. And in the most popular measures of overall vehicle performance (such as quarter-mile elapsed times), the lead has switched back and forth between Mustang and Camaro many, many times through the years.

Having pointed that out, it is interesting to note that in the model car kit industry, kit coverage of Camaros in recent decades has been far superior to that of the Mustang. Some modeling industry executives maintain that Chevrolet kits will always sell better than Ford kits, and if you look at the situation today that would seem to be the case. The model car builder can choose from reasonably well done to superbly accurate *modern-era* kit tooling of the Camaro for each model year from its 1967 introduction to its 1970½ peak.

Conversely, the 1964½ to 1973 Mustang kit world is a hodge-podge of original (and horribly outdated) recycled annual kit tooling along with a number of Wave 2 variants with their roots in early 1980s model kit technology, plus one early 1990s era kit tooling that continues to be compromised by several body accuracy errors. This would certainly seem to present a business opportunity to the kit manufacturer that chooses to replicate the first-generation Mustangs with modern kit tooling and showroom stock replicas. They could start with new kits of the 1968 Mustang GT, 1969 Mach 1, 1969 Boss 429, and 1971 Boss 351, at the very least. I think you'll agree that the original and definitive pony car deserves nothing less.

Missing in Action

Mustang and Camaro pony cars yet to appear in a 1/24th-1/25th–scale kit

- 1967–1968 Mustang hardtop and convertible
- 1969 Boss 429

Mustang/Camaro pony cars that need a new/modern kit offering

- 1964½ Mustang hardtop and convertible in 1/25th scale
- 1966 Mustang convertible and GT 2+2 in 1/25th scale
- 1968 Mustang GT with 428 Cobra Jet
- 1969–1970 Mustang Mach 1 with 428 Cobra Jet
- 1970½ or 1971 Camaro SS396
- 1971 Mustang Mach 1 with accurate 429 Cobra Jet Ram Air/Drag Pack
- 1971 Boss 351 with accurate 351 Cleveland
- 1971–1974 Camaro Z-28
- 1972 Mustang Mach 1 with 351 Cleveland Cobra Jet or HO

Car Model Kits Scale Showroom

The following models show how several of the model kits mentioned earlier in this chapter look when assembled by experienced adult model car builders. (Photography and models are by the writer unless noted otherwise.)

Revell's 1966 Mustang GT-350 kit forms the basis of this heavily detailed model project. Note the added engine detail and the carefully painted tire sidewall lettering. (Builder: Bill Coulter)

Revell's kit formed the basis of this heavily detailed Code Z Grabber Green 1970 Boss 302; it was the subject of a two-part buildup article in the December 1999 and January 2000 issues of Scale Auto Enthusiast *magazine and a feature in the May 2001 issue of* Mustang Monthly *magazine.*

The 1968 Z-28 is built from the original AMT-Lesney kit of the early 1980s, while the 1969 Z-28 is based Revell's superb 1969 Camaro kit series first offered in the early 1990s. They are both 100 percent kit-based other than swapped wheels and tires.

Both of these Camaros are based on AMT-Ertl's 1970½ Z-28 kit. The Z-28 was built with late-in-the-model-year COPO 9796 large rear spoiler upgrade and Code 52 Sunflower Yellow paint. The Code 65 Hugger Orange Camaro in the foreground was converted to a factory stock SS396.

The Code 72 Hugger Orange COPO L72 hardtop and the Code 76 Daytona Yellow SS396 convertible were both built from Revell's 1969 Camaro kit series. The convertible's hound's-tooth interior is courtesy of seat inserts printed on the kit's decal sheet. (Builder/Photographer: Mike Hanson).

The Code 79 Rallye Green Metallic 1969 Yenko S/C Camaro coupe contrasts with a SS396 convertible. Both were built starting with Revell's 1969 Camaro series kits. (Builder/Photographer: Mike Hanson)

The Pony Car Brigade, Part 2

Everything Else

Between "annual kits" and much later kits from Revell, Monogram, and AMT-Ertl, most of the pony car competitors have been reduced to the popular 1/24th and 1/25th scales. In this chapter, I'll cover key kits of the Plymouth Barracuda, Mercury Cougar, Pontiac Firebird, AMC Javelin, and Dodge Challenger from 1964½ through (where applicable) 1974.

If you come late to the party, you better make a big entrance. That's the story, in a nutshell, of all the other pony cars that competed in the sport compact segment. I'll cover them in the order of their entrance into the marketplace. That makes the Plymouth Barracuda up first, and the Dodge Challenger up last.

Barracuda: A Fish out of Water or Vicious Aggressor?

Most automotive historians note that the Barracuda actually beat the Mustang to the marketplace by a few weeks.

While the initial Mustang was in some ways a stunningly re-bodied and brilliantly marketed Falcon derivative; the Barracuda was basically a Valiant Signet with a large glass-covered fastback roof and a modified front end. No one was fooled as to the Barracuda's Valiant origins. The Barracuda was not a truly viable Mustang competitor until the 1967 model year.

Nonetheless, the Barracuda has its own unique appeal, not the least of which was the versatility of its fastback body style that ran through 1969. The 1970 and 1971 versions then went on to define perhaps the most outrageous expression of the original pony car genre, a trait that has made the Hemi 'Cuda from those two years now among the most valuable American automotive collectibles of all time.

1964½–1966 Barracuda: First out of the Gate

Maybe it was that I was already a young Mopar fan, but I recall considerable excitement about the introduction of the new Valiant Barracuda. It featured what some called the largest rear window ever at the time of its introduction, complemented by a versatile interior with a fold-down rear seat and open access to the trunk area. The roof design first appeared in Chrysler Design Studios as a proposed special model of the new 1962 Plymouth Fury to be called the "Super Sport." It translated surprisingly well to the compact Valiant below-the-beltline sheet metal. The first Barracuda grille treatment was also highly attractive, and the leading edge of

AMT's Barracuda kit (Wave 1/) featured a mild custom treatment from Gene Winfield on the box top, along with a showroom stock illustration on the box ends depicted in Code AA-1 Barracuda Gold Metallic. The "Bonneville Racing Version" on the side panel was said to include a "Dodge" (not Plymouth) 426 Hemi Head Engine.***

the front fenders was slightly revised from the Valiant version. A new 273 V-8 arrived just in time for the introduction, too.

For the 1965 model year, the "Valiant" nameplate was dropped, otherwise the Barracuda carried on in its initial form. A high-output version of the 273 V-8 rated at 235 hp soon followed. In 1966, a new grille, new bumpers, and new front and rear fenders (better integrated with the bumpers) were the primary means of delivering a freshened Barracuda appearance.

Given its earlier Valiant annual kits, AMT was the logical choice for a model car kit of the Barracuda. Its kit carried over into 1966 with the minor changes of the real car. The body tool was then permanently altered to facilitate a kit of the rear-engine drag car originally campaigned by Tom McEwen. As a result, I've seen no reissues of these original Barracuda annual kits.

*A mild drag racing version took prime place on AMT's 1967 Barracuda kit box top. The side panel showed a mild custom from George Barris. Inside the kit, hobbyists found the same standard Slant Six and optional (non-factory) 426 Hemi engine dating from AMT's 1965 Barracuda kit. For 1968, the same AMT kit tool, with minor updates, was now marketed with MPC's distinctive box art, instruction sheet, and decals (both: Wave 1/**).*

1967–1969 Barracuda: A Somewhat Different Approach

It didn't take long for the marketplace to deliver a clear verdict that the Mustang solution had a much wider market appeal than the fastback Barracuda. The Plymouth design studios knew the correct response, which was that it was a breathtaking proposal eventually billed as the "Barracuda SX." It was later shown as an auto show concept vehicle (Mopar fans, look it up and weep!), but the design called for a lower cowl height than could be achieved with the Barracuda's Valiant/Dart platform roots, and Chrysler was not able to source the required new body into its existing manufacturing base.

A more modest 1967 Barracuda was introduced slightly later in the model year than the rest of Plymouth's 1967 products, and the eventual design repeated a bit of the "SX" flavor. But it lacked the long hood/lower cowl height/short rear overhand proportions that made the Mustang, and its other new marketplace competitors, so appealing. On the other hand, the fresh new fastback with a smaller rear window was joined by two-door hardtop and convertible body styles.

Very mild front- and rear-end tweaks made for a very appealing 1968 freshening. The big story, however, was a new small-block performance V-8 derived from the 1967 redo of the Mopar 318 V-8 with Wedge heads and thin-wall casting techniques. Available only in a high-performance version, the new 340 Wedge was a legend in the making.

AMT tooled a new body shell to capture the contours of the 1967 fastback, but kept the engine/chassis layout of its circa-1965 1/25th-scale Barracuda annual kit largely unchanged. A major change for 1968 was that the Barracuda annual kit now came from MPC instead of AMT. But in one of those odd and unexplained model kit occurrences, inside the box were those same, and now aging, AMT kit parts, albeit slightly updated to the 1968 Barracuda's appearance.

By the 1969 model year, as noted in the last chapter, the supercar world was starting to heavily influence the pony car marketplace. Plymouth responded with new 'Cuda 340 and 'Cuda 383 packages. It was a kind of Road Runner–esque value approach to go along with the continued availability of the Formula S version. The 340 and 383 engines were joined near year-end with a 440 V-8 option. A new hood (later donated to the 1973–1976 Dodge Dart) enabled a slightly more stylized front-end layout, and the rear taillamp option changed a third time.

MPC's 1969 Barracuda annual kit was reissued in 1988 (right) with a newly tooled 383 V-8 to go along with the kit's Hemi V-8. Round 2 repackaged the kit in 2015 with a box top (left) that visually duplicated the original 1969 annual kit release (both: Wave 1/).*

The Barracuda annual kit stayed with MPC for 1969. The kit was reissued several times in the 1970s in street machine-flavored form (no stock parts), but fortunately it was returned to showroom stock form for a 1988 reissue from AMT-Ertl. This version has seen several reissues.

The first two attempts at a modern 1970 'Cuda kit (background left and right, both Wave 2/*) were greatly compromised by inaccurate body proportions, and collectors are counseled to avoid them. Revell's all-new kit in the foreground (Wave 4/*) is by far the most detailed third-generation Barracuda kit ever. Its body is in some areas more accurate than the original MPC kit, but overall still doesn't look quite as "correct" to most experts as did the original MPC annual kit.

1970 Barracuda: Plymouth Finally Gets It Right!

For 1970, the Barracuda finally achieved the separate platform with true pony car proportions that it had needed since the beginning to be fully competitive with the Mustang and the cars that it inspired. The new body shell and chassis shared many components with the new-for-1971 Mopar B-Bodies (which had originally been scheduled to also appear a year earlier in 1970).

While the Barracuda had a new in-house competitor in the Dodge Challenger, the Barracuda retained its own sheet metal, design theme, wheelbase, and most of the interior styling. Only the cowl area, front windshield, and instrument panel/clusters were visibly shared between the two. Engines from Chrysler's Slant Six all the way to the 426 Street Hemi were available in volume through the factory option system. The 'Cuda AAR joined the lineup at mid-year; this allowed homologation of Plymouth's Trans-Am racing team entry. Myriad appearance, performance, and luxury options were exciting to read about in the sales catalogue, but created a nightmare of factory assembly complexity.

This was not a particularly detailed kit, but among all the 1970 Barracuda kits that have been produced, this MPC annual kit (Wave 1/**) is considered the "Gold Standard" for best capturing the subtle details of the body sculpture from Plymouth Design Studio Manager John Herlitz and his team. MPC even molded the kit in a styrene color that was a convincing copy of the factory code FJ-5 Limelight High Impact paint.***

Then, the pony car marketplace was completely redefined in February 1970 with the introduction of the second-generation Camaro and Firebird, and the startling drop in sales of supercars of all brands was becoming painfully obvious about the same time. Plymouth finally had achieved the right answer, but it was relevant for just a few months before the world moved on. Still, in my studied opinion, no other car better reflects the merging of the original pony car idiom and supercar movements than does the 1970 Plymouth 'Cuda in its 340, 383, 440, and Hemi versions.

MPC continued as the producer of Barracuda model kits, and its 1970 'Cuda kit really captured the excitement around the new Plymouth pony car. In addition to the showroom stock Hemi 'Cuda version, the kit offered three additional building options: Super Stock, Barris Custom, and High Rise (that attempted to capture the Street Freak/Street Gasser flavor that was popular at the time).

The team at Revell has subsequently made three attempts to produce a modern kit of the 1970 'Cuda. The first two tries in 1997 and 2007 were hopelessly compromised in that they were based on the incorrect longer wheelbase of its previous 1970 Challenger T/A kit. An all-new Hemi 'Cuda kit introduced in 2013 did a superb job of replicating many of the factory options a 1/1-scale 'Cuda buyer could choose back in 1970.

1971 Barracuda: Getting Carried Away

By the start of the 1971 model year, it was obvious to all that the age of the pony car, at least in its initial form, had passed by. Plymouth's then-controversial Barracuda freshening, comprising a complex grille including quad headlamps, extraneous fender vents, and optional rear quarter-panels covered with several cubic feet of matte black tape, probably didn't help. Ironically, today these same design eccentricities now help to make the Plymouth's 1971 pony car among the most valuable of all muscle car–era collectibles (when equipped with the Six Pack or Hemi V-8s). MPC and, more than a decade later, Monogram produced kits of the 1971 'Cuda.

MPC offered a 1971 annual kit of the Barracuda (top, Wave 1/). Monogram later produced a 1/24th-scale kit of the 1971 Hemi 'Cuda (Wave 2/*) as part of its focused early 1980s effort to return to market relevancy. A derivative of this kit with a new convertible body and a different interior trim (Wave 2/*) was introduced in 2003 with a license related to the popular*** **Nash Bridges** ***TV show.***

1972–1974 Barracuda

The Barracuda received another minor freshening for 1972, with a return to dual headlamps and a grille theme that was an evolution of the original 1970 theme. But all the big-block V-8s and the convertible body style were gone. The 1973 changes continued with discreet (compared to the competition) 5-mph front bumpers, which were expanded to the rear for the final 1974 model year. Also for 1974, the then-unsung E58 360 Wedge added some new excitement for those in the know, but by April 1974 the very last Mopar E-Body pony cars came down the line as their former assembly plant was converted to produce more of the super-hot Dusters and Darts of the day.

The MPC Barracuda annual kit extended through the 1972–1974 model years (all: Wave 1/**). MPC missed a bet by failing to update the kit's powertrain choices beyond the now-discontinued 426 Hemi engine. Note that the 1973 and 1974 graphic theme included detailed feature call-outs on the box top illustration.

MPC adopted a pseudo-Pro Stock theme for some of its 1972 annual kits. While the decal sheets matched the exterior livery of certain well-known drag strip competitors of the day (Sox and Martin, in this case), the kits were not authentic Pro-Stock replicas. The competition flavor continued with the 1973 and 1974 annual kit updates, in this case adding a Gasser-style front frame and suspension clip. MPC's Barracuda tool was later altered to a dirt track–style car, and later returned to a somewhat compromised street machine version. A later unassembled promo-style kit was offered. (The original 1970–1974 annual kits remain much preferred for their overall accuracy).

Cougar: The Thunderbird of Pony Cars

Mercury's Cougar created a very special niche in the pony car marketplace. The new Cougar was the only pony car product to be primarily marketed toward the luxury side of this new and developing range of competitive products. Automotive writers have surmised that the Cougar's design brief could be summarized as "a new car half way between the Mustang and the Thunderbird," presumably meaning the size of the former and the exterior/interior accouterments of the latter.

1967–1968 Cougar: Mercury's New Image Leader

Debuting in the fall of 1966 alongside the Mustang's first major marketplace change, the Cougar quickly established its own territory in the automotive market. The mid-year edition

*AMT's 1967 Cougar annual kit (Wave 1/****) was packed in a smaller box, which sold for $1.70 retail (versus $2.00 for most of its kits by then). Inside was a ton of detail and content, including a wild ram-tube option for the 390 FE V-8. Gene Winfield was credited with the styling of the handsome custom version.*

*Now in a $2.00 box, AMT's 1968 Cougar kit (Wave 1/***) was a minor update to the kit it debuted a year earlier. As has been noted before, the quality of artwork on AMT's 1968 annual kit boxes was of museum quality. AMT's talented Art Department personnel had much to be proud of that year.*

of the European-influenced XR-7 series further focused the brand's imagery. Magazine tests mentioned similarities to Jaguar's very tony sedans as often as to Ford's own Thunderbird. In addition, it became the image leader for the entire Mercury product range, under the umbrella of a now–politically insensitive "The Man's Car" tagline.

Cougar's body shell appeared completely different from the Mustang, enhanced by the hidden headlamp grille and wall-to-wall taillamps, along with a finely tailored bodyside featuring a very curvaceous side section. Unlike the Mustang, the Cougar featured only V-8 powertrains, and only a two-door hardtop (no convertible or fastbacks to be found). Although Ford's 289 2-barrel was standard, one suspects that many of the cars that left the local dealership were actually equipped with the optional 289 4-barrel, or perhaps more likely, the 390 4-barrel powertrains.

AMT had been the exclusive kitmaker for Mercury since the dawn of the 3-in-1 annual kit business, most recently featuring the 1965–1966 Park Lane and 1966 Cyclone GT as its annual kit offerings. For 1967, the kit flag was tossed to the Cougar, and AMT's kit definitely met the challenge. The body was meticulously replicated, along with the 390 FE engine and a far more detailed chassis and suspension than was found under most annual kits back then.

The 1968 model year brought detail refinements and the most obvious visual change, the addition of federally mandated side marker lights on the front and rear fenders. The new 302 V-8 replaced the 289, and two versions of the FE-based 390 were now offered. A number of special editions were marketed in 1968, including the GT-E with an optional 427 V-8 rated at 390-hp and a very imposing but non-functional hood scoop. The 427 was discontinued mid-year to make room for the new 428 CJ (Cobra Jet) engine. On the scale shelves, AMT's 1968 Cougar kit was updated accordingly, but otherwise carried over all the key features of the previous-year annual kit.

1969–1970 Cougar: Preening the Cat

The 1969 Cougar underwent a comprehensive update throughout, corresponding to a major upgrade to the Mustang that was engineered on the same timeline. The Cougar added a very Buick-like side sweep to its profile view, while the headlamps were now hidden by a horizontal grille of reduced height, along with the loss of the body-colored center grille split applique. A convertible body style was added for the first time. The standard powertrain was upgraded for the third year in a row, to Ford's new 351 2-barrel Windsor V-8. The still-new 428 CJ offering quickly developed a wicked street rep. A dedicated muscle series, the Cougar Eliminator, offered a standard 351 4-barrel Windsor V-8. But the ultimate expression was achieved by Eliminators that were powered by Ford's new Boss 302 introduced at mid-year. Reputable sources now document that four Boss 429 Cougars (using the same offsite production approach as the Mustang Boss 429) were also built.

AMT's 1969 Cougar kit proudly displayed the new body and interior, this time in XR-7 guise, but underneath was the same engine and chassis as before, only this time the factory stock air cleaner went missing. This was to be AMT's last Cougar kit, it seemed, but the kit was reissued once in 1978 as part of AMT's Countdown Series catalog offering. A couple of years later, AMT-Lesney added in a Boss 429 engine and marketed the resulting street-machine themed kit.

AMT-Ertl's 1990s reissues of the AMT 1969 Cougar annual kit (both: Wave 1/*) (above) were moderately reworked with new interiors and engines. Of the many pony car and supercar kits originally tooled during the annual kit era, these two adapted AMT-Ertl kits remain among the best in overall kit design and detail.

*For 1969, AMT's annual kits were "reproduced from Official Factory Blueprints" and carried a Blueprint-themed instruction sheet, complete with a signoff date (November 21, 1968) and signature (K.A.T.). The year 1969 also marked a move away from 100-percent showroom stock replicas for some AMT annual kits; this one (Wave 1/**) offered only super stock, drag, and custom versions. The Countdown Series reissue (Wave 1/*) is on the right.*

MPC's surprise kit of the 1969 Car Craft *Magazine Super Cat (Wave 1/***) replicated a project car built by Dyno Don, featured in the April 1969 issue of the magazine, and later awarded as the grand prize in Coca Cola's National Thirst Eliminator sweepstakes. The kit featured excellent detail and building options.*

As it turned out, more life was left in the old AMT 1969 Cougar kit. When AMT-Ertl was combing the combined AMT/MPC tooling bank in the early 1990s, they decided to revisit the 1969 Cougar tooling, with the result being two new kits. Both these kits were tweaked to remove the XR-7 exterior identification and the interiors were changed to the mid-level Interior Decor Group spec. AMT-Ertl then produced a newly tooled Boss 302 engine in an "Eliminator" kit. The other kit used the highly detailed 428 Cobra-Jet tooling from the MPC tooling bank to create a 428 CJ kit. Both the Eliminator and CJ-428 kits have seen multiple reissues.

But wait, there's still more! With the 1970 model year approaching and an offer from MPC to produce annual kits of the all-new Cyclone plus hardtop *and* convertible kits of the Cougar, Mercury's model car kit allegiance transferred away from AMT for the first time. However, before I get to the 1970 MPC kits, one more surprise was in store for 1969. A flyer targeted at hobby store owners was distributed early in the 1969 model year, announcing an all-new MPC (not AMT) kit of the 1969 Cougar *Super Cat*. The merchandising was tied into a drag-racing promotion run by *Car Craft* magazine with participation from Lincoln-Mercury Division and drag racing driver/builder Dyno Don Nicholson. The kit included both a highly detailed, newly tooled 428 CJ (yep, the same tooling that found its way into the AMT-Ertl CJ 428 kit more than 20 years later) plus one of the very first scale replicas of Ford's all-new Semi Hemi Boss 429. This kit's optional engine was interesting in that it had a number of features not seen on the series production Boss 429. It was probably tooled up based on a pre-production or race-tuned engine in Ford's development labs.

*MPC's 1970 Cougar annual kits (Wave 1/***) were derived from the 1969 Super Cat release shown earlier, and continued to include both highly detailed 428 Cobra Jet Ram Air and non-factory Boss 429 engines. MPC always showed extra creativity in its convertible annual kits. Note the racing windscreen and roll-bar top on the box top illustration here.*

The Cougar saw detail refinements in 1970, with the return of a body-colored center grille divider and the vertical grille graphics seen in the 1967 and 1968 Cougars. The special series continued as per 1969, with the Cougar Eliminator playing the lead role for Mercury in the performance-themed marketing environment in the auto industry that year.

MPC updated its still-new Cougar kit to the 1970 specs, and in a surprise, introduced a convertible kit to sell alongside the hardtop kit. This was to be the only Cougar convertible kit ever offered in 1/25th scale.

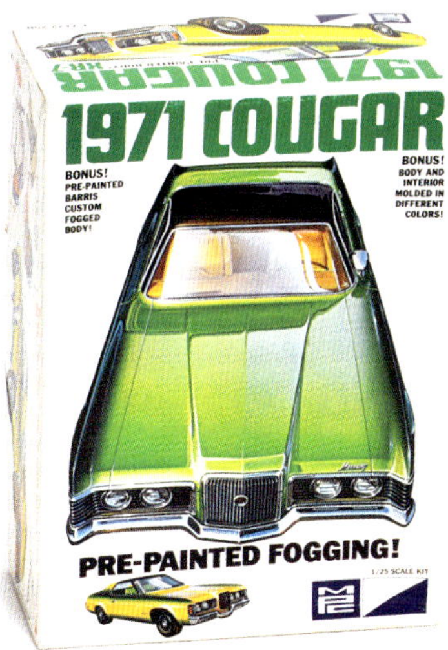

*MPC's 1971 and 1972 Cougar kits (Wave 1/**) reflected the new exteriors and interiors of the real car, while continuing the now-out-of-date engine and chassis from its earlier 1969–1970 kit tooling. The 1971 kit was one of several MPC offerings that year with a factory-applied "edging" paint finish, in this case credited to George Barris.*

1971–1973 Cougar: Last Years as a Pony Car

The all-new 1971 Cougar was actually perfectly timed for the rapid movement away from performance vehicles in the early 1970s. The larger, wider, heavier, and more luxurious Cougar fit perfectly with evolving public preference away from pony cars toward more personal luxury-themed vehicles such as the Chevy Monte Carlo. However, look closely enough and there were still plenty of goodies for the performance car buyer.

The 1971 Cougar continued in base and XR-7 forms, but for the first time it lost the trademark hidden headlamp front-end treatment. A new GT Appearance Package replaced the Eliminator. When it was combined with either of two new powertrains (a 335 series 351 Cleveland 4-barrel or a 385 series 429 Cobra Jet/429 SCJ with or without Ram Air), the Cougar could still be a formidable street warrior.

For 1972, the 385 series engines were gone, and the 351 Cleveland was tweaked to accommodate the new low-lead/no-lead gasoline, but otherwise remained a very interesting product. By 1974, when the Cougar was changed to a midsized Torino-based luxury car, the Cougar completed a move away from my muscle car definition that causes me to forego further coverage here.

While the underbody and engines of the real 1971–1972 Cougar were mostly new, MPC's kits for these two model years continued the engine/chassis/suspension tooling of the previous-year kits. This meant that the new models included two totally incorrect engines: the discontinued FE 428 CJ and the Boss proposition.

This is one of the reissues of the MPC 1973 Cougar annual kit (Wave 1/). These reissues would be far more appealing if they were returned to the 1971–1972 Cougar configuration and the engine choices were changed to the correct 351 Cleveland or (for 1971 only) 429 SCJ factory stock applications.*

The 1973 Cougar wore a visibly larger front bumper in line with federal requirements, but otherwise was little changed. MPC updated its tooling to the 1973 spec, and that annual kit has been periodically reissued since. (For the modeling kit-basher, periodically available aftermarket sources allow back-dating the 1973 kit reissue to the earlier 1971–1972 versions, at least from an exterior perspective.)

Firebird: Was It the GTO of Pony Cars?

Firebird . . . the hottest, swingingest, wildest, and newest sports car . . . from the same people who made GTO the only letters in the alphabet for American youth. Those are the words from model kitmaker MPC's hobby store flyer entitled "The Hot New Sports Machine from Pontiac," announcing the arrival of the new Firebird (with just a little extra MPC hyperbole added on top).

Pontiac's entry in the pony car sweepstakes arrived in 1967½, some three years after the Mustang's marketplace debut. It was a somewhat hastily conceived spinoff of the Camaro, but it was generally well received due to its innovative front-end styling and general refinement of the Camaro's basic bones.

1967½–1968 Firebird: The Magnificent Five

The very first Firebird had front vent windows and front turn signals more centrally located below the bumper to distinguish it from the soon to arrive 1968 update. It was cleverly marketed as five different versions, each distinguished by its powertrain configuration.

MPC had owned the Pontiac promotional toy business since 1966, so it was the logical model company to market the 1/25th-scale Firebird kit. MPC's aforementioned hobby store flyer declared "Special! Kit offers versions of the Magnificent Five, just like the original full-scale Firebird." As expected, the kit included the Firebird 400 V-8, but also in the box was a highly detailed replica of the OHC-inline-6 that Pontiac debuted in the 1966 Tempest. MPC's kit replicated the Sprint version of the inline-6, complete with its 4-barrel carb and dual exhaust manifolds.

The 1968 Firebird that followed a half year later was almost unchanged except for the turn signals moved to the lower front fender corners, the ventless side door glass, and the rear side marker lights. For 1968, MPC's kit was updated to reflect the minor tweaks of the real car.

Meanwhile, down at the local hobby store, another Firebird kit appeared as part of the AMT "for 1968" lineup. This hardtop/convertible kit was a thinly disguised takeoff on AMT's "for 1968" Camaro kit, itself only a guess as to how the real 1968 Camaro would appear. The customized execution was perhaps handsome in some elements, but not at all accurate to the showroom reality. The same kit was joined by a 1/25th Kindsvater-hulled V-drive drag boat and trailer, marketed as the *Quarter Master*. Both these AMT kits should be avoided unless their oddity overrules the lack of authenticity.

Decades later, Revell introduced an all-new 1968 Firebird kit that hit the market in 2001. This kit was unexpected and a real surprise to the modeling community that intimately follows "leads" and "leaks" from sources both legitimate and nefarious regarding future kit introductions from the domestic model kitmakers. Given the last time anyone could buy an

*MPC's 1967½ Firebird kit (Wave 1/***) showed the close relationship between MPC and the Pontiac Division at the time, as the kit side panel promoted Pontiac's Magnificent Five marketing campaign. Also emphasized was ". . . the only overhead cam six in kits . . ." in addition to the kit's Pontiac 400 V-8.*

*MPC's Firebird kit (Wave 1/**) continued into 1968 with both OHC 6 and V-8 engine options. The five Firebird models and the OHC inline-6 engine option were again mentioned, along with side panel illustrations of a somewhat unusual "customized" Firebird on the side panel. MPC also added its unique "Hollow Baloney Tires" to this kit.*

AMT's "guess" at a 1968 Firebird kit (Wave 1/*) resulted in this non-accurate convertible/hardtop kit featuring custom and drag building versions only (no "stock" version). This thinly disguised variant of AMT's similar 1968 Camaro kit is notable today only for its collectability, not its accuracy. The same fictitious Firebird kit was also part of this very rare Quarter Masters *Drag Boat combination kit (Wave 1/**), also issued in 1968.*

Revell's all-new 1968 Firebird 400 hardtop kit (Wave 3/) prompted observations from some modelers about the simplified assembly versus Revell-Monogram's previous series of 1969 Camaro kits, but in reality, it was a fine model kit that suffered only for the inaccuracy of some nonimportant street machine version parts like the ill-proportioned blower/intake manifold assembly.*

accurate 1967½ or 1968 Firebird assembly kit was back in, well, 1968, this nicely detailed Revell kit was well received by the model builders and kit collectors.

1969 Firebird and Trans Am: Refining the 'Bird

When the 1969 Firebird broke cover, it featured mostly new sheet metal that was shared with the Camaro from the front cowl/door rearward, but with a unique front fender/hood/grille treatment all its own. At mid-year, a new model debuted, the first-ever Trans Am. Older car enthusiasts will recall how the automotive press back then discarded the Trans Am as little more than a paint and spoiler package. Today, of course, a 1969½ Trans Am is a highly desirable collectible, especially if it is one of the RA-IV equipped hardtops or the few convertibles that were factory assembled.

MPC's revised Firebird kit captured the 1969 changes. MPC also surprised everyone very late in the model year with a kit of the 1969½ Trans Am.

Up until this point, no factory stock Firebird convertible kit had been produced in 1/25th scale, and that would remain the case until 1982 when MPC dusted off the upper body dies of its 1969 Firebird convertible promo and combined these

*MPC's 1969 Firebird (Wave 1/**) continued with the previous engine and chassis tooling, but featured a new body and updated interior. With the addition of an optional Turbine engine (also shared with MPC's 1969 Camaro annual kit), the kit now featured three engine choices. A second production run of this kit in August 1969 (Wave 1/***) dropped the Turbine engine but added the new Trans Am exterior features and fresh box art.*

MPC's 1969 annual kit is the most reissued first-generation Firebird model kit of all. These reissues of the hardtop kit date from 1979, 1993, and 1996 (all: Wave 1/*). In 1982, MPC adapted the convertible body of its 1969 Firebird promo to the kit form, resulting in this Firebird convertible kit (Wave 1/**), which, other than wheels and tires, could be built in factory stock form.

with the remainder of the 1969 Firebird annual kit to produce the Sundancer assembly kit. Even the Sprint OHC inline-6 and Trans Am exterior parts (other than graphics) survived the transition, offering the hobbyist a number of potential build variations. Since then, both the MPC 1969 Firebird hardtop and convertible variants have seen occasional reissues in more recent times, the more recent ones updated with a different interior upholstery pattern.

MPC's 1970½ and 1971 Firebird kits (both: Wave 1/***) featured the Formula 400 configuration and were well detailed for the time. The 1971 Firebird refinements (fender louvers and high-back bucket seats) were faithfully captured by MPC, which was not always the case for domestic annual kits in the 1970s.

1970½–1974 Firebird and Trans Am: An Italian Exotic at a Fraction of the Price?

As a Mopar fan back then, I was pretty buzzed about the new E-Body Challengers and 'Cudas introduced in the fall of 1969. But when I saw the breathtaking new 1970½ Firebird six months later, even I had to admit that Pontiac had pulled off a stunning coup.

The new Formula 400 coupe in its unadorned purity was breathtaking; an affordable take on a mid-1960s Ferrari coupe that in some ways was even more visually appealing than the Italian exotic itself. And the bespoilered new Trans Am with its rear-facing Ram-Air induction Shaker hood scoop looked like nothing more than a racing Trans-Am circuit competitor that missed the turnout to Pit Road and went through the grandstand tunnel to the streets outside. Even today, the original second-generation Firebird still catches the eye, and they were so well conceived that the basic design lasted 12 model years and achieved record nameplate sales late in its model cycle, which was the exact opposite of most pony cars both then and now.

The 1971 Firebird was mostly a carryover design, but two visual signals helped classify the update. First, the low-back front buckets with headrests were replaced with a high-back design derived from the new Chevy Vega. Under the hood, the newly retuned 455 HO engine with its "Tractive Force" design approach could be ordered for the Formula 400 and Trans Am. Finally, all but the Trans Am received simulated louvers on the front fenders between the wheelwells and the doors. The 1972 version was again little changed, with the adoption of a grille insert composed of a hexagonal honeycomb screen being the most evident.

MPC remained the producer of Pontiac model kits into the early 1970s, so it was ready with a new Firebird annual kit that went down its Mount Clemens factory production line in April 1970. Per past practice, building versions included showroom stock, mild custom, and "race" versions. The latter included decals inspired by the previous year's *Tin Indian* stock class drag racer campaigned by Knafel Pontiac in Akron, Ohio. MPC also produced the 1971 Firebird kit.

While the Trans Am was the clear image leader of the second-generation Firebird, model builders would not see a kit of that Firebird until mid-1971, when a Trans Am version returned as part of the MPC annual kit lineup. Given the historical nature of the 1970½–1971 Trans Am as setting the pattern for what

*MPC's 1971 Trans Am annual kit (Wave 1/***) was one of several MPC kits introduced in the middle of that year that featured manufacturer-supplied photography of real vehicles rather than an illustration of the kit on the box top. This Monogram 1970½ Trans Am (Wave 1/*) was actually a less-than-completely successful retooling of its original 1980 Turbo Trans Am kit.*

eventually became one of the most iconic of all Pontiac nameplates, and the fact that the MPC early second-generation Firebird annual kits have never been reissued, one would have expected at least one newly tooled, modern era kit of these cars to have appeared during the next 45+ years. This was not to be the case. The closest was Monogram's retooling of its early 1980s Turbo Trans Am kit into a 1970½ Trans Am. However, this was a compromised effort, both in that the subtle contours of the front end were not fully captured in scale, and that the 455 engine was adapted, not very authentically, from the Pontiac 301 V-8 that was standard in the 1980 Turbo Trans Am.

*MPC's Superteen Firebird (Wave 1/**), an opportunistic derivation of its 1968 Firebird kit tooling. Additions included a "Custom TV/Stereo Console," a cantilevered roof with gull-wing–style upper windows and roof panels, and customized front and rear ends.*

The 1972 Firebird was little changed. After a near-death experience due to an extended UAW strike and slow sales, the Firebird returned in 1973 with minor tweaks to meet the new 5-mph front/2½-mph rear bumper impact requirements, and far more significantly, an optional and now-iconic 455 Super Duty engine. For 1974, the Firebird received all-new front and rear treatments designed to both update the car and meet the now 5-mph front and rear bumper impact standards, and the 455 Super Duty persisted for one more model year.

MPC's 1972–1974 Firebird kits captured these changes with varying degrees of accuracy. The 1972 box top featured a drag version, this time with Royal Pontiac livery. The 1973 box top showed the Formula 400 version once again, but with added Trans Am front spoiler, front wheel spats, and rear spoiler, plus an interpretation of the Trans Am Firebird graphic, resized to fit between the Formula dual hood scoops.

Special Interest Firebird Kits

Before I leave the Firebird model kit range, I want to mention two side notes of interest. First, the 1968 Firebird *Superteen* Firebird was a custom variation of the 1968 Firebird, designed by Harry Bradly and built by George Barris Enterprises. A cross-promotion involving Pontiac Division, a film production company owned by Robert E. Peterson (of *Hot Rod* magazine fame), and the ABC television network, eventually three *Superteen* Firebirds were built as prizes for the associated talent search. With the close connections between Barris, the auto industry, and MPC's President George Toteff, an MPC kit replicating the *Superteen* Firebird was pretty much a given.

The second note revolves around the market awakening of the 1976 Trans Am black and gold Special Edition and the subsequent editions of this car through the late 1970s. When combined with the optional WS-6/W-72 suspension and powertrain options, these BlackBirds became a huge marketplace success, further aided by the association with the *Smokey and the Bandit* movie series. MPC captured this magic in scale, and its various kit iterations of the BlackBird eventually achieved wholesale unit volume that some industry experts claim was among the top three best-selling MPC kits of all time!

Javelin: Joisting for Position in the Pony Car Market (and Creating a New Image for American Motors)

American Motors in the 1960s was very much a company in transition. Having enjoyed impressive growth and influence

JoHan's 1969 annual kits were modified to the now–industry-standard box size, and among them the Javelin kit (Wave 1/) was exceptionally well turned out. Due to its relatively low volume production run and increased overall interest in the first-generation Javelin itself, this series of JoHan first-generation Javelin kits are highly valued collectibles today.***

in the auto industry in the late 1950s and very early 1960s as a company focused on compact cars and practical transportation, the company soon fell out of favor as other manufacturers expanded their own portfolios of compact-sized cars, and the market itself resumed its preference for more flamboyant and performance oriented automobiles.

AMC's mid-1960s recovery plan is beyond the scope of this book, but just let me say that the 1968 introduction of AMC's pony car, the Javelin, was important not only as an entry in the industry's fastest growing market segment at the time, but also a way to help reposition the entire American Motors brand proposition.

As such, AMC pulled all the levers available to them and turned out a very competitive product. As the last major brand to enter the market (other than Dodge's Challenger), AMC planned to best all the competition in key areas. And to a significant degree, it met its design brief. The 1968 Javelin was unlike any other AMC product to date. The styling and proportions were leading-edge contemporary, and the interior accommodations were well turned out. AMC's new lightweight V-8, in 343 and (soon thereafter) 390-ci versions was competitive with comparable engines from the others. The car enjoyed modest sales success, but probably of even more importance was its role in actually changing the public's perception of the brand. (A very edgy advertising campaign from AMC's new agency of record, Wells, Rich, and Greene, also played a key role in this accomplishment.)

Also noteworthy is that the Javelin was engineered to allow a second, derivative product, the two-seat AMX, to be introduced six months after the Javelin's debut. The two-seat AMX is covered in Chapter 12.

Model maker John Haenle and JoHan models had been the sole producer of Rambler and AMC products since the beginning of the modern assembly model kit business in the late 1950s. AMC's loyalty to its supply base assured JoHan of the kitmaking opportunity provided by the new Javelin. Its Javelin kit was full of value (just like the real car, one might note). The showroom stock version featured the V-8 engine (more of which in a moment), while the custom version was very tastefully done along the genre of a factory-commissioned auto show feature. The third version was a funny car, but unlike the annual kits from other model brands, JoHan included a full Logghe Stamping Company tubular chassis and interior tinwork, along with a setback, blown AMC V-8. JoHan's distinctive long and shallow flatbox was in its last year of production, and JoHan's artists made the most of it with a Javelin funny car illustration that adapted the distinctive livery of the Grand Engineering 1967 Rebel SST funny car to the new Javelin body design.

The Javelin entered its second model year with very modest tweaks, among them the addition of a bulls-eye target graphic in the driver's side grille panel opening, replacing the Javelin script of the previous model year. The mid-year introduction of AMC's three Big Bad colors (green, orange, and blue) was actually a half model year ahead of the aggressive 1970 color programs from Ford (Grabber) and Mopar (High Impact). JoHan's Javelin kit continued with no changes other than the exterior updates, and new box art to complement JoHan's move to a box size commensurate with those of other model makers.

For the Javelin's third year in the market, a slightly more ambitious freshening program provided a new front grille and hood/air intake design, along with new taillamps and a revised instrument panel. JoHan's annual kit followed along, retaining the showroom stock and funny car versions, and replacing the custom version with an oval track racing version inspired by Jim Paschal's real car. (JoHan also issued a racing-only replica of the Penske/Donohue 1970 Javelin Trans Am entry).

1971–1974 Javelin AMX: A Trans-Am Series Champion for the Street

A very aggressive mid-cycle restyling brought a striking design with exaggerated fender flares/humps (reportedly again influenced by the Javelin Trans Am racing series entries), and for the new top line AMX series (ostensibly a replacement for the discontinued AMX two-seater), a flush-fit grille design. A T-stamping in the roof panels seemed to foreshadow the visual dimensions of the soon-to-appear Firebird T-Top phenomenon, and this feature also served to frame the vinyl roof layout for buyers so inclined. All this was accompanied by the slightly enlarged 401-ci V-8 with Ram Air induction. A slightly more elaborate taillamp treatment arrived for 1972. The roof stamping was simplified for the 1973 and 1974 model year run, along with a different rear panel featuring quad rectangular taillamps.

*If original and untouched, this box art should reveal inside a product-correct 1971 Javelin AMX (Wave 1/***), with the plain horizontal taillamp treatment from that year and a body with the T-top–style roof depressions, along with a raised center section connecting to the C-pillars.*

With benefit of hindsight, evidence suggests these 401-powered cars were highly competitive entries in terms of performance even though they were largely ignored by muscle car buyers back in the day.

JoHan produced annual kits from 1971 to 1974. Its own JoHan-branded annual kits ran during the 1971 to 1973 model years, while its 1974 kit Javelin was a simplified, unassembled promo type offering. The 1971 Javelin was also offered as a funny-car only kit (no showroom stock version). As part of JoHan's late 1960s and early 1970s tool sharing program with AMT, a 1971 Javelin model replicating the Mark Donohue Trans Am racer appeared under the AMT label. The 1974 model year full assembly kit (including a showroom stock version) was also an AMT-branded exclusive. Finally, JoHan produced a kit version ostensibly replicating the George Follmer Trans Am Racer.

*The JoHan kits on the left (Wave 1/**) feature a 1972 Javelin/AMX on the box top (note the taillamps and depressed roof panel sculpting) but chances are that one may find a 1973–1974 version (with the quad taillamps and the clean roof panel) inside. Other versions using this same box art may include different contents inside, so carefully review any second-generation Javelin kit before spending your money. The box on the right is a promo-style (no engine) 1974 Javelin (Wave 1/*).*

The kit buyer has to be extremely careful when considering any potential 1971–1974 Javelin kit purchase. Through the remainder of the 1970s and the 1980s, JoHan produced several runs of these kits, with varying levels of accuracy and in differing box art treatments. To the auto enthusiast and model car collectors, the 1971 and 1972 Javelins are the most desirable, while JoHan seemingly produced many more of quasi-1973 and 1974 kits (with the simpler roof stamping), although the box art top of some of these kits incorrectly portrayed the 1972-specific horizontal egg-crate–style taillamp treatment. You simply cannot rely on the box art or kit number printed on the side panel to judge the interior contents. Instead, you need to carefully inspect the contents (particularly the roof area and rear bumper/taillamp panels) to confirm exactly what you are buying, particularly if you intend to collect or build a 1971 or 1972 Javelin showroom stock replica.

Before I leave the JoHan/Javelin story, I want to note that the one major drawback of all these kits was that JoHan never tooled up an accurate replica of the new AMC lightweight V-8 first introduced in 1966½ and eventually produced in multiple displacements, including 343, 390, and 401 versions. JoHan did attempt to disguise the V-8, with its origins in the original 1950s AMC V-8 configuration, with updates such as the Ram-Air–style air cleaner and other tweaks, but to an AMC enthusiast the compromises were, and remain, highly visible. This, combined with the lack of 1968–1970 Javelin reissues and the potentially compromised production of the 1971–1974 versions, makes the AMC Javelin a prime target for a new generation of contemporary model car kits.

Challenger: The Sports Car with the Big Difference

That's the tag line from the first Challenger brochure published in August 1969. The brochure went on to further explain, saying, "Somebody had to build a little bigger, bolder, hotter sports compact at a price people could afford. Dodge Did. This is Challenger."

Dodge's Challenger was the last entry in the pony car brigade. By the time it arrived for the 1970 model year, the pony car segment had already experienced the most success it would achieve, at least until the very late 1970s when the Camaro, Firebird/TransAm, and the all-new Fox-based Mustang together would sell 850,000 units in 1979.

Today's model builder looking for a 1970 Challenger kit will probably find reissues of these two kits dating from the early 1980s. AMT-Lesney's 1970 R/T (Wave 2/) is the only kit that replicates the Challenger's convertible body style and 440 Six-Pack engine. Monogram's 1970½ T/A (Wave 2/*) is likewise the only kit of that Challenger sub-brand. Buy the most recent reissues of these kits you can find, as they contain far more detailed and accurate decal sheets.*

1970 Challenger: "The Six Pack. It snarls, it quivers, it leaps vast prairies at a single bound."

If you're the last to the party, you better make a big entrance. And that's exactly what the Challenger did. Originally conceived as a luxury sports compact to compete against the Mercury Cougar, by the time it arrived on the market the Challenger had become the pony car/muscle car with more. More length, more space, more power, and (to an extent) a bit more luxury. Its exterior design was highly differentiated versus the sister Barracuda, and beyond the instrument cluster and console, the interior treatment was also unique from the 'Cuda.

Beyond the underbody components, the Challenger also shared the Barracuda's nine powertrain choices, right up to and including the 426 Street Hemi. There's the 440 Six Pack that generated the brochure headline. Beyond that, the lineup also included the base Challenger hardtop, a Challenger with the 340 package, the R/T with a choice of 383 Magnum, 440 Magnum, and 426 Street Hemi power, and the S/E luxury hardtop in both base Challenger and R/T versions. At mid-year, Dodge added the 340 Six Pak–powered Challenger T/A to homologate its Trans-Am series entry.

Having produced Dodge's model car kits since the 1965 model year, MPC was the choice to offer Challenger model kits. Its new kit was introduced in October 1969, and featured the Challenger R/T with the TorqueFlite Automatic. While almost every other model introduced during the annual-kit era included at least one optional engine configuration (some included two complete engines), this kit pretty much stands alone in offering just a single choice: the now-legendary 426 Hemi with no kit options. MPC molded its first run of this kit in a purple styrene that was an attempt to duplicate Dodge's Code FC-7 Plum Crazy High Impact paint color. At least one later production run that year was molded in white styrene.

*MPC's 1970 Challenger kit (Wave 1/***) was a relatively straightforward offering, with less of the extra "sizzle" MPC usually employed to move its kits off the hobby shop shelves. Still, the kit included a large decal treatment to reproduce the "Plum Crazy" graphic shown on the box top illustration, and added the U-Haul–style utility trailer first introduced in MPC's 1968 Coronet R/T kit.*

MPC's 1970 Challenger annual kit was never reissued in its original form, but in 1981 AMT, during its brief ownership by U.K.-based Lesney-Matchbox, introduced an all-new kit of the Challenger R/T convertible. For its era, the kit was pretty well done. Under the slightly out-of-scale Air Grabber scoop poking through the hood was a 440 Six Pak Wedge. MPC had entirely omitted the real car's delicate inset surrounding the wheelwell flares, but the new AMT-Lesney kit over-emphasized this feature in its kit tooling (halfway between the MPC and AMT executions would have been just about perfect). A second street machine kit version was marketed as a hardtop, but the roof was a separate piece for the convertible body that lacked in realism. Both these AMT-Lesney kits have been reissued multiple times under AMT-Ertl branding.

In 1984, Monogram countered with a 1/24th-scale kit of the 1970 Challenger T/A. This kit was well designed, and, apart from some slightly off kilter front-end proportions and somewhat simplified underbody content, it is probably the best overall of the scale kits replicating the 1970 Challenger. Like the AMT-Lesney kit, this one has been reissued multiple times. (There is also a recent 1970 Challenger kit that was derived from die-cast metal replica tooling, but the appearance is too compromised to be considered by serious modelers and kit collectors.)

1971–1974 Challenger R/T and Rallye: Changing with the Marketplace

A modestly revised front grille and taillamp treatment comprised the most significant changes for the Challenger in its sophomore year. The Challenger R/T convertible, T/A and S/E

MPC's 1972 and 1974 Challenger annual kits (both: Wave 1/**) prominently featured drag racing versions on the box art. The 1972 kit included optional High Riser rear suspension parts, while the 1973 and 1974 kits included parts for a Gasser-style straight axle front clip. Palmer Scale Models' 1972 Challenger kit (Wave 1/*) has reappeared more recently in a non-stock Lindberg kit reissue.

versions were discontinued. The R/T picked up an obviously added-on dual louver treatment on the rear quarter-panels, and 340-equipped Challengers joined the R/T lineup this year along with optional elastomeric front and rear bumpers in several colors.

In the model car world, MPC's Challenger kit continued for 1971, with the addition of (offensive to some serious modelers) spoof optional body parts. Palmer Scale Models (a division of Palmer Plastics) was known by serious modelers back then as a kitmaker to avoid at all costs. An exception to this rule was Palmer's 1/25th-scale 1971 Challenger kit, which was actually pretty decent. It appeared to be patterned directly off MPC's Challenger kit (for the most part).

For 1972, Dodge dropped the R/T badging at the very last moment and substituted very generic Rallye series nomenclature instead. The convertible was gone, too, along with all the big-block engine options. A very handsome mid-cycle freshening treatment featured a fresh front-end treatment that recalled the 1960 Chrysler 300F, and added quad taillamps in back that repeated the trapezoidal grille shape. The fake side panel louvers from 1971 were resized and moved to the front fenders, with a trailing segmented tape treatment comprising the Rallye series exterior differential to base Challengers. The changes carried over to the 1973 and 1974 model years, with the addition of larger bumper pads in the latter two years, along with the E58 360 high-performance Wedge replacing the 340 for the final run of 1974 Challengers.

MPC's annual kits continued for the 1972–1974 model years with the appropriate external updates, but they never revised the kit's Hemi powertrain to the now-mandatory factory small-block Wedge V-8s. Palmer's kit was updated to 1972 form and eventually reissued in recent times under the Lindberg brand. It's not entirely accurate to the production 1972 Challenger, though. MPC's Challenger tool was modified for a series of Pro-Stock and funny car kits, and it has never been returned to factory stock form.

Unlike Chrysler's Plymouth 'Cuda, the Challenger nameplate later returned to the marketplace, first as a rebadged Japanese import, but more important, as a new product in recent years to once again challenge the new Mustang and Camaro on the street and in the car sales race. Therefore, while the Challenger was late to the original party, unlike most of its original pony car competitors, it is now enjoying relevancy in the automotive marketplace once more. Perhaps in this case "be late, be big" worked out in the long run after all!

MPC's 1971 Challenger R/T annual kit (Wave 1/**) was consistent with MPC's annual kit theme that year, featuring outsized spoof parts like the hood scoop, hood locks, and rear spoiler seen here. Palmer Scale Models' 1971 Challenger kit (Wave 1/**) was actually a semi-respectable kit, though the model inside was actually a factory-incorrect non-R/T 426 Hemi, not the 440 Wedge Six Pac R/T promised on the cover. (Palmer Kit Courtesy of Chuck Helppie)

Missing in Action

Other pony cars yet to appear in a 1/24th-1/25th–scale kit

- 1967½ Firebird convertible
- 1967–1969 Barracuda hardtop and convertible
- 1969 (with CJ-428), 1971 (with 429), and 1972 (with Cleveland 351 HO) Cougar convertibles
- 1970 'Cuda convertible with 426 Hemi or 440 3+2 Wedge

Other pony cars that need a new/modern kit offering

- 1964½–1966 Barracuda
- 1967–1968 Barracuda Formula S Fastback
- 1967–1968 Cougar XR-7 and/or GT-E (1968 only)
- 1968–1970 Javelin with 390 V-8 and Go Package
- 1970 'Cuda AAR
- 1970½ Firebird Formula or Trans Am with correct 400 R/A IV V-8
- 1971 (R/T), 1972–1973 (Rallye) Challenger hardtop with 340 V-8; 1974 Challenger Rallye with E58 HO 360 V-8
- 1971 Firebird Formula or Trans Am with correct 455 HO V-8
- 1971–1972 Cougar hardtop with GT Appearance Package
- 1971–1974 Javelin AMX with correct 401 V-8
- 1973–1973 Pontiac Firebird Formula or Trans Am with correct 455 Super Duty V-8

Muscle Car Model Kits Scale Showroom

The following models show how several of the model kits mentioned earlier in this chapter look when assembled by experienced adult model car builders. (Photography and models are by the writer unless noted otherwise.)

AMT was the only source for first-generation Barracuda 1/25th-scale assembly kits. These 1965 (right) and 1966 (left) models were built to showroom stock specifications. (Builder: Dean Milano)

This model was built from a rescued and restored JoHan 1968 Javelin promotional toy. It's finished in Code 46A Laurel Green Metallic, with 1969 Javelin-type side tape stripes added. (Builder/Photographer: Bob Downie)

The 1969 Trans Am Firebird was built from an early 1980s MPC kit with Fred Cady decals. The 1968 Firebird 400 is based on Revell's modern kit replica and painted in Pontiac-exclusive Code Q Verdoro Green Metallic.

Until just a few years ago, builders constructing a fully accurate 1970 Hemi 'Cuda had to find MPC's hard to locate and very expensive annual kit. Now Revell produces an all-new 'Cuda kit, shown here in Code K2 Vitamin C as well as X8 Black Velvet with a Code P6B5 Blue Vinyl Interior.

This 1969 Mercury Cougar XR-7 kit was constructed from the late 1970s Countdown Series reissue of AMT's original annual kit; it wears 1969 mid-year Code 9 Yellow paint and runs a 390 4-barrel FE V-8.

This intricately detailed 1970 Challenger T/A is based on Revell's kit. Added details include full engine compartment wiring, rain runoff tubes on the Six-Pack air cleaner pan, and a builder-opened trunk with a patterned floor mat, taillamp wiring, a tire jack, and space saver spare. (Builder: Scott Kilgore)

Revell's T/A kit also formed the basis of this 1970 Challenger R/T Hemi. The hood was converted to the dual-scoop R/T form, and the trunk lid was cut apart and hinged. The intricately detailed engine compartment features 46 builder-fabricated pieces in the Hemi valvetrain alone. (Builder: Juan Escalante)

This 1971 Firebird Trans Am annual kit was finished in Code 26 Lucerne Blue Metallic and includes the new Honeycomb wheel option and the factory-correct Firestone Wide Oval tires. It's posed in front of a scale dealership diorama constructed by Kim Pershall. (Builder/Photographer: Mike Hanson)

CHAPTER 10

Smaller in Stature, but . . . the Story of Junior Supercars

"The little car that could. And so it came to pass, from the System that generated the Road Runner, the country's first low-cost Supercar: a new scheme, another mind-blowing plan. Plymouth would introduce the Duster 340, the industry's first real Super Compact." These exact words came from a dual page print spread in the November 1969 issue of *Car and Driver* magazine. Although they are specific to the Duster 340, I think they nicely summarize the whole idea, as well as the cultural zeitgeist, behind the junior supercar movement of the very late 1960s and early 1970s.

Back in the day, there were various interpretations of junior supercar. For many, this referred to the idea of a small-block V-8 in an intermediate-sized car. Think of an Olds 350 W-31 in the 1969 Cutlass or the 340 Wedge plopped in the engine compartment of the new 1971 Road Runner.

Others take the view that I do for this chapter. That is, a powerful engine installed in a compact-sized body shell (instead of intermediate-sized), yielding a power to weight ratio that provided acceleration comparable to a traditional supercar, but with a lower purchase and operating cost.

By this definition, the first truly legitimate junior supercar might be the 1966 Chevy II Nova SS L-79. But there were precedents, as early as 1961, and I want to touch briefly on those before proceeding to the main topic.

The Roots of the Junior Supercar Movement

If the two key enablers of junior supercars were a small, lightweight car and a powerful V-8, the first enabler was the introduction of compact cars from the domestic Big 3. The Ford Falcon, Chevy Corvair, and Chrysler Corporation Valiant were perfectly timed products for a society taking a big breath after the boundless optimism and middle class economic growth during the mid-1950s had been tempered by the stark reality of Sputnik, the ongoing threat of nuclear war, and an economic recession. The Falcon was a huge hit, and the Valiant and Corvair were also popular choices for car and cost-aware households.

While the primary marketing premise of these new compacts was practicality and economy, it quickly became evident that a portion of compact buyers also wanted a dose of sportiness with their purchase. It started with the Monza 900 upgrade for the Corvair, and by the 1963½ model year, bucket seats, floor shifts, convertibles, and two-door hardtops, were major selling features found in compact car showroom displays across America. Upgraded powertrains followed, with increased horsepower options for the Corvair, the 1963½ introduction of the 260 small-block in the Falcon and Comet, and the debut of small-block V-8s in the Nova, Valiant, and Dart during the 1964 model year.

As became typical of each segment of the 1960s automotive market, a power war continued with the Sprint option for the Falcon (adding a less restrictive air cleaner and exhaust to the 260 V-8), the turbocharged Spyder and Corsa Corvair, a performance-themed Cyclone variant of the Comet, the addition of the 327 V-8 to the Chevy II option list, and a 235-hp version of the 273 Wedge for the Mopar contingent. Studebaker took an even more aggressive posture with its R1 Lark and R2 Super Lark (and thus achieved the strongest foreshadowing yet of the eventual junior supercar movement.) In addition, partway through the 1966 model year, Dodge unveiled the D-Dart, more officially known as the code D66-HP-1 Maximum Performance 273 Engine Dart Drag Package. While all of these were power-amended compacts, none of them (other than perhaps the R2 Super Lark) could seriously challenge a GTO or 426 Wedge at the drag strip, nor on the street for that matter. That would soon change.

Model Car Kits of the "Roots Behind" Period

Given the societal attention devoted to the new Big 3 compacts, no one should be surprised that they were the subject of yearly kit introductions from SMP/AMT, Revell, and JoHan. Recently, Asian kitmaker Trumpeter and domestic newcomer Moebius have also joined the compact car kit parade. As a result, nearly every significant car of the 1960s compact car era (other than the 1963–1967 Dodge Dart) has been produced in 1/25th-scale kit form. Not to be forgotten, the premium compact Pontiac Tempest, Olds F-85, and Buick special model kits are covered in Chapter 4.

Here is a visual summary of model car kits covering this era:

First-generation Corvair kits included simplified assembly kits of the SMP 1960 Corvair sedan (lower left) and 1961 Corvair Monza, and AMT kits of the 1962–1964 Corvair including the 1964 Monza Spyder (not shown). AMT produced full detail annual kits for the 1965–1969 Corvairs (shown at the upper left and center column) including the high-performance 1965 Corsa. (All: Wave 1/**.) Some reissues of the 1969 Corvair kit (right column) include most of the 1965 Corsa powertrain pieces. The latest Round 2 release repeats the original 1969 box art. (Reissues: Wave 1/*.)

AMT's kits of the first-generation Chevy II included these kits of the 1962 Nova convertible and 1963 Nova hard-top (both: Wave 1/**). AMT skipped the 1964 model year but returned with a 1965 Nova SS in simplified Jr. Trophy Craftsman Series form. Within the last decade, Trumpeter, a China-based producer of well-regarded scale armor kits, released two highly detailed 1/25th-scale kits of the 1963 Nova hardtop and convertible (Wave 4/*).

Ford's first generation of compact cars was well represented with annual kits for each model year of the Falcon and Comet, including these representative kits (left, all Wave 1/**). Even the 1961 Ranchero was kitted. The Ranchero was reissued a few times, including these 1977 and 2013 issues (Wave 1/*) with a non-stock big-block Chevy engine. Note that the Ohio George licensed kit includes a grille backdated to the 1960 Ranchero.

AMT produced annual kits of the performance-themed Falcon Sprint for 1964 and 1965 (Wave 1/**) in both convertible and hardtop form. According to the kit assembly sheet, AMT's 1964 Sprint included parts to deliver "an exact replica of the winning Falcon Sprint entered in the 1963 Monte Carlo Rally." In AMT's 1965 kits, these Rallye parts were displaced by new drag racing accessories. Within the last decade, Trumpeter unveiled 1/25th-scale kits of the 1964 Falcon Sprint hardtop and convertible, and a 1965 Ranchero (Wave 4/*).

A 1964 Comet Caliente from AMT (Wave 1/*) was a simplified Craftsman Series snap-together kit with no engine. It has seen a number of reissues, including this 2005 Model King (Wave 1/*) private label kit. Meanwhile, the 1965 Comet Cyclone was edging ever closer to a bona fide junior supercar, but it still took more than 50 years and the birth of a new model kit company for a kit of this Cyclone to reach the market. Moebius Models, a very small but dedicated team of model kit industry veterans, is responsible for this highly regarded kit of the Cyclone (Wave 4/*) released in 2016.

AMT affiliate SMP offered kits of the 1960–1961 Valiant, while the AMT brand appeared on simplified kits of the 1962–1965 Valiant Signet two-door hardtop (all: Wave 1/**). Revell produced annual kits and Metalflake reissues of the 1962 Valiant V-200 four-door sedan (Wave 1/**) and Dodge Lancer GT hardtop (Wave 1/***). Revell's Lancer kit included parts for the rare "Hyper-Pak" Dealership parts-counter Slant Six performance upgrade.

JoHan was the source for simplified assembly 1961–1963 Rambler Americans in two-door sedan (all three model years) and convertible (1962–1963 only) kits. The 1961 issue (Wave 1/**) is shown here. With the introduction of an all-new Rambler American in 1964, JoHan introduced equally new full assembly kits (with engines) in hardtop and convertible form, which continued through the 1965 and 1966 model years (all: Wave 1/**).

The only kit of the compact Studebaker Lark was this simplified-assembly annual kit from JoHan that replicated the 1962 Lark (Wave 1/**). While billed as 1/25th scale, most experts rate it as more like an oversized 1/23rd scale. It was reissued years later as part of JoHan's snap-kit series (Wave 1/*). The most-desirable of all compact Studebakers, the R1 Lark and R2 Super Lark, have never seen 1/25th-scale model kit form.

The Junior Supercar Arrives

As alluded to earlier, the first true junior supercar was probably the 1966 Chevy II with the 350 hp L-79 installed under the hood. On the basis of power to weight ratio, this one was a killer (if somewhat compromised by its single leaf rear suspension and narrow tires). The only thing it lacked was a sexy name and image (like that of the "GTO").

The junior supercar movement gained momentum in the 1968 model year, with the introduction of Dodge's GTS Dart with the new Hi-Po 340 Wedge, and the new-from-the-ground-up Chevy II Nova SS with standard 350 small-block power. The junior supercar movement grew further with the addition of several versions of the 396 big-block to the Nova lineup, and with the 1969 intro of the Dart Swinger 340 (and the very limited production 440 Wedge GTS). Fresh new front and rear sheet metal further increased the appeal of the 1970 Swinger 340. By this point, the junior supercar was becoming another success story in the muscle car marketplace.

It could be argued that the 1970 intro of the Plymouth Duster 340 was the ultimate expression of the junior supercar. Plymouth seemed to imply this in the advert headline quoted at the beginning of this chapter. The Duster was a market coup at the time. No one expected it to enter the market, but a strange combination of the staid 1967–1969 Valiant front sheet metal and Dart Swinger-derived hardtop doors, combined with sleek new windshield/roof/rear-quarter-panel/trunk stampings, along with the catchy "Duster" name (playing off the cartoon imagery of the Road Runner) was the perfect car for young buyers. Add in the high-winding 340 Wedge and the Duster became a great package for performance enthusiasts on a budget. The Duster and Duster 340 were huge hits for Plymouth and a key factor in the make's third-place finish in the 1970 sales race (displacing Pontiac for the first time in many years).

Backtracking a bit to the spring of 1969, another true budget junior supercar entered the market. Yes, the 1969½ AMC SC/Rambler. An outgrowth of the earlier Hurst/American Motors collaboration on the AMX Super Stock drag project, this collaboration resulted in a production run of the American Motors Rogue hardtop with the 390 AMC V-8 inserted into the engine compartment and a beefed-up chassis to handle the power. An outrageous (even for 1969) raised hood scoop and equally outrageous red/white/blue introductory paintjob topped off this very serious junior supercar segment entry. AMC introduced the all-new compact Hornet for the 1970 model year, replacing the American (and ending production of the SC/Rambler), but 1971 brought the introduction of the Hornet SC/360. When optioned with the 4-barrel version of the 360 and Go Package equipment, this was a very interesting proposition for junior supercar prospects. Unfortunately, sales reflected little marketplace willingness to convert that interest to hard sales.

The Junior Supercar Market Crashes

Then, just like the overall car marketplace, the junior supercar movement suffered with the advent of a recession, the continuing impact of the Vietnam War, and new emissions and bumper laws. The Nova lost its 396 big-block, Dodge dropped the Swinger 340 (but added a Duster-340-derived Demon 340), and AMC dropped the SC/360. Plymouth and Dodge swam against the tide and continued to offer the Duster/Demon 340 through this period, with the added practicality of a fold-down rear-seat option starting in the 1973, along with a switch in nomenclature from Demon to Dart Sport the same year. In 1971½, Pontiac joined the fray with a badge-engineered Nova called the Ventura II. The Sprint option was the equivalent of the Nova SS, and it briefly offered an optional Chevy-sourced 350 V-8 and 4-speed manual transmission.

The 1974 model year brought a brief glimmer of hope. First was the addition of the torque-fest that was the Mopar E58 Hi-Po V-8, extending the performance market relevancy of the now-renamed Duster 360 and Dart Sport 360 for three more years. Second was Pontiac's repackaging of its Nova-based Ventura with a 350 Pontiac V-8, a Trans Am–style rear-facing Shaker hood scoop, and fresh GTO graphics. Unlike the Chrysler twins, this was just a single model year offering. Then, it was over. The junior supercar was dead.

Model Kits of Junior Supercars: Filling the Gaps, Eventually

Unlike most categories of kits in this book, model kit coverage of the junior supercar has been very disjointed, and it took several decades to fill in some of the biggest coverage gaps. The kit story jumps back and forth in time; hold on for the ride.

To start, let's go back in time to when the 1966 annual model kits were introduced at your local hobby or department store. What's this? There was no kit of the new second-generation Chevy II, much less the Nova SS with the L-79 option. This omission of the Chevy II/Nova from the kit world would continue right through until the early 1970s. Later in the decade, also missing were kits of the Dart GTS and Swinger 340, the AMC SC/Rambler, and others. These omissions really, really offended the modeling community.

As many kit builders of the 1960s reached adulthood during the 1970s and 1980s, they became much more organized and vocal in pointing out kit topic oversights to the model

The initial box art was more than a little boring, but inside that AMT-Ertl box was an outstanding replica of a 1966 Chevy II Nova with the L-79 350-hp 327 V-8. The 1988 kit introduction also included parts for a street machine, and a separate 327 long-block on an engine stand. Round 2's 2013 kit reissue adds all-new box art patterned after AMT's original 1966 annual kit graphic theme, and additional parts to recreate Bill Junkins's Grumpy's Toy *A/Stock drag racer (both: Wave 3/*).*

kitmakers, who at that time still considered model kits a childhood rather than an adult hobby. And right at the top of the omitted kit list (and the associated modeler lobbying) remained that 1966–1967 Chevy II.

Thus, the 1988 debut of AMT/Ertl's 1966 Chevy II Nova SS kit (yes, with that L-79 under the scale hood) was a subject of huge celebration in the adult model car hobby. The kit was very well done, too, far better than it would have been had it been part of the original 1966 AMT annual kit lineup. Moreover, it proved that the adult modeling community could be influential in the choice of specific new kit introductions from the model kitmakers.

Throughout the 1960s, one of the most successful compact cars of all, the Dodge Dart, had been summarily omitted from 1/25th-scale annual model kit offerings. Hobbyists interested in building a Dart GTS or Swinger 340 model car had no alternative but to try to find MPC's Dart funny car kits. Even with that head start, only the most talented builders could even contemplate successful achievement of using these kits to achieve a showroom-stock Dart junior muscle car replica.

*Revell's 1969 Dart GTS kit (Wave 3/**) was the first-ever 1/25th-scale showroom stock model kit of Dodge's highly successful compact car nameplate. In 2000, it was mildly revamped to replicate the 1968 GTS (and the Mr. Norm's 440 Magnum-powered GSS). Two drag racing themed kits followed in 2005 and 2010 (both: Wave 3/*), both still allowing a showroom stock replica as well. The Hemi kit included many of the parts needed to replicate the famous Dodge/Hurst Super Stock drag racing conversion.*

This lack of showroom stock Dodge Dart model kits was finally resolved with an excellent 1969 Dart GTS kit from Revell that was introduced in 1995. Several later iterations of this kit were revised to the 1968 model year GTS.

In the mid-1970s JoHan took its old Rambler American annual kit tool and made some modest revisions to approximate the 1969½ SC/Rambler. In yet another disappointment, the 1971 Hornet SC360 never made showroom stock kit status. Someone wanting to duplicate this would have had to

*Back in the day, MPC's 1969 Charlie Allen and 1970 Ramchargers funny car kits (Wave 1/***) were the only possible sources for bodies replicating the Dart Swinger 340. In both cases, the bodies had non-stock, repositioned wheelwell openings. Exterior and greenhouse moldings were omitted (although the Dart badging remained), and the headlamps were blanked out.*

AMT-Ertl's 1966 Nova SS Kit: The Inside Story on One of the Most Requested Kits of All Time

The late 1980s introduction of AMT-Ertl's 1966 Nova SS kit was a very important event for the hobby. During the first half of that decade, requests for development of a 1966–1967 Chevy II Nova model kit became the subject of an organized campaign by the now-adult model car building community. Then to add fuel to the fire, readers of *Scale Auto Enthusiast* magazine voted a mostly scratch-built model of the 1967 Nova by Ohio model builder Tom Dillion to be model of the year. The possibility of a Nova kit soon became the subject of relentless rumors about future hobby products. For some behind-the-scenes insight into how the decision to produce the kit actually took place, I contacted John Mueller.

By way of background, Mueller joined AMT Corporation in 1963, eventually becoming a project engineer at the company. He remained at AMT through the 1978 sale to Lesney-Matchbox, and then moved to Fundimensions/Craftsmasters (owners of the MPC kit brand) in New Baltimore, Michigan. In 1987, he was recruited to relocate to Dyersville, Iowa, to join the combined AMT-Ertl-MPC product development team. Mueller remained there through 2000 when Racing Champions (which had purchased AMT-Ertl several years earlier) conducted a downsizing that included the ill-advised laying off of the entire model kit product development team. At that point, he retired, but he has remained very busy since then as a consultant on various projects for all the domestic kit manufacturers.

Not long after Mueller joined the team in Dyersville in 1986, he was asked to join a new kit brainstorming meeting along with Dave Carlock, Tom Walsh, and John O'Neil (all well-known names to hobby kit industry insiders). When asked to name the one new kit idea he'd recommend, Mueller promptly voiced the 1966–1967 Chevy II Nova.

"Why *that* car?" Mueller was quizzed? Well, during his 25 years at AMT in Michigan, Mueller had regular dealings with its customer service department, which at the time was the primary AMT contact point with model kit purchasers. Among its duties was to keep a file on customer suggestions for future kits. As Mueller related to the AMT-Ertl team, for several years the 1966 and 1967 Chevy II Nova was near or at the top of customer suggestion lists. Plus, the real 1966 Nova SS with the L-79 engine nearly matched the horsepower of the top carbureted Corvette small-block at far less money, making it a popular Q-ship purchase choice for savvy, budget-minded street warriors and drag racers back then. Its reputation only grew during the following decades.

"OK, if this was such a great kit idea, why wasn't it included in AMT's original 1966–1967 annual kit lineup?" Apparently, AMT's leadership team had been informed that the new Chevy Nova would only have a two-year product cycle, and it would be replaced for the 1968 model year. AMT's finance team didn't want to invest in a tool that would be good for only two annual kit production runs. Plus, the observation of the AMT team was that 1/1-scale car buyer interest (and kit builder interest as well) was rapidly migrating toward big-block intermediates. All this was enough to kill the Nova as a 1966 annual kit entry. Once the Nova was dropped, it was never to return to AMT's annual kit lineup (although the 1972 Nova kit eventually debuted as part of AMT's Trophy Series).

"If we could only do one kit, either the 1966 or the 1967, which one would it be?" The tone of the questions suggested the kit was now under serious consideration. In the end, Mueller picked the 1966 version. It was always good to lead with the first product of a series. In addition, it was the only one with volume production of the L-79 option (although a very small number sneaked out during the 1967 production run). The 1966 Chevy II Nova SS with the L-79 engine it would be.

Once approved, kit engineering began. Mueller and the AMT-Ertl product development team located three actual L-79 Novas nearby, one a pristine restoration, and another partly disassembled, providing valuable reference material on the kit's optional headers and the extra 327 long-block mounted on an engine stand. The actual cutting of the metal tool was outsourced to Asia, and Mueller reports that the work done was of very high quality. But timing and political concerns resulted in it falling behind schedule, so the partly finished tool returned to North America and was split up for finish work among two trusted Canadian tooling shops.

I asked Mueller how it sold. "Sold like gangbusters." Not only that, but the kit received rave reviews in the modeling community and helped establish a more positive reputation for the still relatively new, combined AMT-Ertl-MPC product development team. As Mueller related, "AMT-Ertl had arrived as a kit designer and manufacturer."

One more question: "*What was the second kit subject on Mueller's list back in that 1986 product development brainstorming session?*" No hesitation in his response. "The 1962 Bel Air 409 Bubbletop." As model builders know, this AMT-Ertl kit idea came to reality several years later, and it too was an overwhelming success for AMT-Ertl and another great kit for the adult model building community.

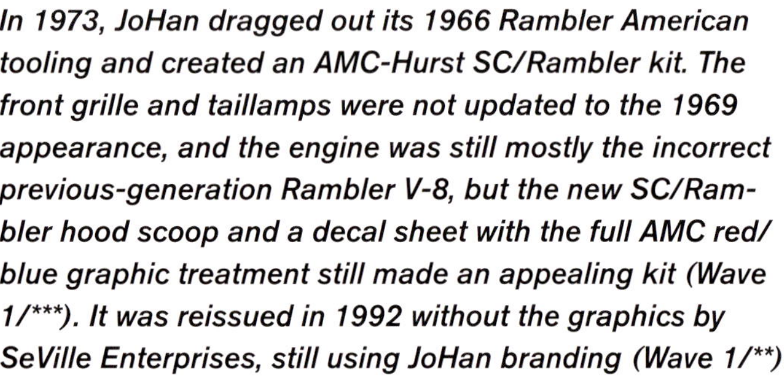

*In 1973, JoHan dragged out its 1966 Rambler American tooling and created an AMC-Hurst SC/Rambler kit. The front grille and taillamps were not updated to the 1969 appearance, and the engine was still mostly the incorrect previous-generation Rambler V-8, but the new SC/Rambler hood scoop and a decal sheet with the full AMC red/blue graphic treatment still made an appealing kit (Wave 1/***). It was reissued in 1992 without the graphics by SeVille Enterprises, still using JoHan branding (Wave 1/**).*

find JoHan's Hornet funny car kit body and then do lots of scratch-building.

Following some very pointed early 1970s commentary from *Car Model* magazine's Hank Borger (perhaps the most popular model car magazine writer of the era), AMT finally introduced a Trophy Series–style kit of the 1972 Nova SS. It proved immensely popular, having remained in nearly continuous production for decades after its introduction.

Just in the last decade, Revell introduced several new kits of the 1969 Nova SS, both in small-block (introduced in 2008) and big-block form (2011), helping to fill out the third-generation Nova kit choices. These new Revell kits are wonderfully detailed but lose some accuracy points for their incorrect treatment of the inward-sloping Nova taillamp panel and slightly misshapen rear wheelwell openings.

AMT cleverly designed the 1972 Nova kit with separate front fenders to allow two other kits to use the same basic body casting: an altered-wheelbase Nova funny car and a showroom stock 1972 Pontiac Ventura II. AMT's Pontiac kit featured the Sprint version of the Ventura with its 350 Chevy V-8 and manual transmission, which meant the powertrain included in the

*AMT waited until 1972 to kit a version of the third-generation Chevy Nova (Wave 1/**). Rendered in advanced Trophy Series form instead of an annual kit format, it included a showroom stock 1972 Nova SS with the 350 V-8, and a big-block Chevy setup for drag racing. Revell is responsible for the first-ever 1969 Nova kit in 1/25th scale, including an SS350 version (the engine appears to be a non-stock LT-1), and a COPO version with a 427 big-block (both: Wave 4/*).*

*AMT produced a one-time kit of the 1972 Pontiac Ventura II Sprint (Wave 1/***). Other than the front-end clip, rear taillamps, decals, instructions, and some box art, the remainder of the kit was AMT's 1972 Nova SS kit.*

Nova kit could be legitimately carried over intact. The separate front fenders made the Ventura kit, as well as the Nova, somewhat fiddly to assemble correctly.

Starting in 1971, MPC did its part to address the lack of junior muscle car kits when it introduced an annual kit of the Duster 340. The Duster version of this tool was updated each year through the 1975 model year. The 1975 and 1976 versions of this tool were also produced as a Dart Sport. MPC used this same tool to produce a very rare 1971 mid-year annual kit of

*MPC was responsible for annual kits of the Duster 340/360, starting in 1971 and running through 1975. The 1971 annual kit (Wave 1/***) shows the stock and spoof versions, but the stock version graphics are omitted on the decal sheet. For MPC's 1973 annual kit (Wave 1/**), a 426 Hemi joined the 340 Wedge. AMT-Ertl's all-new 1971 Duster 340 kit (Wave 3/*) added considerable interior/engine/underbody detail, and finally included the appropriate external markings on the decal sheet. Note the subtle difference in the layout of the two boxes.*

*If there was a contest for the rarest kit of a junior supercar, this one would be a prime contender. In December 1970, MPC produced a second run of its new Duster 340 tool, with the minor changes needed to recreate the new Demon 340 (Wave 1/****) introduced by Dodge just a few months earlier. Unlike many annual kits back then, this one had a decal sheet with the correct side graphics.*

the Demon 340. The kit incorrectly used Duster front fenders (while the real Demon used the different Dart front fenders with their unique wheelwell openings), and the Dart-specific hood strakes in the kit were shallow versus the real car. This kit has never been reissued.

Just before the turn of the century, AMT/Ertl again revisited the Mopar junior muscle car portfolio to produce a highly detailed all-new kit of the 1971 Duster 340. I've recently heard occasional news flashes about a new Demon 340 kit, but it has yet to materialize.

With the very recent attention paid by Moebius to the compact car segment with its kit of the 1965 Cyclone, adult model builders are hopeful to see the remaining gaps in the world of junior supercars addressed soon by new full-detail model kits. A very good place to start might be that rumored 1971 Demon 340. In addition, it now appears likely that there will be an all-new Moebius kit series featuring the first-generation Chevy II, starting with a 1964 Nova SS V-8 hardtop.

Missing in Action

Junior muscle cars yet to appear in a 1/24th-1/25th–scale kit

- 1963–1964 Studebaker R1 Lark and R2 Super Lark
- 1966 Dodge Dart with "Maximum Performance 273 Engine Dart Drag Package" (aka "D-Dart")
- 1967 Chevy II Nova SS
- 1970 Dodge Dart Swinger 340
- 1970 Duster 340 (produced as a spinoff of AMT-Ertl's 1971 Duster 340 kit)
- 1971 AMC Hornet 360 S/C, with 360 4-Barrel and Go Package
- 1974 Pontiac GTO

Junior muscle cars that need a new or modern kit offering

- 1965 Chevy Nova SS with 327
- 1971 and 1972 Dodge Demon 340

Muscle Car Model Kits Scale Showroom

The following models show how several of the model kits mentioned earlier in this chapter look when assembled by experienced adult model car builders.

Revell's first Dodge Dart kit was this 1969 GTS, equipped with the optional 383 Magnum V-8. This Code F8 Dark Green Metallic model features Mopar's infamous 1969 early production "recall" cast-aluminum wheels (sourced from MPC's 1969 Barracuda kit).

This 1970 Duster 340 is a clever conversion of AMT-Ertl's 1971 kit. It includes a 1970-style grille and side graphics, as well as 1970 mid-year Code M3 Moulin Rouge High Impact paint. (Builder: Ken Dawson)

AMT-Ertl's 1971 Duster 340 kit was also the source of this 1971-spec project. It includes full engine compartment wiring and detailing, and additional graphics from The Last Detail (sadly, no longer produced). (Builder: James Tester)

This Nova, based on AMT's 1972 SS kit, has been backdated to 1968 model year specs, with Code V Sequoia Green Metallic and the L78/375-hp V-8. The rear view emphasizes AMT's more accurate lower tail panel slope versus the later Revell Nova kit. (Builder/ Photographer: Mike Hanson)

Flash, Space, and Grace

The Family Supercar

"A New Breed of Scat" (1963½ Mercury Marauder S-55 427)
"Where the Action Is" (1964 Olds Jetstar 1)
"The Velvet Brute" (1965 Galaxie 500 XL 427)
"Irresistible force . . . in an irresistible object" (1965 Impala 409)
"A flying machine for people who can't stand heights" (1965 Pontiac 2+2)
"Stop telling me I'm beautiful. Love me for what's inside." (1965 Pontiac 2+2)
". . . the Smoothest Brute on Wheels" (1966 Galaxie 7-Litre)
"Do Not Tease" (1966 Impala SS427)
"For the man who'd buy a sports car if it had this much room" (1967 Impala SS427)
"Big Brother" (1967 Pontiac 2+2)
"Horizon Grabber" (1968 Ford XL Fastback)
"The Michigan Strong Boy" (1969 XL GT)
"The Executive Branch of the Rapid Transit System" (1970–1971 Plymouth Sport Fury [and GTX])

These headlines from magazine car ads and brochures suggest that the full-sized muscle car was very much on the minds of Detroit's Product Planning and Marketing Teams back in the 1960s.

Starting in the 1950s, the idea of placing a company's largest and most powerful engines in cars otherwise designed for family use saw limited but continued use in the automotive industry. A great example would be the Chrysler 300 letter series cars starting in 1955 and continuing into the mid-1960s.

But once the auto industry began to understand the appeal, and more important, the sales potential of intermediate-sized supercars, the assumption was that large engines in large cars could also enjoy more success if packaged and marketed more aggressively based on the recent supercar lessons learned.

Some of these were continuations of earlier efforts, while others were newly conceived entries: Pontiac's 2+2, Ford's Galaxie Seven Litre, Chevy's SS427, and late in the decade, Plymouth's Sport Fury GT and Mercury's Marauder X-100. These cars mimicked the successful supercars. They added high-performance big-block engines, buckets, consoles, better-handling suspensions, beefed-up chassis, and generally added exterior/interior eye candy.

It should have worked. Through the 1960s, each brand's full-sized cars were the sales leaders and the image leaders as well. A company's most aggressive and new design themes debuted on the full-sized cars, then later migrated to the other carlines in the brand portfolio. Chevy's 1965 Impala was clearly the design lead for the brand, with the midsized Chevelle a year or two behind in copying those themes. The same applied with the full-sized Pontiac versus the intermediate LeMans and its GTO derivative. Thus, shouldn't a company's most aggressive and innovative products also benefit from the supercar formula that was working so well on its intermediate product lines?

Well, no. The much heavier bodies of the full-sized cars tended to sublimate any performance advantage from the use of larger engines. Pontiac's 421-powered 2+2 did not have a real world performance advantage compared to the 389-powered GTO. Moreover, these full-sized cars were significantly more expensive than the affordable intermediates. Not to mention that full-sized cars had grown so large during the preceding decade that they were starting to lose relevancy for some American families.

Then, during the second half of the decade, companies began migrating their most aggressive and innovative styling themes away from full-sized cars toward their intermediates. In 1968, for instance, the Dodge Charger clearly became Chrysler's most stylish vehicle, largely leaving the full-sized C-Bodies in the dust. At General Motors, the 1968 Pontiac GTO's rakish new proportioning and body-colored Endura front bumper unarguably stole the Pontiac design lead away from the full-sized Catalina and Bonneville. This further lessened any full-sized muscle car's appeal for current intermediate-sized supercar owners who were looking to replace that car with a slightly larger, more luxurious, and yet still stylish automobile.

In spite of all this, the full-sized muscle car was given a good deal of model car kit coverage in the 1960s and early 1970s. As I said earlier, for almost all auto brands, full-sized cars were the image and sales leaders. It was only natural that those were the

This image gives just a glimpse of the model car kit coverage of the large, family-sized performance cars of the mid-1960s to early 1970s.

cars that their marketing departments would contract with the kitmakers to produce as 1/25th-scale promotional toys. In addition, as seen before, those promo tools soon begat assembly kits for the hobby shelves.

As a result, most major brands enjoyed an entire decade of annual model kit replicas of their full-sized cars. That complete coverage also means that there have been very few newly designed, contemporary kit introductions for these muscle behemoths (unless your brand name happens to be Chevrolet). Therefore, the story of full-sized muscle car kits in scale is much different from those of the intermediate-size supercars I have just covered.

Just as I did for the preceding chapter on junior supercars, I'll cover the entire product segment (that is, all makes of full-sized performance cars) in a single chapter. I'll discuss each brand separately, sequentially by model year. Many of these original annual kits of the full-sized performance car kits have not been reissued, which makes them valuable collectibles. Where there are reissues, I'll give an overview of those at the end of each brand's section.

This coverage starts with the 1964 model year, except for Oldsmobile (1963) and Ford/Mercury (1963½). Why 1964? It was the introductory year of the textbook supercar (the GTO) that inspired the proliferation of full-sized performance cars based on a similar marketing approach. From a model kit perspective, 1964 was also the year that kits adopted differentiated and personalized box art differentiation. For kit coverage of family-sized performance cars prior to the 1964 model year, refer back to Chapter 3.

1964–1972 Chevy Impala SS (409/396/427/454)

For the entire 1960s, the full-sized Chevy Impala was the style and value leader for all family-sized cars. It was also, by a wide margin, the best-selling Chevy product. In each of these years, the Impala included at least one powertrain option that would qualify it as a bona fide muscle car. Starting with the 409, moving to the 396 and then quickly to the 427 and 454, Chevy featured Impalas using these powertrains in advertising for the product line, even if the volumes were comparatively tiny when compared to the overall Impala production each year.

In addition, the Impala SS became a separate series in 1964 and ran through 1967. Though orderable with any Impala engine, advertising featured the biggest optional V-8s. The SS427 became a separate option introduced in 1967 and was produced through 1969. The SS was a strong image leader for Chevrolet and its full-sized car lineup, and a logical home for customers that ordered top-end performance powertrains.

All the major muscle Impalas have been reproduced in 1/25th-scale annual model car kits, and many have reappeared either as reissues or all-new kits during the subsequent decades. All years were produced as hardtop kits, and many model years also included convertible kits. AMT handled the original

AMT's 1964 Impala hardtop and convertible kits (Wave 1/) included components to equip the model with operating headlamps and taillamps. The Advanced Customizing Kit subtitle on the box top was AMT's language for multiple customizing options. Performance fans cared more about the optional 4-71 blown version of the 409 V-8.***

AMT's 1965 Impala SS convertible (Wave 1/***) was still promoting Advanced Customizing features including a bubble top and a separate front clip. The box art emphasis moved to racing themes for the 1966 and 1967 annual kits (both: Wave 1/***), and both were equipped with new Mark IV big-block V-8s. The 1966 kit even added optional headers and a cowl-induction setup patterned after the 1963 Daytona 500 Mark II 427 "Mystery Motor."

annual kits for model years 1964–1967. The 1964 and 1965 kits featured the 409, while for 1966 AMT tooled the new big-block 396 to replace the W-blocks. The all-new body design of the 1967 SS prompted a new body tool from AMT, featuring the distinctive domed hood that was unique to the new SS427 option that was replicated by the kit.

For 1968, MPC took over the Impala promotionals contract, and as a result also produced assembly kits of the SS427 Impala in hardtop and convertible form that year. As a result, AMT was left without access to the 1968 Impala design changes. Unwilling to walk away from a market, and without fully amortized tooling from the 1967 updates, AMT's art and engineering departments developed a factory "auto show custom" type of execution, which it marketed as "for 1968" rather than as a complete factory stock replica. Still, many buyers of the kit were surprised when they opened the box and only found a custom body with the entire rear window opening blanked out in styrene!

Gorgeous box art aside, AMT's 1968 SS427 kit (Wave 1/**) was a guess rather than an accurate kit that allowed the builder to replicate a showroom stock Impala that year. Check out the blanked rear window on the end cap illustration; that's the way the body inside was molded. Also note the "AMT for 1968" wording on the box stop and end cap. It sounds like a "get out of jail free" card from AMT's legal department!

In 1969, the Promos contract returned to AMT, but both AMT and MPC retained access to the all-new body design of the 1969 Impala SS427. Thus hardtop (AMT and MPC) and convertible (MPC only) annual kits emerged from both the AMT and MPC factories for this last year of the Impala SS nameplate (at least until the 1990s). For 1970, AMT and MPC again marketed kits, this time with the AMT kit replicating the mainstream Impala series hardtop equipped with the stand-alone 454 engine option, while the MPC kit was still formatted as an SS version even though there was no such real car that year.

Impala annual kits for 1969 (all: Wave 1/***) and 1970 (all: Wave 1/**) were produced by both AMT and MPC. By this point Chevrolet offered its large performance cars with the sport coupe and the slightly more formal custom coupe hardtops, but both the AMT and MPC replicated the custom coupe body style.

*MPC's 1971 Impala (Wave 1/***) shared the Mild and Wild merchandising themes found on other MPC annual kits that year, including the out-of-scale spoof and the Street-Freak–style High Rise versions. Underhood was a 454 V-8 with an optional turbocharger version.*

Revell chose the 1964 Impala SS as the basis for a showroom stock/low rider kit introduced in 2000, and later reissued it with Chip Foose licensing in 2013; it includes a 327 4-barrel underhood. AMT-Ertl's 1967 Impala SS427 had all-new tooling from 1997; Round 2 reissued this kit in 2016 with fresh box art inspired by (but not a copy of) AMT's original 1967 Impala SS box art (all: Wave 3/).*

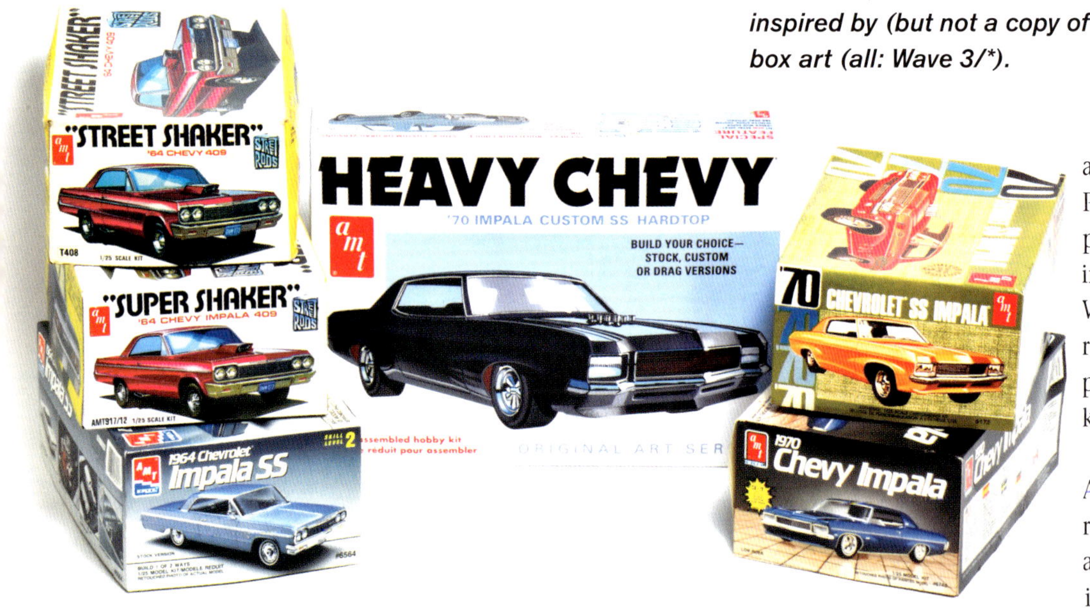

This is a representative sample of the many reissues of AMT's 1964 and 1970 Impala hardtop kits (all: Wave 1/). Many of these kits contained nearly all of the optional parts that were in the original annual kits. The most recent reissues include much-higher-quality chrome plating and far-superior decal sheet lithography. Note the subtly altered title in Round 2's 2015 reissue of the circa-1974* Street Rod Series Street Shaker *version of the 1964 Impala (middle and top left, respectively).*

Wrapping up the original Impala annual kit story, MPC took over the Promo contract for 1971 to 1972 and produced assembly kits of the Impala in hardtop form for those two years. While MPC continued with big Chevrolet annual kits through 1976, AMT permanently exited the Impala annual kit business after the 1970 model year.

Of the above annual kits from AMT and MPC, the only ones to see reissues have been the AMT's 1964 and 1970 Impala hardtop kits. According to *The Directory of Model Car Kits, Seventh Edition*, there have been at least 10 reissues of AMT's 1964 Impala SS hardtop kit during the last five decades, and 9 reissues of its 1970 Impala Custom coupe kit.

In more recent years, kitmakers have begun revisiting the Impala as

The 1965 Impala SS convertible was a premium kit first marketed under the Monogram label in 1996; it included the new mid-year 396 engine. The same basic kit returned in 1998 under Revell branding with a hardtop body and the early 1965 409 V-8. Further additions to the kit tool in 2010 yielded a new 1966 Impala SS with the 396 V-8. The Chip Foose 1965 hardtop kit dates from 2014 and includes all the parts for a showroom stock replica, in addition to the Foose Design version on the box top (all: Wave 3/).*

a topic for fresh kit tooling. Revell introduced an all-new 1964 Impala (albeit with 327 4-barrel power), and a highly detailed 1965½ Impala SS hardtop with the new 396 V-8 under its Monogram brand. Later came a 1965 Impala SS convertible with the early 1965 409 W-Block with Revell branding and a 1966 Impala SS396 convertible. AMT-Ertl countered with an all-new 1967 Impala SS427. All of these new kits have superb underbody detail, while in some cases certain minor elements of body detailing have prompted some criticism from hard-core kit experts.

1970–1972 Monte Carlo SS454

The 1970 Monte Carlo was a new choice for car buyers who might have otherwise chosen an Impala or Caprice for their automotive purchase. The Monte Carlo also finally gave General Motors a response to 15 years' production of profitable Ford Thunderbirds. Like the all-new Pontiac Grand Prix introduced one year earlier, the Monte was a re-skin of GM's A-Body intermediate with a longer coupe wheelbase, with the extra length added to the front clip of the car. But unlike the Grand Prix, which lived on an exclusive 118-inch wheelbase, the Monte Carlo adopted the 116-inch wheelbase already used for the Chevelle four-door sedan, four-door hardtop, and wagon. The Monte used a dual-headlamp treatment, the only GM intermediate to do so at the time of its introduction. A front bumper was similar to that of the Chevelle, but it featured circular lamps below the headlamps (the bumper was also shared with the El Camino that year). A complete instrument panel with full gauges was derived from the Chevelle SS396/SS454, though for the Monte it featured a wood-look background versus a functional looking "camera black" background for the SS Chevelles.

More germane to the topic of this book, the introductory Monte Carlo also included a performance-based subseries called the SS454 (ostensibly replacing the discontinued SS427 Impala that year). No Chevelle or Camaro hood and deck paint stripes for this one, just a discreet SS454 nameplate low on the front fender on top of the intricate rocker panel moldings. Inside, buckets, console, and the full instrumentation checked all the boxes for the performance buyer who also wanted some real

*AMT's 1970 Monte Carlo kit box art omitted any reference to the model year. Build options included showroom stock, custom, and a drag version with a Moon Cross-Ram intake and Weber carbs (Wave 1/***). AMT-Ertl's all-new tooling dating from 1998 (Wave 3/*) was only buildable as showroom stock, but included a far superior drivetrain, chassis, and interior detailing, along with the correct SS454 badging missing from the original AMT annual kit. The new kit also included separately molded rear fender skirts.*

luxury. Under the hood, the SS454 featured the 360 hp variant of the 454 big-block (though some suggest a few LS5 and LS6 big-blocks might have escaped the Chevrolet plant system under the Monte's long, graceful hood).

The 1971 Monte Carlo was little changed from 1970, but the expert would notice the horizontal themed-grille bars (versus the earlier fine-textured grille bisected by two thin bars), the movement of the dual front headlamps to a location farther outboard of the grille, rectangular (versus circular) turn signal cutouts in the front bumper, a stand-up hood ornament, and additional chrome-accented lines in the vertical taillamp lenses. The 1972 version had slightly more obvious changes, with the turn signals moving up beside the headlamps and incorporated in the grille surround moldings. The SS454 version continued for both years, although by 1972 it was clearly an afterthought for Chevrolet, its dealers, and its customers.

Surprisingly, model builders have been graced with excellent kits of all the SS454 Monte Carlos, as AMT produced well-detailed annual kits of all three model years. Some 30 years later, AMT-Ertl produced an all-new kit of the 1970 Monte Carlo SS454. This new kit carried far superior underhood and chassis detail, and is many times more affordable than paying the high price to acquire an original annual kit these days. One minor note, for both the original annual kits and the newly tooled AMT-Ertl version, the builder has to apply a chrome-like finish to the headlamp surrounds to achieve the appropriate appearance. A second note, more from the marketing perspective, compare the compelling and action-oriented original 1970 annual kit box art illustration, versus the sterile and heavily airbrushed photo of an early test shot on the AMT-Ertl box art.

AMT followed Ford's 1963½ fastback introduction with its annual kit (Wave 1/**). The engine compartment still had the now-outdated 406 tri-power engine, though. AMT's 1964 Galaxie 500 XL annual kits (Wave 1/) featured a unique internally lit headlamp and taillamp system, shared with its 1964 Impala kit also shown in this chapter.***

1963–1969 Galaxie 500 XL/7-Litre/GT

Among the mainstream large car offerings, no one was more aggressive than Ford in terms of offering high-performance powertrains and in the promotion of it during the mid-1960s. While the 406 FE engine and the XL series upgrade (with its bucket seats and console) were introduced in 1962½, the real push began in 1963½ when Ford introduced a second two-door hardtop with a fastback C-pillar and backlight treatment, and the 406 was replaced by the famous 427 Wedge V-8. As the image leader of Ford's new Total Performance marketing campaign, these Super Torque Fords would also enjoy considerable racing success during the next several years. The 1964 Galaxie 500 XL Fastback repeated the roof and engine features, but employed virtually all-new sheet metal below the beltline for perhaps the finest design iteration of the entire 1957–1964 Ford platform.

The 1965 Ford full-sized lineup debuted on an entirely new platform. A new LTD series augmented the XL series with a luxury-themed persona. The two 427 production engines continued, with a number of refinements introduced at mid-year including the expanded "side oiler" lubrication features on the lower left side of the block. For 1966 the big news was the introduction of the 7-Litre" series, a derivative of the Galaxie 500 XL, with a new standard engine. It was a 428-ci derivative of the FE big-block, designed for low- and mid-range torque and quiet performance instead of daunting acceleration and top-end speed. Meanwhile, the 427 engines remained available.

The 1967 Galaxie 500 XL and 7-Litre wore all-new exterior sheet metal, yielding a very handsome car with a subtle curvaceous theme. The move away from performance to luxury continued in 1968, with a single 427 offering at 390-hp, only available with a C6 automatic. A new GT equipment group included stripes, badges, and selected underbody tweaks.

The last stand for Ford's performance-themed full-sized cars took place in 1969. The GT Equipment Group continued and was featured in advertising as the "The Michigan Strong Boy." The 427 FE was replaced entirely with a new 429-ci derivative of the 385 series V-8 that debuted in 1968½ on the Thunderbird and Lincoln products. The full-sized Ford lineup topped out at slightly more than 1 million sales that year, but performance-themed Galaxies were now a small fraction of that total. The XL persisted for one more year, but there was no GT Equipment Group for 1970. The era of the full-sized performance Ford had drawn to a close.

From 1964–1970, AMT had a lock on the Ford promotionals business, and it offered kit versions of the high-performance

*After a one-year stint with a highly detailed annual kit of the 1965 Galaxie 500 XL hardtop and convertible, AMT returned to a more typical annual kit format for its 1966 lineup of full-sized Fords (all: Wave 1/**). It also added a SOHC 427 engine setup for 1966, while also carrying over the 427 Wedge with dual-quads from the 1965 annual kit. Unlike most annual kits in this book, these were one-year products (i.e., they were not retooled for the following years' changes in the real cars); thus, they remained available for future reissues in its original kit form.*

Galaxies during this same period. Two-door hardtops were featured during all the years, and while the convertible promotional toys continued through the entire period, convertible assembly kits were dropped after 1967.

As would be expected, showroom stock annual kits from AMT replicated the Total Performance Galaxie 500 XL Fastbacks from 1963½ and 1964. The year 1963 represented the last year for AMT's generic annual kit box art; starting in 1964 each annual kit had its own personalized top, side panels, and end caps.

The all-new 1965 Ford led the AMT team to produce a one-time-only, highly detailed annual kit with features such as a multi-piece rear suspension and opening trunk with spare tire tools, added details that would normally only be found in AMT's premium Trophy Series kit lineup. Moving on to 1966, Ford emphasized the new 428 FE-powered 7-Litre series in its advertising, so AMT dutifully added "7-Liter" nomenclature to its hardtop annual kit box top, and the associated badging to the kit's body, while still continuing the 427 FE-based powertrains inside the box.

The swoopy 1967 XL fastback prompted a much-liked AMT kit that many would love to see return today. Featuring an image of a NASCAR-equipped Galaxie racer on the box top, AMT's art department gave fans a glimpse of what the race series might have looked like had NASCAR *not* agreed to make intermediate-sized race cars legal for the 1966 race season. This year, 1967, was also the last year for an AMT annual kit of the Galaxie convertible. AMT updated the hardtop body for its 1968 annual kit, again featuring the 427 Wedge and the non-stock 427 SOHC race engine options. The 1968 AMT kit also appeared under the FROG/AMT label for a European market release of the kit.

By the late 1960s, the model car companies were starting to get a little lazy on underhood engine accuracy, so while the top version of the 1969 Galaxie XL featured the new 385 series 429 engine, AMT's annual kit introduction maintained the previous FE-based engines, thus making the AMT kit a non-stock execution. AMT's kit also omitted the real car's GT version front fender louvers and GT nomenclature.

AMT announced a 1970 Galaxie XL fastback kit but never actually produced it. Concurrently, AMT's promotionals contract for 1970 called for the LTD four-door to be the featured

*AMT's Galaxie annual kits for 1967 (Wave 1/****) and 1968 (Wave 1/***) continued with a performance theme on the box tops. I, for one, would have loved to see Ford's 1967 race season entries look like this XL hardtop illustration (instead of using the smaller Fairlane body shell). These kits have not been reissued, though many modelers would love to see that 1967 hardtop return to kit form.*

Do you recall ever seeing a real 1969 Galaxie set up as a drag racing machine like the one pictured on the box top of AMT's kit here? Me neither. Model kits of full-sized cars were becoming slow sellers by this time. Therefore, AMT added the competition flavor to increase the hobby store appeal of its 1969 Galaxie annual kit (Wave 1/**). This included the injected SOHC 427 engine depicted on the side panel.

application, but back then a four-door, full detail assembly kit would have been dead on arrival on the hobby kit shelves. AMT instead tried a simplified un-assembled promo four-door sedan kit as part of its 1970-only Motor City Series. It later tweaked the kit to the lower Galaxie series exterior trim, added a non-factory stock Boss 429(!) engine from its 1970–1971 Torino kit tooling, and remarketed the kit as a "Police Interceptor" full detail kit starting one year later. In this form, the 1970 kit has seen sporadic reissues since.

Unlike the Chevy Impala story, there have been no newly tooled kits of any full-sized Fords after the annual kit runs. Fortunately, AMT has seen to periodically reissue the 1964 kit (first in the original stock/custom/drag annual kit form for a 1969 misnamed kit release called Daytona Sportsman, then later with reissues based on a second Craftsman Series/unassembled promo tool). The 1965, 1966, and 1969 annual kits have also seen multiple reissues, along with the 1970 Police Interceptor kit. Fans of the 1967 and 1968 XLs, though, have no option but to track down some very rare and expensive original annual kits of these cars.

There have been multiple reissues of AMT's Galaxie annual kits from the model years 1963½ through 1970, some of which are shown here. Other than the 1964 reissues (upper left and top right), the kits shown here contained many features of the original Galaxie annual kits. At the bottom of the two center rows are Round 2's latest reissues, which restore almost all features of the original annual kit releases, and reprise the original annual kit box art and decals. As for the 1964 reissues shown here, they were based on the simplified Craftsman Series Galaxie 500 tooling (all: Wave 1/*).

1964–1968 Pontiac Grand Prix, 1964–1969 Bonneville, and 1964–1967 2+2

Pontiac was, along with Oldsmobile in 1964 and 1965, the only full-sized brand that offered two distinct full-sized performance car series in the mid-1960s. Those series were the 2+2, based off the mainstream/high-volume Catalina, and the Grand Prix, which combined top-end Bonneville-style trim and equipment level with a unique greenhouse/C-pillar treatment and the Catalina's shorter wheelbase. The 2+2 ran from 1964 to 1967, while the Grand Prix continued through the remainder of the decade, eventually switching to GM's intermediate platform in 1969.

The only model car kits of the pre-1969, GM B-Body-based Grand Prix were AMT annual kit releases of the 1964 and 1965 versions. The 1965 kit has seen periodic reissues through the decades that followed. The 2+2 was not kitted until the 1990s, when a very inaccurate spinoff of AMT's 1965 Bonneville annual kit was released.

Not only did Pontiac offer the 2+2 and Grand Prix, but savvy car buyers could also order the luxurious, longer wheelbase Bonneville two-door hardtop with a 421 performance V-8, along with bucket seats, console, and even a 4-speed manual transmission.

AMT included just such a Bonneville in its 1964 and 1965 annual kit lineup, while MPC engineered the same car (with the 428 eventually replacing the 421) in its 1966–1969 annual kit lineups. MPC even kitted the 1970 Bonneville, though by that point the top-line full-sized Pontiac's styling had strayed

*Pontiac's top line Bonneville was covered by kits from AMT through 1965, and then MPC for the remainder of the decade (1964 and 1966–69 kits: Wave 1/***; 1965 kit: Wave 1/**). These kits contained all the top performance options you'd want, from the largest engine option with a manual transmission to bucket seats and console (the last two items replaced with a bench seat in the 1969 and 1970 kits). MPC erred, though, by maintaining the tri-power setup as the kit engine even engine after it was discontinued by Pontiac starting in 1967.*

*Pontiac Grand Prix sales grew rapidly after the 1962 introduction and the breakthrough styling of the 1963 edition. Meanwhile, AMT was slow in getting a Grand Prix kit to the market, waiting until 1964 to introduce its first annual kit replica (Wave 1/***). The all-new 1965 Grand Prix prompted a follow-up AMT model kit for that model year (Wave 1/**). These kits were entirely separate tools from AMT's Bonneville kits of the same model years, sharing little in terms of content and kit accessories.*

AMT's 1965 Grand Prix and Bonneville kits have been reissued multiple times with most of the original goodies intact, including the examples shown here. Counterclockwise from the upper left are releases dating from 1978, 1987, 1990, and 1975. The 2+2 on top is a makeshift kit from 1995 that was incorrectly based on the longer wheelbase Bonneville tooling, and best avoided as a result (all: Wave 1/).*

far away from any performance car appeal. Among these MPC kits, and somewhat sadly, only the 1970 Bonneville kit has been reissued.

1969–1972 Pontiac Grand Prix

As mentioned above, the original 1962–1968 Grand Prix was a sub-series of the basic Pontiac B-Body large car line. But after a superb 1963 model run of more than 70,000 sales (the Riviera only sold 40,000 that year), the family car derived–Grand Prix sales never again reached that level, instead tacking on a generally downward trend throughout the decade. Perhaps in explanation, the Grand Prix itself played down the original European Formula 1–inspired appeal of its nameplate in favor of luxury as each subsequent model year progressed. While the 1968 evolution of the original Grand Prix concept was still a very attractive vehicle, the automotive market's attention had largely turned to midsized supercars, leaving the full-sized Grand Prix as an afterthought.

In retrospect, John DeLorean's decision to support a then-radical proposal to produce the next generation 1969 Grand Prix on a lengthened version of the GM intermediate A-Body was one of the most consequential product decisions of the late 1960s. With its exclusive 118-inch wheelbase and what was billed at that time as the industry's longest hood length, it was a stunning product. While the first year sales did not even remotely approach that of the first Mustang, it far exceeded initial projections and reportedly made a ton of money for Pontiac and General Motors in the process. More important, with hindsight you can see that the 1969 Grand Prix became the blueprint for many other midsized cars such as the Chevrolet Monte Carlo, Chrysler Cordoba, and late 1970s intermediate-based Thunderbird, not to mention the 1970–1987 Oldsmobile Cutlass Supreme, which eventually went on to became the best-selling individual carline in the entire industry for several years.

But back to the performance story, the 1969 Grand Prix was designed with performance in mind from the get-go. With much lighter weight, the standard 400 4 barrel V-8, and the driver-centered "command center" with its instrument panel center stack and console angled toward the driver, this made for a very appealing and stylish muscle car in its standard form. Spec up to the Model SJ with its standard 428 4-barrel, or maybe even to the optional 390 hp 428 HO and 4-speed manual transmission, and you were stylin' to the max in the context of 1969. So appealing was the overall product offer that it continued to sell all the way through the 1970 model year with not much more than a minor revision to the grille texture and in increase in displacement for the larger engine from 428 to 455 ci.

With MPC being Pontiac's model kitmaker of choice since 1966, it received the go-ahead for a 3-in-1 assembly kit of the new Grand Prix. Offered in traditional 3-in-1 annual kit form, this kit featured an interesting "Ski" version in lieu of the then-expected drag racing build option. The kit continued for 1970 with very few changes.

For 1971, Pontiac started to stray (again) from the Grand Prix's successful performance emphasis, with a new front design including somewhat contrived dual (versus the earlier quad) headlamps along with a more complex bumper, and a stylized boat-tail theme to the rear deck. The design continued for 1972 with the slightest of tweaks. MPC slightly revised its Grand Prix kit to capture the changes for each of these two years. After the 1972 annual kit run ended, MPC made what are probably irreversible changes to the tooling for two spoof models (*Sweathog's Dream Machine* and the *Grand Superfly Custom*). Accordingly, no model kit reissues of the 1971–1972 Grand Prix kit, much less the more desirable 1969–1970 Grand Prix, have been seen.

With the advent of the Colonnade era for the 1973 model year, the Grand Prix lost its exclusive wheelbase and the product differentiation associated with that feature. Still, the product skewed back a bit to the

With MPC's merchandisers always looking for a new marketing angle, its 1969 Pontiac Grand Prix annual kit (Wave 1/) included "a going skiing machine" version. A scale rescue sled, emergency stretcher, snow shovel, ski boots and holders, and rear snow tires were all inside the kit box. MPC's 1970 Grand Prix kit (Wave 1/***) featured a custom version credited to George Barris, complete with Duesenberg SJ-type side exhaust pipes.***

performance with luxury story that made the 1969–1970 products so appealing. Had any 1973 Grand Prix cars actually been produced with the planned SD-455 powertrain option, they would be extraordinarily collectible cars today. The 1974 version carried the necessary revisions to comply with that year's more restrictive 5-mph front- and rear-bumper impact standards, but kept most of its appeal. Sadly, no assembly kits of this generation of Grand Prix have ever been produced.

*AMT's 1965 Olds Dynamic 88 kit (Wave 1/***) was chock full of detail and building options, particularly for a kit priced at $1.50 retail. While a Starfire or Jetstar 1 might have been a better subject for the kit, it is still well worth tracking down for Oldsmobile enthusiasts. It was reissued only once, in 1969, with a politically inappropriate box art theme (Wave 1/**). The tool was later irreparably altered as part of AMT's Modified Stocker Series kit for its 1971 catalog.*

1963–1966 Oldsmobile Starfire, Jetstar 1, and Dynamic 88

Oldsmobile played a major part in the 1960s' large car muscle marketplace. Its 1961½ introduction of the convertible-only Starfire, with its Olds 98 interior and powertrain packaged in the smaller GM B-Body, actually presaged the introduction of the 1962 Grand Prix that adopted a similar package strategy. The 1962 Starfire added a hardtop version (while reaching nearly 40,000 unit sales that year), while the 1963 Starfire shared the unique Grand Prix C-pillar treatment. The 1964 Starfire continued to add luxury to go with the performance of the 394 Olds Starfire Rocket V-8 with its 345-hp rating that carried over from the previous Starfire model years.

The 1964 model year brought a second performance model to the full-sized Olds lineup, the Jetstar 1. This was a performance-themed derivative of the mainstream entry series Jetstar 88, using the same V-8 as the Starfire. It was analogous to the Catalina 2+2 (while the Starfire continued to compete against the Grand Prix). The all-new and spectacular 1965 body styling, along with a standard 370 hp version of the all-new Olds 425 V-8, made the Starfire and Jetstar 1 even more appealing that year. The Starfire alone continued for one more year in 1966, but its place in the Olds lineup was largely superseded by the new Toronado. Oldsmobile actually tried one last time to market a performance-themed full-sized car with the largely unknown W-33 Performance Package that included a 390 hp 455 V-8 for the full-sized 1970 Delta 88.

Unfortunately, Olds fans suffer from the least complete representative of model car kits of any of the full-sized brands covered here. The only 1/25th-scale kits of full-sized Olds performance cars were JoHan's 1963 Starfire hardtop and convertible annual kits, and AMT's 1965 Dynamic 88 hardtop full detail annual kit. The AMT kit was reissued only once in stock form, while the JoHan Starfire hardtop was as part of JoHan's USA Oldies kit series in the mid-1970s.

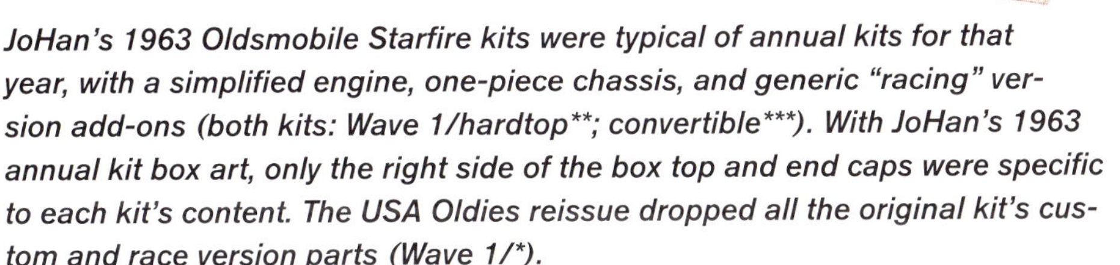

*JoHan's 1963 Oldsmobile Starfire kits were typical of annual kits for that year, with a simplified engine, one-piece chassis, and generic "racing" version add-ons (both kits: Wave 1/hardtop**; convertible***). With JoHan's 1963 annual kit box art, only the right side of the box top and end caps were specific to each kit's content. The USA Oldies reissue dropped all the original kit's custom and race version parts (Wave 1/*).*

1964–1970 Buick Wildcat

Performance was a key storyline for the Buick Wildcat, which was introduced at 1962½ as a limited production response to Pontiac's Grand Prix and Oldsmobile's Starfire. In 1963, it became a full lineup of models and replaced the mid-series Invicta lineup in 1963 (except for the wagons that retained Invicta nomenclature that year). Then the 1964 Wildcat marked the debut of the "Super Wildcat 465." This 425-ci version of Buick's 425-ci Nailhead V-8 incorporated dual 4-barrels for the first time, generating a factory rating of 360 gross horsepower.

GM's all-new 1965 B-Body car was perhaps the apogee of full-sized car design progression, and the Buick versions were right there in the hunt with Pontiac and Oldsmobiles for industry design leadership that year. The Wildcat remained Buick's performance-oriented full-sized series, distinguished by features including optional bucket seats and console, tachometer, and the continued availability of the 360-hp dual-quad Super Wildcat V-8.

The 1966 Wildcat (along with the all-new Riviera) was, in many ways, the poster child for Buick's advertising campaign that year: The Tuned Car. A new Wildcat Gran Sport option paralleled the performance-themed offerings in the Riviera and Skylark lines. The Wildcat's Code A9 Gran Sport High-Performance Group included the 340-hp 425 V-8 (with the single 4-barrel carb) plus a chrome-plated air cleaner, cast aluminum valve covers, dual exhaust, heavy-duty suspension, and Positraction rear differential. As if that were not enough, reportedly there were 21 Buick Wildcats that year built with an optional Y48/Code A8 Gran Sport Performance Group. This added dual-quad carbs to the aforementioned A9 Gran Sport High-Performance Group content.

The 1967 and 1968 Buick Wildcats were evolving away from performance, and features such as standard rear wheel skirts certainly reinforced that message. The GS package was gone, even though the all-new Buick big-block V-8 now displaced 430 ci, was rated at 360 hp (gross), and was now the standard and only engine for the Wildcat.

Performance returned to a modest degree with the slimmer and trimmer 1969 Buick Wildcat. Fully radiused rear wheel openings and a new side sculpture theme were conceptually similar to the sporty 1969 Camaro. After several years of sharing the longer 126-inch wheelbase of the Electra chassis, the 1969 version returned to the LeSabre's shorter 123-inch dimension. Meanwhile the same 430-ci V-8 remained. A slightly blockier front-end theme then characterized the 1970 Wildcat, which

*AMT's 1965 Buick Wildcat annual kit (Wave 1/***) came only in hardtop form this year, with stock, racing, and custom versions (the latter was styled by the Alexander Brothers). Updated as a 1966 Wildcat (Wave 1/**), the box art stated that the kit was now customized by George Barris even though the parts inside appeared much like the year before.*

*AMT's 1969 Wildcat (Wave 1/***) was the last full-detail big Buick annual kit it would design. Optional parts included a dual Ram Air setup for the engine and a hidden-headlamp custom front end with two grille choices. The instruction sheet was laid out in AMT's official blueprint 1969 annual kit format, showing a signoff/approval date of November 30, 1968.*

*AMT's 1964 annual kit lineup included the Buick Wildcat in hardtop and convertible form (both: Wave 1/***). Included was a Nailhead V-8 upgrade with a 4-71 supercharger and a sidesaddle carb location, along with aftermarket valve covers, headers, and air cleaner. These kits have never been reissued.*

Since both AMT's 1966 and 1970 Wildcat kit tools were dead ends that were not subsequently modified, model builders have enjoyed sporadic reissues of both the 1966 3-in-1 type and 1970 unassembled promo-style kits. Shown here are 1966 reissues dating from 1987 and 2001, and the Model King private label reissue from 2007 (all: Wave 1/*).

would be the last year for the nameplate in the Buick full-sized catalog.

AMT produced the kits of the full-sized Buicks for most of the 1960s (with the exception of 1967–1968), but up until 1964 the top-line luxury Electra 225 was the Buick subject that was reduced to 1/25th scale. Starting in 1964, the AMT lineup began featuring the Wildcat instead.

The all-new 1965 Wildcat saw an all-new AMT full detail annual kit. That tool was revised to replicate the 1966 Wildcat, although kit experts note that the interior tooling was not updated from the 1965 appearance.

Hasegawa's 1966 Buick Wildcat kit is best considered as a collectible oddity rather than a detailed assembly kit. The body and grille/taillamps are very accurate, but the rest is a combination of generic and inaccurate components. First released in the late 1980s, shown here is a 1996 reissue of the kit (Wave 2/*).

After the 1967–1968 Buick annual kit gap, given the slight skew back to a more performance-branded premise, AMT returned with a full-detail 1969 Wildcat annual kit offering. This tooling was updated for the last Wildcat annual kit ever in 1970, but this version was a simplified unassembled promo-style kit (no engine and simplified chassis) marketed as part of AMT's Motor City Stocker kit series that year. With the conclusion of Buick's Wildcat series at the end of the 1970 model year, so also concluded AMT's long run of offering 1/25th-scale Buick assembly kits.

In the mid-1980s, Japanese kit manufacturer Hasegawa offered a 1/25th-scale 1966 Wildcat kit. It is widely believed that the body of this kit is patterned off the original AMT annual kit. This was part of a series of mid-1960s GM kits that included a shared generic interior and chassis, making this kit a compromised endeavor.

1963–1966 Mercury Marauder/S-55/Park Lane

The notion of performance in a full-sized Mercury could be traced at least as far back as the extremely rare, and extremely powerful Super Marauder version of the 1958 Mercury. Powered by the new Mercury/Edsel/Lincoln 430 V-8, this limited-production offering carried the flag for the most factory-rated horsepower (at 400) for any domestic car produced during the 1958 model year. However, with the onset of the 1958 recession and the growing sales of compact and economy cars during the next several years, performance at the Mercury brand took a back seat from 1959 to 1962.

A thaw started in mid-year 1962 with the introduction of the S-55 series, debuting in two-door hardtop and convertible form, and offering the new 406 version of the FE engine family rated at 365 hp with a 4-barrel, and 405 hp with the tri-power upgrade. Still, the very conservative styling of the 1962 big Mercury tended to limit the performance car appeal of the new S-55.

The 1963 lineup dawned with the continued availability of the S-55 package, but the unusual reverse C-pillar hardtop design (called Breezeway in Mercury marketing parlance) again didn't sway many performance car prospects. At mid-year, the cavalry arrived in the form of a fastback two-door hardtop design called "Marauder." Combined with the new 1963 below-the-beltline sheet metal based on the Ford Galaxie (but visually differentiated by some cleverly designed add-on sheet metal stampings), this mid-year S-55 Marauder fastback finally checked all the boxes for a very appealing medium-priced muscle car. And that's not even counting the introduction of the 427 Wedge, which replaced the 406 at mid-year in two versions generating either 410 or 425 hp.

For 1964, apparently the S-55 nomenclature took a temporary hiatus, but all the goodies it contained remained available

AMT's 1963½ Mercury fastback kit (Wave 1/**) included the 427 FE big-block engine, and the body wore engraved Marauder and S-55 badging. The two optional build versions were custom and advanced custom versions. AMT's 1964 kit (Wave 1/**) replaced the advanced custom version with a modestly executed NASCAR-like racing version. (Note: The 1964 kit shown here is AMT-Ertl's 1995 Buyer's Choice reissue that replicates the original 1964 annual kit box art).

The fastback Mercury Park Lane was the subject of 1965 and 1966 annual kits from AMT. The 1965 kit (Wave 1/ included an interior with a separate, removable rear seat and a racing instrument cluster, along with other well-executed NASCAR-themed racing options. For the 1966 kit (Wave 1/**), these parts were mostly replaced with a street-custom version. The 1966 kit has been reissued at least five times, including the 1977 (Wave 1/**) and 2004 (Wave 1/*) reissues shown on the right.***

with a properly spec'd factory order. Meanwhile, a new front and rear clip kept the big Mercury lineup looking fresh in the showrooms.

Like its Ford stable mate, the full-sized Mercury was almost all-new for 1965. Mercury once again returned to totally unique sheet metal (other than the greenhouse stampings above the beltline), and the styling (and the marketing to go with it) took on a very formal, Lincoln Continental–inspired tone. Performance remained a supplemental selling point, and the fastback roof on the two-door hardtop yielded a very handsome car by any standard. The one major carryover from 1964 was the performance powertrain options.

The S-55 returned to the lineup for 1966, featuring the new 428 version of Ford's venerable FE engine family. The body styling remained largely unaltered except for revised front and rear design themes, and a new sweeping curve to the two-door's fastback roof line and backlight. Mercury continued the S-55 (but as an option rather than a stand-alone series) on the nicely massaged new sheet metal gracing the 1967 offering. But sales were slow and there was no S-55 when the 1968 lineup debuted.

The Marauder nameplate returned briefly for 1969 and 1970, gracing a shorter wheelbase version of the all-new Marquis luxury series. A "tunnelback" roofline borrowed from the 1969 Galaxie and the hidden headlamp front end of the Marquis made it quite a looker. Two models were offered; the XL-100 upgrade added flat black paint in the tunnelback area and fender skirts for the rear wheelwell opening. It was essentially the original Pontiac Grand Prix formula applied to the Mercury carline. Much like the fading sales of the full-sized 1967–1968 Grand Prix, the new Marauder didn't move the market either.

As with the Ford brand, AMT had a lock on the Mercury promotional and assembly kit business in the 1960s. The first real performance-themed Mercury assembly kit was AMT's 1963 Marauder hardtop kit. While the 1963 Marauder enjoyed notable success in racing that year (both in oval track racing and at the Pikes Peak Hill Climb), regrettably no such racing version was found in the kit. AMT updated the tool to 1964 specs, with the kit replicating the new top-line Park Lane series, while continuing the Marauder fastback roof and fender badging.

AMT's 1965 Mercury annual kit repeated several themes from its 1964 kit: the choice of the Park Lane series (Mercury's equivalent of the Pontiac Bonneville) for the kit replica, the three build versions (showroom stock, custom, and racing), and bucket seat/console interior configuration. Unlike the AMT Galaxie 500 XL kit for 1965, this Mercury kit had a very simplified chassis layout, typical of most 1960s annual kits. AMT updated its Park Lane kit for 1966, adding a non-stock dual-quad induction system as the only engine assembly choice, and eliminating the racing option, making for 2-in-1 versus the earlier 3-in-1 kit format.

No assembly kits of the 1967–1970 full-sized Mercury have been produced, with the lack of 1969–1970 Marauder X-100 kits being a particularly notable omission.

1965–1968 Plymouth Sport Fury

With the benefit of hindsight, Chrysler's decision to downsize the Plymouth Fury for the 1962 model year largely shut them out of the full-sized low price market segment, which at that time was by far the largest volume portion of the automotive industry. A very effective redesign returned the Fury to a stronger market position for 1963 and 1964, but the car was still notably undersized compared to the Chevy Impala and Ford Galaxie.

All that was rectified in 1965, when Plymouth returned to the full-sized marketplace with its version of the all-new Chrysler C-Body. The new design was handsome, well proportioned, and included the vertical quad headlamps that appeared (at least at that time) to be sweeping the industry. The Sport Fury continued as the bucket seated/floor shifted image leader. The Fury received a minor freshening of the front and rear for 1966.

For 1967, new exterior sheet metal continued the previous design theme with an added, modest rear fender kickup. Two different two-door hardtop designs were now offered. For 1968, another minor change to the front and rear clip completed the changes for the four-year run of the C-Body Fury. Top end performance engines were offered each year, including the 426 Wedge in 1965, the 440 4-barrel in 1966, and the upgraded 375 hp 440 in 1967 and 1968.

Chrysler's fuselage era for its large cars began in 1969, and Plymouth shared with a straightforward design theme. For 1970–1971, new wraparound front and rear bumpers made the design far more contemporary. A new Sport Fury GT offering added a hood with twin power bulges, unique exterior graphics, and most important of all, a standard 440 in 4-barrel in 350 hp form along with a 375-hp three–2-barrel upgrade. The 1971 continued with the 370 hp 440 Golden Commando replacing the previous 440 offerings. These GTs are cult favorites with good reason. Some would argue that they were the ultimate (as well as the last) expressions of the full-sized muscle car story of the previous decade.

The model kit world followed right along with the 1965–1968 Sporty Fury developments. JoHan continued its association with Plymouth, providing pre-assembled promotional and assembly kits for each Sport Fury during this four-year period. These kits include a rather unusual feature. While the kit interiors replicated the Sport Fury with its bucket seats and console, the exterior body ornamentation reflects the mainstream Fury III series. Chrysler's dealer promotionals order explained this each year, specifying the higher-volume Fury III (along with its bench seating), while the model kit market preferred the top-line Sport Fury. As exterior tooling had to be shared between the promo and kit products, the Fury III exterior took precedence.

There have been no assembly kits developed for the 1970 and 1971 Sport Fury GT, although they frequently appear near at the top of modelers' wish lists for newly tooled future kit releases.

1965–1966 Dodge Monaco, Custom 880, and Polara 500

Dodge also returned to the full-sized market with full force in 1965, after having pieced together a temporary 1962½ to 1964 offering based on the 1962 Chrysler Newport. The new C-Body lineup included a Pontiac Grand Prix competitor wearing "Monaco" nomenclature. The full line upper series was called Custom 880, while the Polara range was an entry-level medium price series facing off with the Pontiac Catalina. The Polara 500 was the bucket seat/console derivative, sort of an Impala SS recipe applied to the Polara lineup. Performance powertrains were not a major selling feature for the big Dodges, but both the 413 and 426 Street Wedge engines were offered in 1965, and the new 440 Wedge replaced both of them for 1966. Further, a 1966 Street Hemi option was originally planned, and then later dropped from the product cycle plan.

Dodge conjured up a particularly handsome mid-cycle freshening for the 1967 and 1968 model years. The series lineup continued, but now the top engine option was a Magnum

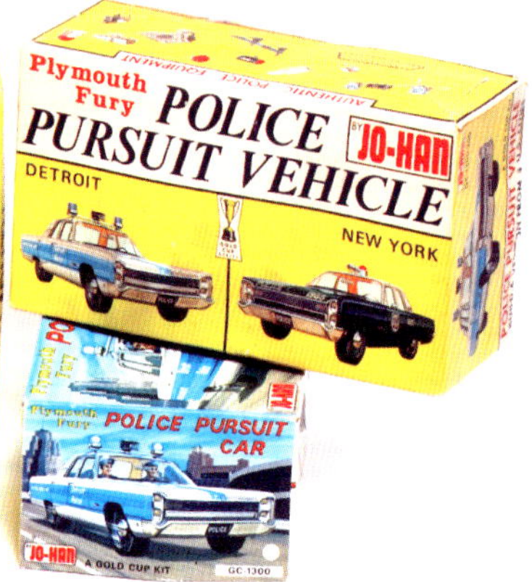

*JoHan's Sport Fury annual kit lineup ran from 1965 to 1968, including 1966 and 1967 annual kits shown here (both: Wave 1/***). These kits had only one engine choice: a 426 Hemi (instead of the Wedge-head engines found in the showrooms) that was based on the 1964 onward competition-only cross-ram A864 Hemi, rather than the 1966–1971 Street Hemi. JoHan later modified its Sport Fury tooling to replicate a 1968 Plymouth Police Cruiser, shown here in its original and reissue kit livery (both: Wave 1/**).*

version of the 440 Wedge. Dodge then participated in the new fuselage 1969 C-Body program, with sheet metal vaguely derived from the 1968 Charger side sculpture theme. The Monaco 500 was now an option package rather than a series. While the 440 Magnum continued into future years, 1969 was the last year of the specific sporty C-Body Polara 500 and Monaco 500 offerings.

For 1965, MPC replaced JoHan as the new Dodge promotional and kitmaker (remember that MPC designed and produced the 1965 Dodge Coronet 500 kit even though it was marketed under the AMT label). That year MPC also produced Monaco hardtop and Custom 880 convertible kits sold under its own brand. Its 1966 Dodge offerings continued with the top line Dodge hardtop (now called Monaco 500), but the convertible kit was changed to a Polara 500. After the annual kit product runs, none of these kits were ever reissued in their original form, as MPC irreparably modified its Dodge C-Body kit tool to produce a Magnum II bubble-topped show car kit.

No model kits have been produced for the 1967–1969 C-Body Dodges (although an extremely well executed 1967 Polara 500 trans kit was offered for several years by two resin casters). This required the purchase of a companion JoHan or MPC Mopar C-Body kit for the engine, chassis, tires, and wheels needed to construct a complete finished model.

*MPC produced full-sized Dodge kits for 1965 and 1966 (all: Wave 1/***). These kits featured a factory stock Mopar B-Block Wedge V-8. The 1965 Custom 880 kit, however, included a 426 Hemi engine option. Just as with its Coronet 500 kit (the engine tooling was shared by both kits), the Hemi was an A864 replica rather than a copy of the upcoming 1966 Street Hemi. Note the rapid evolution of MPC's box art graphics from the 1965 to the 1966 product lines.*

There was never a mass-produced 1/25th-scale kit of the 1967 Dodge Polara 500, but resin trans kits were produced by All-American Model and R & R Vacuum Craft, both based on a superbly accurate "master" built by Finnish modeler extraordinaire Juha Airio. Neither trans kit is currently in production, but unbuilt examples sometimes show up on auction sites. Be prepared to pay accordingly!

1965–1968 Chrysler 300

Some could claim that Chrysler started the series-specific full-sized performance car market with the 1955 300. They might just be correct. The 1955–1964 Chrysler letter series model kits are covered in Chapter 3.

We'll pick up the Chrysler 300 story here with the 1965 model year. By this time, the letter series had largely been diluted by the mainstream 300 series and the availability of letter series engines as options on lesser Chrysler series offerings. Nevertheless, Chrysler introduced the 300-L in the all-new C-Body guise. These were beautifully designed and ornamented products, with a level of interior quality, materials, and execution that Chrysler would not equal again until decades later. The 300-L was distinguished by series-specific side moldings with a red insert and a standard 360-hp version of the 413 Wedge.

For 1966 the 300 series had its best sales year ever, seemingly unaffected by the loss of the letter series 300 this year. (A 300-M was temporarily in the 1966 product plans but later dropped; it was to be powered by the 426 Street Hemi.) A TNT version of the new 440 Wedge, rated at 365-hp in 1966, was the top performance option. Chrysler's 1967 and 1968 versions of the 300 wore a mid-cycle freshened body. The TNT 440 Wedge engine option was uprated to 375 hp for 1967 and for 1968 remained the top powertrain for the 300 series.

Chrysler's new fuselage body shell played host to one of the finest designs ever for the 300 series: the 1969 iteration. From the architectural hidden headlamp grille to the simplified body sides graced with triple pinstripes and individual letters spelling THREE HUNDRED across the rear-quarters, this was the ultimate expression of all the Chrysler Fuselage Era C-Bodies. Minor freshening for 1970 and 1971 (the last year the 300 was offered) lost a touch of the purity of the 1969 design, but they remained very

*JoHan produced both hardtop and convertible kits of the 1965 and 1966 Chrysler 300 (all: Wave 1/***). The bodies in these JoHan kits are considered works of art by many kit collectors due to their crispness, scale accuracy, and superb engraving. The one-piece promo-style chassis in these kits are inferior, however, when compared the more fully detailed C-Body chassis setups found in the MPC Dodge C-Body kits discussed earlier.*

*These are some of the last Chrysler annual kits JoHan produced. Shown are the 1967 300 hardtop and convertible (both: Wave 1/***), and JoHan's 1984 reissue of its 1968 300 hardtop (Wave 1/**). While JoHan's mid-1960s box art was overly simplistic in its execution versus AMT and MPC's kit box graphics, experienced modelers knew the kit contents ranked right up there with the best of its competitors.*

attractive products. The standard powertrain for these 300 offerings was the 440 4-barrel, with the 440 TNT a modest $79 to $83 upgrade. A small production run of 1970 Hurst 300 cars featured a scooped hood and spoilered trunk, an Imperial interior and the distinctive white/gold Hurst paint layout.

JoHan continued to produce the Chrysler annual kits, focusing on the 1965–1966 300 series hardtops and convertibles. As in the past, JoHan's bodies were miniature masterpieces. The engines for these kits were interesting; in effect they were a carryover of the tooling from the 1964 kit and included standard 4-barrel, dual quad–4-barrel, and 1960–1964 long ram dual-quad setups. Only the 4-barrel, of course, was showroom correct. For 1966, the 4-barrel version added a second snorkel to the air cleaner to represent the TNT 440.

JoHan continued with assembly kits of the 1967 and 1968 300 series in both hardtop and convertible body styles. Of all these 1965–1968 kits, only the 1968 300 hardtop kit has been reissued by JoHan, marketed during the mid-1980s as a late addition to the USA Oldies kit series.

No assembly kits have been produced for the Fuselage-era Chrysler 300s. As is the case for a number of other cars mentioned in this chapter, there have been aftermarket resin kits produced for the 1969 and 1970 Chrysler 300.

Missing in Action

Flash, Space, and Grace Muscle Cars yet to appear in a 1/24th-1/25th–scale kit

- 1963 Pontiac Catalina 421 Super Duty
- 1964–1967 Pontiac 2+2
- 1964–1965 Oldsmobile Jetstar 1
- 1964–1966 Oldsmobile Starfire
- 1967 Mercury S-55
- 1967–1969 Dodge Monaco 500 with 440 4-barrel (1967)/440 Magnum (1968–1969)
- 1967–1968 Buick Wildcat
- 1969–1970 Mercury Marauder X-100
- 1969–1971 Chrysler 300 with 440 TNT
- 1970–1971 Sport Fury GT with 440 6-barrel (1970)/440 4-barrel (1971)
- 1973 Grand Prix Model SJ (for extra credit, include the stillborn Super Duty 455 V-8 option)

Flash, Space, and Grace Muscle Cars that need a new/modern kit offering

- 1962 Galaxie 500 XL/406 FE V-8
- 1959–1965 Chrysler 300 D to 300 L
- 1967 (Galaxie) 7-Litre
- 1968 XL Fastback with 428 4-barrel
- 1968–1969 Impala SS427 Sport coupe
- 1969–1970 Grand Prix Model SJ

Muscle Car Model Kits Scale Showroom

The following models show how several of the model kits mentioned earlier in this chapter look when assembled by experienced adult model car builders. (Photography and models are by the author unless noted otherwise.)

Revell's 1965 Impala SS was painted to match Corvette Code F Nassau Blue Metallic, and then finished with kit-bashed American five-spoke mags and wide/wider tires. The chrome trim accents are BareMetal adhesive foil. (Builder: Ken Dawson)

JoHan's 1965 and 1967 Plymouth Fury kits look like this when professionally assembled. While the JoHan kits only contained a non-stock 426 Hemi, many source kits exist for the factory-correct top-line 426S and 440 Golden Commando engines, respectively. (Builder: Dean Milano)

These models were constructed from heavily restored AMT 1967 Impala SS427 pre-assembled promotionals. The Code H Mountain Green Metallic convertible reflects "sleeper" imagery with its whitewalls and full wheel covers, while the Code F Marina Blue Metallic hardtop strikes a more imposing visage with its slotted Rallye wheels and redlines. (Builder/Photographer: Mike Hanson)

The last year for Chevy's stand-alone SS427 series receives a fitting tribute with this 1969 Custom coupe finished in Code 51 Dusk Blue Metallic along with a builder-added vinyl roof and Rallye Wheels. (Builder/Photographer: Mike Hanson)

Dodge's 1965 Custom 880 convertible presents a conservative appearance but could be running a 340-hp 413 Wedge or a 365-hp 426S under the hood. This MPC annual kit was finished in 1965 Dodge Code L Dark Turquoise Metallic. (Builder/Photographer: Mike Hanson)

This 1964 Mercury Park Lane convertible is based on the AMT annual kit, finished in Code D Silver Turquoise Metallic. The kit's FE V-8 engine represents the Code Z 390 4-barrel or the Code Q 427 4-barrel. (Builder: Steve Goldman)

Chevy's Impala design language progressed from overtly muscular (AMT 1967 Impala SS, left) to very formal (MPC 1971 Impala Custom coupe, right) as performance-oriented prospects moved away from buying full-sized family cars. (Builder: Dean Milano)

The 1965 Monaco and 1966 Monaco 500 were offered with Chrysler's biggest Wedge-head V-8s (426 and 440, respectively). MPC produced annual kits of both cars. (Builder: Dean Milano)

The Domestic Sports Car

Some may view the inclusion of sports car model kits to be a stretch given the title of this book. True, back in the day, there was a pretty wide gulf between those who owned a supercar and those who owned a sports car. It wasn't just the income required to support purchasing and maintaining a sports car, but also the utility of a car at a point in our lives when most families had only one car that had to serve multiple transportation roles. Then there were the philosophical differences of the two types of buyers. Suffice it to say that sports car owners as a whole viewed their automotive preferences as more informed choices than those of the remainder of the car buying public.

Today muscle car fans, collectors, and owner/drivers don't face these issues (at least to the degree we did back then), and their broad interests extend to *any* 1960s to early 1970s cars that pushed the performance envelope and had the imagery to go with that. That includes both muscle cars *and* sports cars.

Thus, I've decided to include the performance-oriented, domestically produced sports cars called Corvettes, AMXs, Shelby Cobra roadsters, and, yes, even Studebaker Avantis in this chapter.

Corvette: America's Sports Car

As referenced several times elsewhere in this book, the modern era of model car kits began with the 1958 model year and AMT's introduction of 3-in-1 model kits with one-piece body castings. As any sports car fan knows, America's Sports Car began earlier, with the 1953 model year. Thus, unlike many of the kits in this book, 1953–1957 Corvette model car kits all were introduced at least a decade or more after the real cars debuted. Moreover, because AMT affiliate SMP's annual kit coverage of the Corvette began with the 1959 version, the 1958 Corvette was also missing from the early annual kit world.

Not too surprisingly, model kit coverage of domestic sports cars from this era is among the most complete of all muscle cars. Here you can see the kits of C1, C2, and early C3 Corvettes, along with the Cobra, AMX, and Avanti. With the exception of the more recent 1958 Corvette kit and 427 Cobra kits, the remainder of these kits all date from the 1960s to late 1970s. How many do you recognize?

The C1 Corvettes: 1953–1962

The 1953–1955 Corvettes first appeared in two AMT kits introduced in the mid-1970s. AMT did so in response to many customer requests to the customer service department. Up to that point, some highly skilled modelers had previously pieced together early C1 Corvette models from the ill-defined, primitive promotional toys issued when the real cars were first introduced, but other more casual model car hobbyists were without luck if they wanted to build 1953–1955 Corvette models.

AMT's early C1 Corvette kits were highly anticipated, and very popular when first introduced. But these kits were developed during a period of AMT's history when kit fit/finish and overall accuracy were at a bit of a low point, so they were criticized in several areas by Corvette fans (mostly treatment of exterior trim items). These two kits have seen multiple reissues.

AMT was the first to offer 1/25th-scale assembly kits of the 1953 and 1955 Corvette kits (both: Wave 1/*). These kits were introduced in 1975, and were among the last AMT kits produced with those engaging illustrations of the subject on the box lids (versus the widely adopted imagery of actual built models that soon followed).

During Monogram's "rebirth" as a serious model car kitmaker in the late 1970s, it saw an opportunity to do the 1953 Corvette in a higher level of accuracy than the AMT kit (Monogram's then-president had previously been the president of AMT during the period when its Corvette kit was developed). Monogram's kit was scaled in 1/24th (versus AMT's 1/25th), and was better detailed and finished than the earlier AMT kit. The kicker, however, was that this kit was part of a new Monogram premium series of kits that featured die-cast metal bodies to go along with the remainder of parts that were formed in the expected styrene plastic. Suffice it to say that the die-cast bodies experiment was not a success, but Monogram was able to modify the body tooling to allow the kit to be reissued with a styrene body to go along with the rest of the kit contents, and has done so multiple times since then.

The 1956 and 1957 Corvette saw its first 1/25th-scale kit offerings when a still-new MPC introduced a full detail kit back in 1966. The engine choices were single and dual 4-barrels. At the time of its introduction, this was an excellent kit, compromised only slightly by too-large upper rear wheel openings. MPC later modified the tool to produce various drag and street Gasser kits. Other than that, there was one re-issue in the mid-1980s as part of a combination Corvettes box.

Monogram also introduced a 1/24th-scale 1957 Corvette, sharing a kit design approach with its 1953 Corvette kit but including a styrene body from the very first release forward. This kit features a nicely rendered fuel-injected 283, and is still considered by some to be the pre-eminent early C1 kit offering.

AMT-Ertl entered a period of product development in the mid-1990s wherein it revisited best sellers from its earlier AMT and MPC product lines with new tooling that reflected the advanced kit engineering approaches in place at that time. An all-new 1/25th-scale 1957 Corvette kit was among the results. This kit included the fuel-injected 283 that was missing from the original MPC kit of this Corvette. This is an excellent kit, only faulted by some for the curve of the Corvette "scallop" in the lower door area and its lack of sun visors. It too has been reissued.

The restyling of the C1 Corvette for the 1958 model year coincided with AMT's introduction of 3-in-1 annual kits with one-piece body shells. As mentioned above, it wasn't until 1959 that AMT/SMP expanded its annual kit coverage to include the Corvette. The 1959, 1960, and 1961 annual kits all displayed SMP instead of AMT nomenclature, while the 1962 Corvette adopted the AMT brand.

Monogram's 1953 Corvette kit first appeared in 1977 (as shown here on the right) with a die-cast metal body (Wave 2/**). The kit was later reissued in 1982 with a styrene body (left, Wave 2/*), and also formed the basis of Monogram's 1957 Corvette kit. Both kits included the extra engine parts to build the model as a 1954 as well as 1953 Corvette.

*The 1956–1957 Corvette was MPC's first choice of a 1950s kit to produce in 1/25th scale (Wave 1/**). One of the first kits designed by Budd Anderson at MPC, following his earlier stints at AMT and IMC, it was merchandised offering eight ways to build (1956 and 1957 showroom stock, modified sports drag, Bonneville racer, custom, road racer, rally car, and B/SP drag).*

AMT-Ertl's 1957 Corvette kit (Wave 3/) was all new and ostensibly replaced its earlier 1956–1957 Corvette kit based on the original MPC tool shown (left). Red Corvettes (with white coves, where applicable) were by far the box art colors of choice among 1/24th- and 1/25th-scale kit producers.*

Monogram's 1/24th-scale 1957 Corvette kit (Wave 2/) (left) was first issued in 1977, and included parts for both a showroom stock version with a fuel-injected 283, as well as a late 1970s style street machine. The latter was graced with American 200-S five-spoke mags, a competition-type Z-28 cross-ram manifold, roll bar, and a mid-1970s–style pro-stock hood scoop.*

*These are the 1959 (upper left, lower left, lower center), 1960 (lower right), 1961 (upper right), and 1962 (upper center) Corvette annual kits (all: Wave 1/**). Note the two different sizes of 1959 Corvette annual boxes on the left. The only Corvette ID on these generic boxes was a stamp on the box end (1959), a personalized box seal (1960 and 1961), and a black-and-white photo inset on the box top and end (1962).*

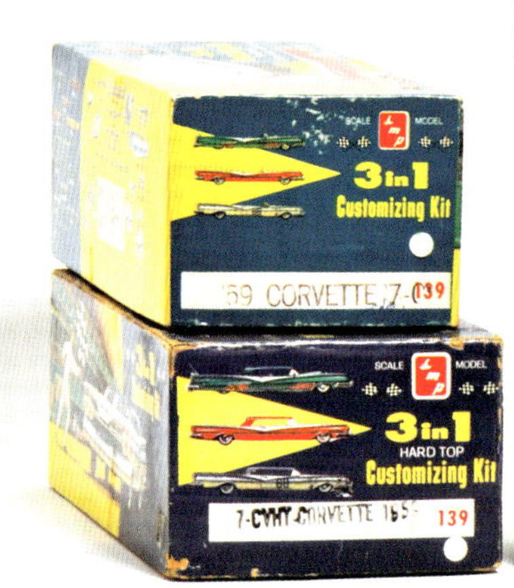

(Kits that wore "SMP" utilized the kit design and manufacturing approach of AMT, and each of the SMP box tops here also shows the AMT name in small print on the lower box sides.) The 1960 SMP Corvette was one of the first annual kits with an operating hood and engine, while the 1961 SMP and 1962 AMT Corvette kits were also distinguished by the addition of opening trunk lids.

Original box art Revell 1959 Corvette kits are extremely hard to locate. Shown here are reissues including the Skip's Fiesta Drive-In Series (Wave 1/) from 1988 and a kit with cardboard diorama motel (Wave 1/*) released in 1998. Both these kits contain multi-piece bodies rather than the one-piece bodies typical of annual kits of this era.*

Revell as a maker of detailed 1/25th-scale models was finding its way during this period, introducing several nicely detailed kits of subjects as varied as a 1957 Ford Country Squire to, yes, a 1959 Corvette. These kits were somewhat ignored by model builders as they contained multi-piece body castings (for example, separate body sides and body tops) that were challenging to glue together without telltale signs of the body joints. Nevertheless, adult modelers today view the Revell 1959 Corvette kit as a pretty competent kit for those that have the skill to assemble it properly. The kit has been reissued multiple times, but it is usually mislabeled as a 1960 instead of 1959 Corvette.

Around 1968, AMT dug out its C1 annual kit tooling and engineered a modest revision of its 1962 annual kit. The choice of optional non-stock building versions was expanded, while the separate trunk lid was dropped and the upper front fender areas were retooled, unfortunately with very evident undersized headlamps as a result. This version, still wearing its annual kit/promo-style one-piece chassis construction, has seen many reissues; most recently in a repop of the late 1960s reissue featuring a Gasser version with psychedelic era graphics.

AMT also located and recycled the SMP 1960 Corvette annual kit tooling, then announced an incorrectly branded 1959 Corvette reissue as an addition to its Street Rod Series offerings in 1974. Like most 1960 model year annual kits, this was an extremely simple kit even though it included an engine. It is best avoided by the serious model builder because other

The first reissues of the SMP/AMT C1 Corvette 1960 (Wave 1/) and 1962 (Wave 1/**) annual kits date from 1974 and 1967, respectively. The 1960 kit is incorrectly labeled as a 1959 for this and several later reissues, while the 1962 kit wears the highly desirable Trophy Series portrait box art format used for a couple of years in the mid-1960s.*

*Posed in the "jumping off the box" position favored by MPC in the late 1960s, its 1960 Corvette kit (Wave 1/**) depicted a period-perfect supercharged drag car. The side panel promoted building versions labeled as stock, drag, custom, road, or rally. Inside, however, the assembly instructions suggested seven versions: stock, Bonneville, modified sports car, wild custom, rally car, road racing, and stock drags.*

1960 Corvette kits are available that are more accurate.

For its 1968 kit catalog, MPC took its 1956–1957 Corvette kit tooling and engineered a 1960 Corvette body addition. The resulting kit replicated the excellent accuracy of its earlier C1 kit, except that MPC forgot to update the interior bucket to the 1960 upholstery pattern and neglected to include the updated 1960 single air cleaner for the dual quads.

In the late 1990s, Revell-Monogram introduced the Pro Modeler brand for a series of premium-priced, highly detailed 1/25th-scale car kits. Included was a terrific 1958 Corvette, the first popular-scale model kit of that C1 to be produced. This kit tool was later modified to also produce a 1959 Corvette, equally well detailed but at a more accessible price point. Both these kits have been reissued.

More recently, Revell introduced an all-new kit of the 1962 Corvette. Featuring a well executed fuel-injected 327 V-8, the kit shares none of the tooling with its 1958–1959 C1 kits. Rather, it adopts a similar parts breakdown and produces a nice replica that is far more accurate than the reissued AMT 1962 Corvette kits.

Revell's 1958 and 1959 Corvette kits (both: Wave 3/) are easily listed among the best detailed C1 model kits you can buy. The body features a separately molded cove. A photo was included to assist with painting two-tones. The fuel-injected engine is a jewel, but a close look and research will reveal that the setup is only 100 percent correct for the 1958 model year (minor but visible changes occurred for the 1959–1961 fuel-injection setups).*

The C2 Corvettes: 1963–1967

As an eight-year-old at the time, I still recall the start of the 1963 model year as something special. Right at the top of my attention list was the new C2 Corvette and the Studebaker Avanti. I didn't think in such terms at the time, but I was witnessing the beginnings of a legacy for both of these cars.

First released in 2012, Revell's all-new 1962 Corvette kit (Wave 4/) was a welcome surprise to the modeling community. This kit clearly shows the advances in model kit design and quality during the four decades since AMT's old 1962 Corvette annual kit.*

*AMT 1963 Corvette lineup included separate kits for the coupe and convertible body styles (both: Wave 1/**). The two kits differed in several ways beyond the body style. For example, the convertible kit featured operating retractable headlamps and a center rear deck fin for the racing version. Only the box end caps showed the Corvette; the remaining box top and side panel graphics were generic images shared with other 1963 AMT annual kits.*

*AMT's 1964 Corvette hardtop and convertible box tops are shown on the right (both: Wave 1/***). On the left are both side panels of the convertible kits. Note the road-racing theme to the kit extras, and the mention of AMT spokesperson Budd Anderson on both box tops.*

Continuing the pattern set with 1958–1962 Corvette kits, AMT drew first straws on the new 1963 Vette, offered in both the hardtop and convertible versions. The convertible kit assembly manual included a small section with customizing hints from George Barris, the Alexander Brothers, Bill Cushenberry, and Gene Winfield. The same decal sheet design was used for both kits, but printed in different colors.

AMT went on with updates of the C2 Corvette for each year through 1967, maintaining the dual hardtop/convertible kit approach. While the chassis casting was simplistic to the max, the optional building versions each year are a three-dimensional record of the leading edge of the 1/1-scale performance and appearance of the aftermarket's evolution during each year.

The Corvette also provided one of the very first business opportunities for the new guys in town, MPC. Its 1964 Corvette hardtop kit was sold with neat merchandising hooks, including a scale drag racing 'chute and working steering. MPC made minor updates to its Corvette annual kits for 1965 through 1967 releases, including a working front suspension setup complete with real coil springs.

Both AMT and MPC eventually reissued some of their C2 Corvette kits. AMT was first out of the gate in the late 1960s with several reissues of the 1967 version. It backdated the hardtop tool to the 1963 status as a lead offering of its 25th anniversary Street Rod Series kits, which debuted in 1973. This kit has seen many reissues, including the latest from Round 2. In the mid-1980s, the AMT 1963 Corvette was reintroduced with a newly tooled convertible body. This version has also seen many reissues.

Meanwhile, MPC kept its tool in the 1967 format and reissued it several times in several mildly altered street machine formats. The various AMT reissues included either the rat engine or both the rat and mouse engines; MPC kit used only the small-block with its reissues.

Decades later, some newly tooled C2 Corvettes were eventually available from Revell-Monogram. The first of these was an evolution of a previous kit tooling project that included customized versions of C2 and C3 Corvettes, updated with a semi-stock 1965 Corvette body and interior tooled up to tie in with

*AMT's 1965, 1966 and 1967 Corvette Roadster annual kits are shown along the bottom, along with the 1966 coupe at top center (all: Wave 1/***). The 1966 convertible had the 327 V-8 in 4-barrel, and no-longer showroom-correct fuel-injected dual-quad setups. The 1966 coupe had both a 327 and a 396 (according the box art and instruction sheet) even though the real car had an optional 427 instead of a 396, and a raised center section hood that was missing from this AMT kit.*

*MPC's 1964 Corvette was the first full detail kit issued by this new kit manufacturer (Wave 1/***). It made quite a statement with features like steerable front wheels, rotating rear halfshafts, and three engine building versions (dual-quads, fuel injection, and 6-71 supercharger). The 1965 annual kit (Wave 1/**) added a four-piece, vacuum-formed parachute to the kit options.*

a very brief television series. Monogram evolved this 1/24th-scale tooling to offer a reasonably correct 1965 hardtop with the big-block 396 under hood.

Next, a 1967 big-block convertible appeared first in an all-new full detail 1/25th-scale kit dating from 1996, followed in 1997 by a big-block hardtop of the same C2 vintage. These were all-new kits, and their tooling produced replicas that far eclipsed any previous second-generation Corvette model. The treatment of the upper fender blister transition into the bodyside is slightly more realistic in the coupe kit, however.

Revell later followed with 1963 Corvette convertible and hardtop kits, but these were brought to market as simple, snap assembly kits with no engine detail, simplified chassis, and stickers instead of decals. While targeted at the pre-adult market, these kits are nicely proportioned and can be made presentable with just a little extra effort. If you look closely at the top of the convertible kit, you'll see Revell-Monogram's late VP of Engineering Roger Harney behind the wheel of his own beloved 1963 Vette convertible that he drove to many of the Woodward Dream Cruise events.

*Several early C2 reissues from AMT and MPC are shown here. The AMT 1967 coupe annual kit (Wave 1/**) was reissued intact in this box art in 1969; it was later retooled into the 1963 body style for the AMT 1973 25th anniversary Street Rod Series (Wave 1/*). The 1963 convertible kit (Wave 1/*) dates from 1988, and is thought to include an all-new tool for the convertible body. MPC's 1967 Corvette annual kit saw its first reissue in this circa 1973 Streaker release (Wave 1/*).*

Monogram's 1965 Corvette kit first appeared in 1987 (Wave 2/) and replicated the featured automobile in a short-lived TV series about a mysterious character known as Sting Ray. With a change of wheels and valve covers and plating for the bumpers (which were body color in the TV series release), a showroom stock 1/25th-scale 1965 big-block Corvette kit emerged in 1991 (Wave 2/*).*

Revell's assembly kits of the 1967 Corvette coupe and convertible (both: Wave 3/*) are considered the most detailed 1/25th-scale C2 kits in the marketplace kits given their level of component breakdown, detailing, and fit and finish. The coupe runs an L36 4-barrel, while the roadster employs a tri-power L71. The 1963 snap-tite coupe and convertible kits date from 2000 and 2002 respectively, and build up as sharp simplified assembly models (both: Wave 4/*).

The Early C3 Corvettes: 1968–1974

Any car guy or gal probably has a favorite among the various generations of Corvettes, and for this writer, the early C3 Corvettes (1968–1972) are at the top of my personal list. For this section, I am going to add the 1973 and 1974 Corvettes, as these pre-catalyst offerings still featured the choice of small and big-blocks, and included true dual exhausts among their equipment. They also debuted the handsome initial versions of the bumperless front and rear ends that would eventually carry the C3 through the rest of its lifecycle. As for 1975 and beyond . . . that was a new Corvette world, one of increasing emphasis on luxury (and growing sales to boot), but one not covered by this book.

For the 1968 to 1974 period, both AMT and MPC offered hardtop and convertible Corvette annual kits for each year except 1968, when AMT offered a combination coupe/convertible kit. AMT's dual body-style kit was a guess as they missed out on viewing the factory blueprints prior to the model year. The result was a caricature of sorts; they guessed correctly on the basic design elements, but certain details, such as the proportions of the body behind the rear wheels, were wrong. This kit also used a recycled chassis from AMT's 1963–1967 annual kits. This kit was later reissued with spectacular drag-themed "accelerator" box art.

Conversely, MPC's 1968 Corvette annual kits were right on the mark from the start. MPC also continued the somewhat problematic working and steering front end with real coil springs from its previous C2 kits.

For 1969, AMT got access to the full body blueprints and its kit was now right on the money. Then, both AMT and MPC

The new C3 Corvette annual kits from AMT (Wave 1/**) and MPC (Wave 1/) both wore compelling box art, but inside, only the MPC had a correct 1968 body. AMT's body was a good guess, but missed the mark in certain areas such as the too-short rear-end proportions. In addition, AMT's separately molded roof and C-pillar was not as accurate as MPC's one-piece coupe body.***

*Both AMT and MPC offered correctly proportioned Corvette hardtops and convertibles for the 1969 annual kit run (all: Wave 1/**). Note the "Reproduced from Official Factory Prints" logo on the AMT box top, perhaps a reassurance to those who purchased its earlier, incorrect 1968 Corvette kit. MPC continued its use of optional Bubble Tops to make convertible kits more attractive to the retail trade.*

*Chevy's modest revision of the Corvette for 1970½ brought the expected new annual kits from MPC and AMT (all: Wave 1/**). Note that MPC included the model year on its kits, while AMT omitted any mention of model year, thought to be a reaction to kit retailers who wanted to avoid drawing attention to outdated kits on their shelves. The AMT boxes shown here are the 1970½ coupe and convertible kits (which were unchanged through the following 1971 annual kit run).*

*Closing out our coverage of early C3 Corvette kits, AMT and MPC continued to produce annual kits of the convertible and coupe body styles (all: Wave 1/**). AMT continued to omit the model year from its C3 box tops and ends, but the side panel revealed the green box to be the 1973 edition, while the orange car was the 1974 kit.*

continued with their offerings each year through 1974, incorporating minor yearly edits to keep pace with the real car. For the model builder, though, once you had built either the AMT or MPC kit, there wasn't a lot to justify buying next year's kit unless you were truly a kit collector or dedicated Corvette enthusiast back then.

Several factory stock and racing-themed C3 reissues have come from subsequent owners of the AMT and MPC C3 annual kit tools, but they were mid-1970s Corvettes rather than the more desirable 1968–1974 Corvettes. (Both the AMT and MPC tools were updated as annual kits only through the 1977 model year; at that point AMT exited the annual kit business while MPC developed all-new tooling for the remainder of its C3 Corvette annual kit run through 1982).

So, for many years thereafter, the only way to get a 1/25th-scale 1968–1974 Corvette model kit was to search out and purchase a collectible annual kit version; asking prices rose rapidly as a result.

Having noted this situation as both a model car builder and journalist, I concocted a plan to get Revell-Monogram, (who in the late 1980s was the premier model maker of that era) to introduce some new kits of the early C3, shark-era cars. In a conversation with one of its senior executives around 1987, I told him that I had heard a very strong rumor that one of the Japanese kitmakers was planning a new kit of the C3 Corvettes if they didn't see a U.S.-based kitmaker enter that market

The most detailed/authentic and affordable early C3 Corvette kits are these Revell kits dating from 1988 (convertible) and 1989 (coupe) and the AMT-Ertl kits both introduced in 1991 (both: Wave 3/*). All of these kits have been reissued multiple times since with new box art and various additions or modifications, but the basic kit contents remain the same as those shown here.

soon. Of course, my "rumor" was 100 percent fabricated, but whether in response to my "planted" info or for whatever other reason, a year later Revell announced plans for a 1968 Corvette convertible, soon followed by a 1969 Corvette coupe. These two kits hit the kit nail squarely on the head, with detail superior to that of the original C3 annual kits and a mainstream purchase price to boot. Both of these kits have seen many reissues in various formats.

Following shortly after Revell's new C3 kits was AMT-Ertl's announcement of a 1970 Corvette hardtop and a 1972 Corvette convertible. Not only that, since Revell had gone the big-block 427 route with its kits, AMT-Ertl researched and tooled the small-block LT-1 for its kit series. In addition, they added in the ZR-1 competition option components as well for the 1970 kit. Experienced modelers have their favorites between the AMT-Ertl and the Revell new-tool C3 kits, but for our purposes, both the brands' offerings are highly recommended for those who actually want to build their C3 Corvette kits.

Corvette Concepts and Factory Racers

Before I move on to America's other 1960s sports cars, several Corvette Design Studies and Concepts have eventually seen kit form, and I want to cite them here. The original Mako Shark concept debuted around 1960, and while it has never been replicated in a full detail kit, in the 1990s AMT-Ertl developed a simplified replica with a pre-finished body.

MPC was responsible for a full-detail kit of the Mako Shark II that inspired the design language of the production C3 Corvette. This kit featured a number of operating features inspired by the 1/1-scale concept, and when it was introduced in 1966, it was by far the most detailed Corvette kit to break cover as of that point. After an initial multi-year run, the kit tool was altered several times to produce non-stock kits, but has never been reissued in its original GM Design configuration.

MPC was also the source of a 1/25th-scale kit replicating the Astro-Vette Concept, which was essentially a streamlined

GM's Mako Shark II Concept was an incredibly popular subject when unveiled in 1965, and that made it an obvious candidate for a model kit. MPC stepped up to the plate with a very well done kit (Wave 1/) with several operable features, and even added a 25-piece transport trailer to the box contents. The tool was modified for the mid- and late 1970s reissues at the right (both: Wave 1/*).***

Revell-Monogram's AeroVette mid-engine concept kit (Wave 3/*) debuted in 1998. Revell and former GM vice president of design Chuck Jordan reportedly enjoyed a good working relationship, so it should not be a surprise that the resulting kit was very well designed and produced.

Accurate Miniature's Corvette Grand Sport is probably still the most detailed kit ever of the Corvettes represented in this book (Wave 3/**). This was the first domestically designed and produced popular-scale kit to include photo-etched components and represented a heretofore unseen level of design detail and fidelity. Revell later released some unused inventory of the original kit run with a different competition livery in a limited 2012 kit offering (Wave 3/*).

1968 Corvette sporting full rear fender skirts and a chopped-down windscreen with integral roll bar feature.

Corvette fans will proudly remember the 2-Rotor and 4-Rotor, Wankel rotary-based mid-engine Corvettes of the early 1970s. Neither of these made the kit world, but GM's further evolution of the 4-Rotor property with a small-block V-8 replacing the original engine did eventually see kit form.

It was rechristened the AeroVette. Recalling the buzz surrounding its unveiling, in *Cars That Never Were: The Prototypes* former GM vice president of design Bill Mitchell notes that the AeroVette was to have been the actual production Corvette for the 1980 model year. The book states that it was approved for series production at the end of the 1977 calendar year by GM chairman Thomas Murphy, with the only change to be one additional inch of headroom, according to Mitchell. It is interesting to speculate on how this might have changed the entire trajectory of General Motors and the performance car world, had the program not been cancelled soon thereafter.

According to a former Revell-Monogram executive, two somewhat simplified assembly kits of late 1980s GM Design concepts (the Sting Ray III and Pontiac Banshee) turned out to be surprise best sellers, eventually topping 500,000 and 350,000 kits each, respectively. Thus it would have seemed natural to revisit the GM Design archives for additional kit topics, and the AeroVette was tapped as a new kit for the Revell-Monogram catalog.

Finally, the Corvette Gran Sport program of 1963 is a much-storied part of Corvette history. This chapter came alive in 1/25th scale in the 1990s with an all-new, intricately detailed Gran Sport kit in several different liveries from a new model kit company named Accurate Miniatures. Staffed in part by several model kit industry veterans and established in Charlotte, North Carolina, with a goal of producing highly detailed airplane and competition-themed automotive assembly kits, its first car kit introduction, the Corvette Grand Sport, certainly lived up to that goal.

The Ongoing Supply of Corvette Kits

While I don't have access to model company kit sales figures, my guess is that Corvette model kits have been and remain among the perennial top sellers for their manufacturers. Not surprisingly, then, the tools that produce these kits are revisited time and time again for production by their owners, resulting in a continuing supply of Corvette kits for the model car builder and collector. Ranging from the multi-piece bodies of late 1950s model kit technology to today's latest products resulting from digital and Electronic Discharge Machining (EDM) tooling processes, your supply of Corvette kits is nearly endless, and is likely to stay that way for years to come.

Among the literally hundreds of Corvette kit tools that have been introduced during the last six decades, many have been run through fresh production cycles with new box art, decal sheets, and (in some cases) minor revisions to the parts inside. This presents thousands of potential kit choices to the savvy model kit collector. Shown here are just a few of the many reissues of Corvette kits covered earlier in this chapter.

Studebaker's Avanti: Trying to Save an American Institution

While Studebaker's stunning Avanti sports car preceded press coverage of the 1963 Corvette introduction by several months, they were together perhaps the hottest news of the entire 1963 model year, and that is going a mile given all the other exciting things that happened in the auto industry that year. While the Avanti was a media sensation, production difficulties and somewhat controversial styling conspired to make the Avanti a failure at its assigned mission to reinvigorate the passenger car business of Studebaker Corporation. Fans of the Avanti got the last laugh, however, as the design continued for several decades as the limited production Avanti II.

Within several years of that star-crossed introduction, scale modelers were fortunate enough to see two entirely different 1/25th-scale Avanti kits come to market. The first was from New York's Aurora Corporation. Aurora is largely ignored in today's modeling world, but in the 1960s by some accounts it was the largest and most successful hobby kit producer in the world. Granted, most of its kits were of non-automotive subjects, but it was highly successful at the time and at one point during this period it reportedly investigated acquiring the entire assets of one of the industry's most successful automotive kitmakers.

Aurora's new Avanti kit was part of a series of 1/25th-scale sports cars replicating the likes of Maserati, Aston-Martin, and Jaguar and road racing efforts from Ferrari, Ford (GT-40), and

*Aurora's Avanti kit (Wave 1/***) was introduced in 1963; it included the most detailed Studebaker V-8 ever placed in a 1/25th-scale kit, and several detailed components not found in AMT's kit (Wave 1/**). On the other hand, the AMT body was more finely engraved, and more realistic in appearance. It also included parts for a tasteful custom version, the revised 1964 square bezel Avanti factory headlamp configuration, and a competition version inspired by Studebaker's 1962 and 1963 Bonneville speed record attempts.*

Chaparral. Its Avanti kit included opening doors and trunk while replicating the basic Studebaker 289 V-8 under the hood. This was a respectable kit, but as with most of its other sports car offerings, the overall body proportions and detail were a bit lacking.

This Aurora kit saw only one reissue, in the mid-1970s. The tooling was eventually acquired by Monogram, and was either lost at the bottom of Lake Erie in transport to Monogram's Chicago factory (a popular war story among modelers), or more likely, scrapped shortly thereafter for tax write-off purposes by Monogram's business-minded management team at that time.

AMT's 1963 Avanti debuted in 1965 with Trophy Series 3-in-1 branding, and was part of a sub-series of internationally themed kits including the 289 Cobra, the 300SL coupe, the Sunbeam Alpine and Tiger, and a stillborn Porsche 911. AMT's version also included opening doors, and offset the lack of the Aurora kit's opening trunk with replicas of both the single Paxton supercharged R2 289, as well as the one-off Due Cento R5 dual supercharged 305 V-8 used in the Avanti's Bonneville Salt Flats assault in 1962 and 1963. Unlike the Aurora kit, AMT's Avanti kit has seen multiple sporadic reissues each decade since.

AMC's 1968–1970 AMX: The Unexpected Sports Car

The story of domestic sports cars of the muscle car era would be irresponsibly incomplete without coverage of the American Motors AMX. Introduced in 1968½, this shorter wheelbase, two-passenger derivative of the Javelin pony car actually made quite a stir in the automotive marketplace of the late 1960s. JoHan developed the tooling for the AMX kit (as it did for all AMC products back then), but the kit itself was sold as an annual kit under the AMT label for the 1968½, 1969, and 1970 model years. Surprisingly, the AMT AMX kit was sold with two different box art treatments in the 1969 annuals kit lineup, and again for the 1970 annual kits catalog.

*The 1968½ and 1969 AMX kits (both: Wave 1/**) appeared in the AMT kit catalog and wore AMT box art, even though they were designed and (most likely) produced by JoHan. These kits were great values as they not only built showroom stock AMX replicas, but also included what was the best (then and now) 1/25th-scale replica of the original Logghe tubular funny car chassis.*

JoHan later did some minor additions to the tool to replicate the Hurst-AMC AMX Drag Racing Super Stock project, including livery that replicated Shirley Shahan's successful quarter-mile stomper. The tooling was returned to 1969 showroom stock status for JoHan's USA Oldies series. Like all of JoHan's late 1960s to early 1970s AMC kits, the engine in this AMX kit was inaccurately derived from the old, first-generation AMC V-8 instead of being a correct copy of the all-new second-generation V-8 engine family that debuted during the latter 1960s.

AMT's Avanti kit has seen at least six reissues since its 1965 introduction (all: Wave 1/). Shown here are (counterclockwise from the upper left) the 2014, 1974, 1989, and 2000 versions. The most recent release restores some parts missing from the other versions. All of these include both the circular and square headlamp bezel treatments of the original Studebaker-built Avanti.*

After a 1970 AMX annual kit run with the new front-end design, JoHan returned the kit to 1969 status and made the minor changes to replicate the Hurst/AMX Super Stock entries. The kit was then issued with the stock parts (except for an incorrect 1970 interior tub and Hurst mags in lieu of the factory-correct Magnum 500–style road wheels) as one of JoHan's USA Oldies kit series (both: Wave 1/*).

Cobra: Carroll Shelby's 289 and 427 Roadsters

The improbably successful story of Carroll Shelby's project to combine a British sports car body with an American-made V-8 has been told thousands of times, and needs no repeating here. Given its outstanding performance, and its quickly developing status as a winner over the C2 Corvette on America's Road Racing courses, it became an obvious candidate for a model kit.

AMT stepped up to the plate with a 1965 kit introduction as part of its premium Trophy Series kit line. I remember this kit fondly, not only for its highly detailed (and fun to build) tubular chassis with its transverse leaf spring front and rear suspension, but as the first detailed kit I successfully assembled as a child to a respectable conclusion, one that is still displayed in my collection today.

Of course, once the outrageous 427-powered Cobras debuted on the road and track, model builders pined for a kit. A Japanese kitmaker attempted a replica, but most builders dismissed it. Not until 1988 did a finely detailed 427 Cobra kit debut, courtesy of Revell-Monogram. Engineered by Jay Adams and the Monogram product development team, ex-Monogram executive Bob Johnson considers this to be his definition of a "nearly perfect" 1/24th-scale assembly kit.

AMT's original Shelby Cobra kit with its 260 Ford V-8 is shown here at center top (Wave 1/**), while Round 2's latest reissue (wearing a rebop of the late 1960s "King Cobra" version release) is directly below (Wave 1/*). Counterclockwise from the upper left are other kit reissues sequentially debuting from the mid-1970s to early 2000s (all: Wave 1/*).

Monogram's first Cobra kit was the 427SC kit on the upper left (Wave 3/**). It was followed one year later by the more streetified version at the lower left (Wave 3/**), which added front and rear bumpers, a dual-quad version of the FE 427 V-8, and a raised convertible top option. Several competition-themed reissues (right) have kept the kit in regular production rotation.

Ford's 1955–1957 Ford Thunderbird: Was It a Sports Car?

The introduction of the two-seat Ford Thunderbird Roadster in 1955 set the auto industry on its ear. In many ways, the Thunderbird actually delivered what the 1953–1954 Corvette promised. With a powerful V-8 and a weather-secured interior compartment with roll-up windows, not to mention then-sensational styling, the Thunderbird was an immediate hit and sold in volumes geometrically larger than the 1953–1955 Corvette. In retrospect, it may have been even more important in that some Corvette historians speculate that the Thunderbird ensured that General Motors would make the necessary investment to evolve the Corvette into a bona fide sports car of its own. In any case, the Corvette responded strongly in 1956, and especially 1957. The future of an American two-seat sports car was now assured.

When the Thunderbird matured into a four-seat, low-slung personal luxury automobile for the 1958 model year, most pretensions of muscle car–like performance went away. Nevertheless, the two-seaters of those first three years of Thunderbirds were sports cars in the context of the era, and thus worthy of mention in a book about performance-oriented model car kits.

The 1957 Thunderbird became the subject of one of AMT's first post–World War II kit entries in its popular Trophy Series kit lineup. This 1962 kit introduction featured a fully chromed Y-Block V-8 and multiple customizing options including extended front and rear ends and a fastback-style roof treatment. Note the smaller kit box on the left, which is considered the most collectible version of this kit (Wave 1/***).

The Directory of Model Kits lists 20 reissues of AMT's 1957 Thunderbird (including a simplified assembly Craftsman version). These four kits date from (counterclockwise from the top left) 1976, 1979, 1989, and 2005 (all: Wave 1/). These kits exclude many of the customizing parts found in the original 1962 kit and its 1960s reissues.*

*The 1956 Thunderbird eventually saw these scale kits. Monogram's 1/24th-scale styrene kit with a die-cast metal body debuted in 1977 (center, Wave 2/**), and was eventually replaced in 1982 with a similar kit molded entirely in styrene (left, Wave 2/*). AMT-Ertl's 1/25th-scale kit with American Graffiti licensing (Wave 4/*) debuted in 2003, and was a fine kit other than the misshaped Y-Block V-8 underhood.*

What about Imported Sports Cars?

From what I recall of the 1960s and early 1970s, sports cars of all geographic origins were subjects of near-universal appreciation among the hard-core enthusiast car owners of America, and that admiration extended to the world of model car kit builders and collectors. Whether the car came from St. Louis in the United States or Germany, England, Italy, or (later in the decade) Japan, what mattered for a sports car was its style, overall performance, and (in many cases) a link to a successful competition record, not where it was designed and built.

Given this interest, it was not surprising that the U.S.-based kit manufacturers occasionally tapped the import sports car marketplace for kit subjects. Of all the kitmakers, Aurora probably placed the most priority on this kit genre. At times, however, AMT, Revell, and (later on, Monogram) all offered kits of import sports cars.

One subject AMT started but never finished was a Porsche 911 scheduled for introduction in 1966 or 1967. It went as far as a completed 1/10th-scale wood master before being cancelled for unknown reasons. I saw it at the AMT headquarters in the mid-1970s. Don Emmons, probably the pre-eminent model car journalist of the 1960s, was also a consultant to AMT at that time. I recently asked him if he knew anything about why the 911 project was dropped. He didn't know for sure, but thought that the somewhat disappointing sales of AMT's Mercedes-Benz 300 SL Trophy Series kit may have been a consideration.

I can't cover this subject extensively in this book, and import sports cars may be straying a bit too far from the muscle car theme, but I wanted to touch on the subject briefly. The point remains that model builders back then, as well as kit collectors today, have a rich choice of import sports car kit material to search out and enjoy.

A cabinet-full of import sports car kits produced in the 1960s through the mid-1970s might look a little like this. The MPC Toyota 2000 GT Roadster was a kit tool shared with U.K.-based Airfix. Aurora's sports car kits date from the early 1960s and saw only one reissue in the mid-1970s under the Battle Aces of the Road banner. Revell's Datsun 240Z kit was highly popular (as was the real car when introduced).

Missing in Action

Domestic sports cars yet to appear in a 1/24th-1/25th-scale kit

- 1973 Corvette 2-Rotor and 4-Rotor Concepts

Domestic sports cars that need a new or modern kit offering

- 1961 Corvette full-detail kit
- 1963, 1964, and 1966 Corvette hardtop and convertible full-detail kits
- 1968½–1970 AMC AMX full-detail kits (with correct 390 AMC V-8)
- 1971, 1973, and 1974 Corvette Kits

Most needed kit restoration and reissue:

- 1965 Mako Shark II (return MPC tooling to original GM design studio concept configuration)

Muscle Car Model Kits Scale Showroom

The following models show how several of the model kits mentioned earlier in this chapter look when assembled by experienced adult model car builders. (Photography and models are by the writer unless noted otherwise.)

These 1957 and 1960 Corvettes are built from AMT-Ertl and MPC kits, respectively. Other than the dropped front suspensions and different wheels/tires, both models were built straight from the box.

Revell kits replicate a wide spectrum of C3 Corvette offerings. The 1963 Roadster is a pre-painted snap-tite quick assembly kit, while the 1967 coupe is a heavily detailed replica wearing Code 976 Marina Blue Metallic.

Kit-bashed 1968 L-46 327 and 1971 LS-6 454/ZR-2 Corvette Roadsters with optional hardtops are based on modern era C3 kits from Revell and AMT-Ertl. Colors are Code 976 Le Mans Blue Metallic and 989 War Bonnet Yellow Metallic, respectively.

Compare the Wave 3 C3 1969 and 1970½ Corvette coupe kits from Revell (foreground) and AMT-Ertl, respectively; note subtle differences in the curve of the upper edges of the "wings" surrounding the rear windows. Paint from MCW Automotive Finishes is Code 983 Fathom Green Metallic and Code 979 Bridgehampton Blue Metallic.

Revell's 1969 Corvette coupe has been kit-bashed to exactly match one of the two or possibly three factory-assembled ZL-1 aluminum block cars. The Code 984 Daytona Yellow replica differs only from the prototype specifications in its use of aftermarket wheels and tires.

These kit-bashed Corvettes were based on AMT-Ertl's contemporary Wave 3 kits. The convertible is a replica of the actual 1970½ L46/350 Code 992 Steel Cities Gray Metallic car in the builder's garage. The coupe is converted to a 1970½ LS5 454 in Code 982 Donnybrook Green Metallic. (Builder/Photographer: Mike Hanson)

AMT and Aurora both offered 1/25th-scale Studebaker Avanti kits, but AMT's offering (shown here) had a more accurate, final finished appearance. Opening doors were included in both kits. (Builder: Dean Milano)

JoHan produced AMX annual kits for sale under the AMT brand, later reissued as JoHan kits. This model has been assembled to replicate the 1969½ Code P-4 "Big Bad Green" option that included painted bumpers. (Builder: Don Sikora II)

Shelby Cobra Roadsters have been continual best-selling subjects for AMT (289 Roadster, left) and Revell (427 Roadster) ever since their introductions to the hobby kit trade in 1965 and 1988, respectively.

Today We Call Them Tuners

However, back then, they were simply awesome.

For most of us, factory muscle cars of the 1960s and early 1970s were everything that was needed and desired, at least at the point that new cars were driven home from the dealership. The same applies to the many outstanding performance cars on the market in the second decade of the 21st century.

Then, as now, there are always those who want the ultimate; even more performance than the best of the factory offerings. Along with this comes a willingness to give up certain things you get from a fully engineered factory muscle car to achieve the ultimate in performance. This can include refinement, a broad range of capability, and a certain degree of affordability. Today the term *tuner* is used to describe both the factory-owned organizations (for example, BMW M, Ford SVT, Mercedes-Benz AMG, FCA SRT) and independent companies with a racing or street performance-based reputation (such as Roush) that provide this capability. In the 1960s and 1970s, this term did not exist, but companies and dealers providing this service certainly *did* exist. These cars offered some of the most colorful back-stories, as well as performance stats, of the entire muscle car era.

Slowly at first, but with far more frequency these days, the model car companies have discovered that these tuned muscle cars provided excellent fodder for scale model kits. In this chapter, I'll show you the kits that capture in miniature the magic of many of these unforgettable cars.

Today's model car companies provided a surprisingly large catalog of 1960s tuner-based muscle cars, but the coverage is most complete for the Shelby Mustang generation. Every model year (except the reserialized 1970 version) is represented in 1/24th- or 1/25th-scale form, and in one case, even in the convertible body style.

Shelby GT350, GT350R, and GT500

When it comes to the tuner cars of the muscle car era, the Shelby Enterprises offerings stood alone. While both early AMT and MPC Mustang kits contained option parts that were suggestive of the GT350 and GT350R, the first fully accurate Shelby Mustang came from AMT in late 1968. After the regular annual kit run of its 1968 Mustang GT, AMT made the necessary exterior and interior changes to duplicate that year's Shelby GT500.

Proving the enduring value of a well-engineered model car tool, AMT's 1968 Shelby GT 500 kit has been reissued at least seven times.

The first fully authentic Shelby GT-500 kit was this release from AMT (Wave 1/). Beyond the well-executed kit contents, a 33 1/3-rpm vinyl record inside the box featured the "Sounds of Carroll Shelby at Riverside." The side panel teases "Hear his voice as he talks you through the turns at the world famous Riverside International Raceway. Hear the roar of the engine, the whine of gearbox, the scream of the tires . . ."***

When Monogram developed its 1/24th-scale 1965–1966 Mustang 2+2 Fastback kit, it was only natural that several Shelby derivatives would follow. The most accurate Shelby kits at the time, releases included a 1965 GT350, a 1965 GT350R, a 1966 GT350, and a 1966 GT350H (the Hertz Rental version.)

In 1988, Revell released a very accurate 1969 Shelby GT500 Fastback kit, based on the wood masters developed for earlier Monogram 1970 Boss 429 kit. This kit has been reissued multiple times, and in 2013 it was joined by a new GT500 convertible kit that shares the engine and chassis of the earlier coupe kit.

Rounding out our coverage of the Shelby GT Mustangs, in 1995 AMT-Ertl released a 1967 Shelby GT350 derivative of the 1967 Mustang GT kit it introduced a year earlier. This kit is the most recent ground-up tooling of a Shelby GT Mustang, and therefore reflects a level of sophistication throughout not seen in the other Shelby kits listed here.

On the top row (left to right) are reissues of AMT's 1968 Shelby GT500 kit dating from 1972 (Wave 1/**) and 1974 (Wave 1/*). On the bottom row (left to right) are the 1978 AMT-Lesney, 1986 AMT-Ertl, and 2003 AMT/Ertl/Round 2 (all Wave 1/*).

The origins of Monogram's 1965–1966 GT350 kits date from 1985 (all: Wave 2/*), and the results reflect its kit engineering philosophy at the time: somewhat simplified parts count and assembly, combined with highly detailed engraving. These kits are well liked by the modeling community.

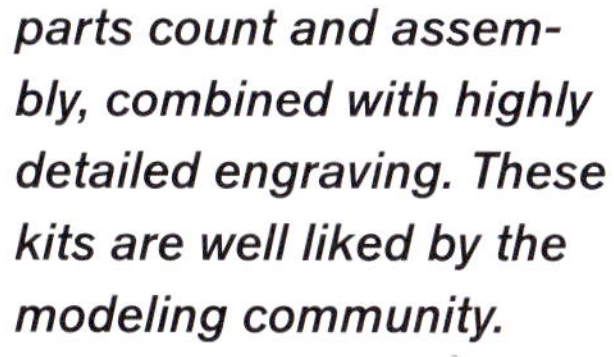

The side panels of the (top to bottom) 1968, 1972, and 1975 issues of AMT's 1968 Shelby GT500 show how AMT's marketing and art departments utilized every inch of box space to inform shoppers and sell kits. Note the enthusiastic wording of the caption on the middle box (often credited to AMT's late Dave Wilder), and a side panel that also repurposed the illustration developed for the box-top illustration of the original kit issue.

Revell's original 1988 release of its 1969 Shelby GT500 kit is at the lower left, followed by reissues dating from 1998 and 2005 (all: Wave 2/*). The convertible kit derivative (the only GT500 convertible ever kitted in the popular scales) debuted in 2013 (Wave 2/*). It includes a highly detailed decal sheet with instrument cluster graphics and woodgrain appliques for the dash and door panels. It also includes a raised roof option, a feature often missing from contemporary model kits.

AMT-Ertl's 1967 Shelby GT350 (Wave 3/) includes what is probably the best "K-Code" 289 Hi-Po in kit form. It also features highly detailed chassis and suspension, a realistic platform-style interior, and the highly desired "outlaw" center fog lamps layout for the front grille.*

Yenko

Don Yenko was among the first car dealers of the 1960s to get into the business of modifying factory offerings and selling them in (relative) volume as uniquely badged products. His first product of this type was a Corvair modified for improved handling/performance and race sanctioning by the SCCA. These were followed by his better-known modifications of first-generation Camaros and, eventually, the third-generation

*AMT's 1967 Corvair annual kit (Wave 1/**) illustrated the Yenko Stinger build version on the box top, and its "for 1968" pseudo-annual kit showed the same car in a rear-three-quarter perspective. The engine featured three induction and six (!) exhaust options as well as the distinctive Yenko hardtop and decklid components. Some of the Yenko version parts have resurfaced in more recent reissues of AMT's 1969 Corvair annual kit (see Chapter 10).*

Revell's 1969 Yenko Camaro kit (all: Wave 3/) is more than a quarter-century old now but compares favorably with the most recent kit tooling, particularly its essentially flawless body proportions. As a general rule, more-recently produced kit reissues (such as this 2003 version, bottom) contain far more complete decal graphics along with a higher-resolution printing of the decals, and are preferable compared to original issue kit versions for that reason.*

"Buyer Beware": A 2003 licensing agreement between AMT-Ertl and The Fast and The Furious *franchise resulted in this reissue of the highly compromised retooling of the MPC 1969 Camaro annual kit (Wave 1/*). Search out Revell's* Fast and Furious *1969 Yenko S/C kit dating from 2016 for an immeasurably better scale replica.*

Nova. Today, there is a surprisingly complete catalog of Yenko offerings in the scale kit world.

When Revell first developed what would eventually be considered the preeminent series of 1/25th-scale 1969 Camaro kits, the initial release was configured as a Yenko 427/SC coupe. This excellent kit has been reissued multiple times.

AMT-Ertl unearthed its inaccurate refurbishment of the original MPC 1969 Camaro kit (discussed in Chapter 8) for yet another run, this time as a *Fast and Furious* licensed Yenko Camaro. As before, I recommend avoiding this kit due to the body accuracy issues.

Revell again revisited the Yenko lineup in 2009, with a Yenko version of its new 1969 Nova kit. Recently Revell renewed its Yenko licensing agreement, and in 2016 issued a

Revell's 1969 Nova tool (Wave 4/) was the basis for this Yenko 427 kit. Yenko hood, side, and headrest graphics were included in this highly detailed kit, which was only slightly compromised by misshaped rear wheelwell openings and an incorrect slope to the lower taillamp panel.*

Fast and Furious version of its 1969 Camaro 427/SC kit, as well as a Yenko dealership C3 Corvette convertible kit.

AMT-Ertl's original 1970½ Camaro Baldwin Motion kit was an intricately detailed kit, but the latest 2014 issue (top) has a far more complete decal sheet that includes the distinctive side graphics missing from the original kit (both: Wave 4/). Note that the latest kit box art cleverly reprises the original 1970 AMT annual kits graphic theme.*

Baldwin-Motion

Revell tied up with Joel Rosen's Baldwin-Motion legacy of modified Chevrolets to introduce several new variations of kits already in its lineup. Starting in 1991, Revell introduced Baldwin-Motion versions of its 1969 Camaro hardtop, 1969 Corvette hardtop, and 1970 Chevelle SS454 kits. (The latter kit was actually a revision of Monogram's old 1/24th-scale SS454, not a 1/25th-scale kit as called out on the box top, and some sources suggest only one real Baldwin-Motion SS454 was ever produced.)

AMT-Ertl developed a second version of its new 1970½ Camaro tool for introduction in the year 2002. Its Baldwin-Motion kit was leaps ahead of the original second-generation Camaro annual kits, but was missing a bit of final refinement when introduced. The latest Round 2 reissue of this kit has addressed some of these issues and is the recommended version to purchase.

Nickey

This famous performance-themed Chevrolet dealership made history with its big-block 427 version of the new 1967 Camaro, engineered by Bill Thomas. Revell recently introduced a second version of its new 1967 Camaro tool, a Nickey RS/SS with the 427 engine.

Revell has referenced the history of Baldwin-Motion modified Chevrolets for a series of kits, including these 427-powered 1969 Corvette and Camaro kits from the 1991 Skip's Fiesta Drive-in Series catalog, and this 2002 reissue of the Corvette kit (all: Wave 3/).*

Revell's all-new 1967 Camaro, by far the most detailed tool yet for Chevy's first-year pony car, forms the basis of this Nickey spin-off version introduced in 2015 (Wave 4/). In addition to the RS trim upgrades, other kit changes include a dual-quad 427 Rat Motor with headers, and some strangely undersized five-spoke mags.*

Royal

Another dealership made famous by its tuning activities was Royal Pontiac, located in Royal Oak, Michigan. Revell's 1966 Royal Pontiac GTO kits are also covered in Chapter 4.

Revell's 1966 Royal Pontiac GTO kit from 1999 was a very precise copy of the two cars that ran in drag strip promotions during the 1966 racing season. A reissue of the Royal Pontiac GTO kit debuted in 2013, though this one was a copy of the contemporary GeeTO Tiger drag strip recreation (both: Wave 3/).*

Hurst

A discussion of 1960s and early 1970s tuners would be woefully incomplete without mentioning the activities of Hurst Corporation. Beginning in 1968, its series of Hurst Olds conversions (based on the Oldsmobile 442) created a special legacy of performance combined with luxury. AMT-Ertl replicated the 1969 Hurst Olds in a kit first introduced in 1989. Revell visited the Hurst Olds lineup for its 2009 release of the 1972 Hurst Olds convertible, another highly detailed and highly regarded kit from the model maker hailing from the Chicago suburbs.

While not fully production vehicles, I also want to mention the Hurst-Olds' role in the 1968 Dart and Barracuda 426 Hemi Super Stock program, and the 1968½ AMC AMX Super Stock project. JoHan's Shirley Shahan *Dragon Lady* AMX kit is loosely based on the drag cars created by Hurst, while Revell's 1968 Dodge Dart Super Stock Hemi kit is also loosely inspired by the famous Mopar dragsters that were assembled with Hurst's help. (The AMC SC/Rambler and Machine were also developed with the assistance of Hurst; kits of those cars are covered in Chapters 7 and 10.)

AMT-Ertl's 1969 Hurst Olds kit was the second release from the tool that produced its earlier MPC-branded 1969 W-30 442 kit. It was reissued recently by Round 2 using AMT 1969 annual kit–inspired box art (both kits: Wave 3/). Revell based its first release of its Cutlass convertible tool on the 1972 Hurst Olds convertible (Wave 4/*).*

*JoHan's AMX Super-Stock kit (Wave 1/**) modifications included a dual-quad cross-ram intake and headers, a hood scoop, Cragar S/S wheels, and Shirley Shahan Drag-on-Lady graphics. Revell's 1968 Dart Super-Stock kit (Wave 3/*) requires the builder to do some modifications (such as cutting out the Hemi-specific rear fender wheel openings), and omits the typical Dodge A-100–style buckets, but is a good basis for a Hurst Super Stock factory dragster project.*

Epilogue

Model builders and collectors should expect to see more kits in the future featuring the cars created by the now-revered tuners of the 1960s and early 1970s. These are generally easy conversions for the kit manufacturers that generate additional volume from existing tooling assets. They also prove to be very popular kits with those adult model builders and collectors who remember these famous offerings from the muscle car era.

Missing in Action "Under the Hood" Edition

As I've noted throughout this book, there are some pretty big holes in the 1/25th-scale kit availability of some of the premier muscle car–era engines. I've summarized the most unforgivable of these omissions here.

Iconic muscle car engines yet to appear in a 1/24th-1/25th-scale kit

- Pontiac RA-III and RA-IV 400 V-8s
- Pontiac 455 HO (1971) and 455 Super Duty (1973–1974)
- Oldsmobile 350 Ram Rod/W-31
- Ford 1971 Boss 351
- Ford/Mercury 1972–1973 Cleveland 351 HO/CJ
- Dodge/Plymouth 1974 E58 360 Hi-Po
- For a truly rare, extra-credit choice: 1958 Mercury 430 MEL Super Marauder

The Model Car Kit Collector

After reading about all these great vintage model car kits, you've decided you want to acquire some of them. What next?

This chapter is intended to give you some guidance on that subject. After some initial advice, I'll pass along some sources of old kits and touch on collecting other types of old model car kit memorabilia. I'll also cover another way to fill in some of the gaps in scale muscle car kit coverage.

Collecting Kits: Advice for the New Kit Collector

The very first step in collecting kits is to *know your subject well.*

My best advice is to acquire the latest edition of the bible of model car kit collectors. This spiral-bound reference is called *The Directory of Model Car Kits with Price Guide, American Manufacturers Only, 1/24-1/25 Scale* by Bill Coulter and Bob Shelton. Compiled by these highly knowledgeable kit collectors and builders, this self-published guide is presently in its seventh edition as this book is written.

The information in these guides is invaluable. Kits are listed by manufacturer, kit category, model year, body style, scale, date of the kit issue, kit number, and suggested value. Like any effort of this sort, there are a few minor errors or omissions, although the writers continue to improve the accuracy with each updated edition. (For purchase information, see Resources.)

The second key piece of advice is to inspect in detail any potential purchase. Be extremely careful if a kit is presented as being in the original shrink-wrap. When originally produced, most model kits of the early to mid-1960s were not shrink-wrapped at the factory. When wrapping came into use, it was often brittle and prone to being torn. With shrink-wrapping machines easily accessible today, it would be easy to box some other contents inside a "factory sealed" vintage kit box.

After opening the box, examine the contents carefully. Look for any missing parts using the kit assembly instructions as a reference. Check the back of the decal sheet, as many vintage kits will have a decal production date printed there. Make sure it aligns with the original kit issue date. Check the chrome parts tree and clear parts for scratches. Make sure the body itself does not show signs of warpage, and that the A-pillars are intact and unbroken. If a kit shows any of these imperfections (and vintage kits for sale these days are often imperfect), negotiate a reduced price with the seller.

Many vintage kits that are for sale also show signs of partial assembly or painting. If you only collect vintage, unbuilt kits, it's a full stop. However, if you plan to build the kit, sometimes these partially assembled kits represent a good value, as they typically sell at a fraction of the price of a perfect, untouched kit.

Another tip is that starting in the 1990s, Revell/Monogram and AMT/Ertl began reissuing kits with reproductions of original kit box art. These reissues are worth much less than the original kits that bear the same box appearance. Look closely at the box art before any purchase. The presence of a digital scan-

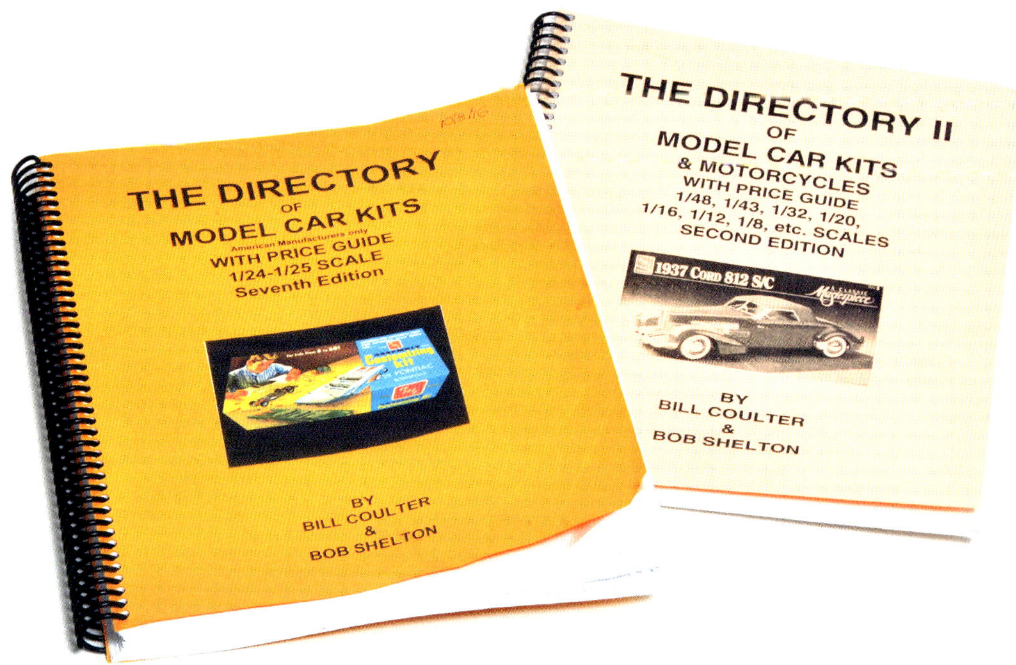

If you plan to do any major purchases of vintage model car kits, your first step should be to acquire the latest edition of The Directory of Model Car Kits, 1/24-1/25 Scale, with Price Guide. *Shown is the seventh edition, with a publication date of 2016. A second, similar guide is available for kits in other scales (1/48, 1/43, 1/32, 1/20, 1/16, 1/12, and 1/8).*

One of these kits is a hard to find original issue, and the other is a relatively common reissue produced 25+ years later. The original issue sells for three times the price of the reissue. You can tell the reissue on the right from the gold Limited Edition sticker, the digital scanning code, the 1996 copyright date, Chevrolet licensing statements on the side panels, and the printing on the box bottom.

Round 2 recently began reissuing its Wave 3 model kits with all-new box art that is inspired by the graphic layout of the original AMT box art graphic for annual kits of a given model year. However, Round 2 has made the boxes visually different enough that you will not mistake the original annual kit with the later, modern tooled kits that are completely different inside. Compare the original AMT 1967 Impala SS annual kit on the left with the all-new box art on the right for the AMT-Ertl 1967 Impala SS kit that was engineered in 1997. Further tipoffs to the newer kit include the copyright date, the UPC scanner block, and printing on the box bottom.

Today's best model car kits allow you to build up a scale muscle car to the exact configuration you would have ordered for yourself in the showroom of your favorite brand back in the day. One of the best examples is Revell's 1970 Hemi-Cuda kit first introduced in 2013. How would you have ordered yours? Now you can build a kit to your exact specifications.

the box art before any purchase. The presence of a digital scanning code, a later copyright date, a licensing statement from the manufacturer of the car being duplicated, and/or printing on the box bottom is a tipoff of a reissue rather than the original.

The last piece of advice is don't be afraid to ask for advice if something seems amiss.

Online model car message boards and forums are great sources for novice kit collectors. A respectful message post asking for advice will often generate multiple answers in less than 24 hours. (See Resources.)

Sources of Vintage Model Car Kits

Purchasing vintage model car kits was a bit of a challenge years ago. Your best bets were once-a-year regional toy shows for collectibles or mail correspondence with advertisers that were found in the classified sections of model car magazines.

Today, the Internet provides instant information and capability to view and complete purchases of your favorite current, recent, or vintage model car kit. Beyond a Google search of "vintage model car kits," here are some suggestions:

Original factory literature from the kitmakers reveals fascinating tidbits about the kits and the hobby. These 1959 and 1960 AMT convertible kit catalogs are actually color reprints of the original documents (as the originals are extremely rare and pricey). Note the pictures of built-up models on the 1960 catalog.

Vintage Kit Specialists

There are three vintage kit merchants that are the longest running and most knowledgeable in the field. All are highly regarded by model car kit experts. See Resources for their websites.

Auction Sites

Many vintage kits are available from eBay and Etsy. As always, read the item description in complete detail (never rely on just the auction title), review feedback of the seller, and compare the actual selling prices of recent similar transactions before making a bid. Most sellers are reliable but, as always, be aware of potential shysters. Typical scams include putting the latest kit reissue contents inside the original box art of a kit release, offering kits for sale at prices much higher than the typical selling prices, and unusually high shipping and handling charges. In other cases, sellers simply do not know what they are selling, and as a result sometimes misrepresent the kit contents. In these cases, contacting the seller will, in most cases, result in an adequate adjustment to the selling price or other mutually acceptable accommodation.

Collectible Toy Shows

John Carlisle produces one of the longest-running toy shows at which vintage model car kits are sold under the name Old Toyland Shows. If you live in the Midwest or Northeast United States, check out one of his shows. The yearly schedules are posted online.

Model Car Events

Many model car contests and model exhibitions (often called NNLs) include a vendor display that frequently feature vintage model car kit sellers. Information on dates and locations is available in *Scale Auto* magazine and other online sources (see Resources).

Other Options: Collecting Box Art, Hobby Dealer Literature, Box Proofs, and Original Art

What if you don't have the budget, space, or inclination to collect unbuilt vintage model car kits, but you'd still like to collect *something* related to the model car kit hobby? I can offer several suggestions.

First, pristine *original box art without the contents* is now considered collectible in its own right. In fact, a portion of the kits shown in this book are collectible empty boxes rather than full kits. These sell for a small fraction of the cost of a, complete vintage kit (although prices are now on the rise). They allow you to admire the box art, revisit memories of building these kits back in the day, and many of the box tops can be folded flat for efficient storage. An online auction search for "AMT Empty Boxes" or "Airboxes" can give you an idea of what is available.

Many hobbyists enjoy collecting the factory literature from the model car manufacturers. Through the 1960s, these mostly four-color catalogs were distributed primarily to hobby shop owners and other retailers, and they are relatively rare today. Some sell reprints of these references. Starting in the 1970s, kitmakers began to make these catalogs available to kit buyers, and they were produced in larger numbers accordingly.

A much more specialized form of collecting is to track down and purchase box art proofs or unfolded box art prints. Kitmakers produced these in small numbers for internal review

This is an original single kit sell sheet distributed by AMT prior to the production run of its 1970 Chevelle SS454 annual kit. Note the full description of the kit features. The kit shipping information box on the lower right reveals that hobby dealers, rather than individual kit buyers, were the primary target audience for this page.

Uncut and unfolded box tops (above) are an interesting collectible associated with model car kits. These can be very hard to locate. They were used by the factory as proofs before final production, or they were simply extras after production finished. The 1941 Plymouth Street Rod box top was provided to the writer by AMT in appreciation for the partially scratch built model he built that was photographed for box top imagery seen here.

AMT's primary competitor during the early annual kit years was JoHan, and it too used sell sheets for its annual kit lineups. Here the 1963 and 1964 kit literature details JoHan's simplified 98 cent kits, along with a further description of the full 3-in-1 1964 kits priced at $1.49. Note that JoHan's flyer was two-color rather than the four-color approach of the AMT retailer catalogs.

Model car kits occasionally documented "planned but later cancelled" real muscle cars from the Big 3. Examples include these AMT and MPC kits, showing a planned Dodge C-Body Hemi option, a SOHC 427 option for the 1966 Galaxie 500 XL, a factory installation of the Boss 429 engine for the 1970 Cyclone (and Torino), a continuation of the Plymouth SuperBird onto the all-new 1971 Road Runner body shell, and a stillborn 1975 Pontiac GTO.

and, sometimes, as a reward for those outsiders who helped make the kit a reality. These sometimes surface on the auction sites and other sources.

The rarest and most expensive non-kit collectibles are the original illustrations/art that were used to produce those great box art treatments. These studio pieces are airbrush, watercolor, chalk, or oil paintings of the subject of the kit, without the lettering, trademarks, and disclosures that were later added in the kit box art production process. If you manage to locate one of these originals, it deserves to be framed and displayed accordingly. As an example, a vice president of design for one of the domestic automakers currently displays the original box art illustration of an AMT kit in his office.

Model Car Kit Fun Facts

Here are some "did you knows?" about model car kits and the model car kit business.

AMT

During the heyday of the model car kit business, the engineering and product development teams worked 58 hours, every week, on a very tight timetable leading to the debut of the next year's 1/25th-scale promotionals in late September or early October, followed by the 1/25th-scale convertible and then hardtop 3-in-1 assembly kits.

AMT announced a number of kits for its 1970 annual 3-in-1 kit lineup that were never produced. These included a Corvair (the real car was dropped for 1970), El Camino, Cougar, Galaxie XL Fastback, Falcon, and Cadillac Eldorado. Today's kit collectors call kits that were announced but never produced "ghost kits."

AMT's iconic assembly plant located at 1225 East Maple Road in Troy, Michigan (a northern suburb of Detroit), still stands today. After AMT left the facility in the very late 1970s, it has served a number of different functions, including a stint as a sub-assembly site for the second generation of Ford GT during the first decade of the 21st century. The facility now wears a new, very modern facade.

SMP

Various model kit historians have brought forward explanations of the close relationship between kitmakers SMP and AMT. One respected source states that a company named Detroit Plastics produced the SMP-branded kits in its factory, while AMT handled the kit design, marketing, and distribution.

Others suggest that SMP may have been a shell company set up by AMT to handle non-Ford branded promotionals and kits. What is generally agreed is that AMT acquired the SMP business sometime in 1961 (though the SMP brand still appeared on some 1962 annual kits).

MPC

MPC grew quickly from its formation in 1963 and first kit offerings in 1964. By 1968, it was selling 8 million promotionals and model kits a year (according to an article in *Dodge News*, a publication for Dodge owners). Approximately 1 million of these sales were Dodge kits.

During the busy summer periods in the late 1960s, MPC's Mount Clemens, Michigan, factory employed 250 workers working three shifts per day.

JoHan

While the rest of its annual kit and promotionals were mostly engineered to 1/25th scale, American Motors reportedly instructed JoHan to produce its Rambler promotionals starting with the 1962 product range in the slightly larger 1/24th scale.

Conversely, some of JoHan's luxury car kits and promotionals were reportedly shortened in length to fit inside its existing model kit and promotionals packaging.

Monogram Models

A highly placed former executive told me it was standard practice at Monogram (and possibly other model makers) to increase the engine size by 10 percent relative to the rest of the kit, to provide a more "realistic" appearance when the model's hood was opened or removed. But to fit the enlarged engine under the hood, it had to be further "sectioned" (a horizontal slice removed) in height through the engine block or oil pan.

Model Car Tools

As of 1968, a kit and promo tool would need to produce more than 300,000 copies reach a financial break-even point, and tools cost a kitmaker $50,000 in 1968 funds. Today, a first kit run of 10,000 copies is often considered a success, and various sources claim a tool runs from $100,000 to $250,000 in 2017 funds.

Wood Masters

Until about 20 years ago, new model kits were developed with three-dimensional 1/10th-scale masters sculpted from basswood and measured from actual automotive factory blueprints. These 1/10th-scale molds made from these Wood Masters were then reduced to 1/25th scale via a 2.5 to 1 pantograph engraving setup.

Model Car Kit Fun Facts *continued*

Perhaps the most complete and clearly understandable explanation of how model kits were traditionally developed can be found in the December 1988 issue of *Fine Scale Modeler*. Most of the kits shown in this book were developed with methods similar to those described in this article.

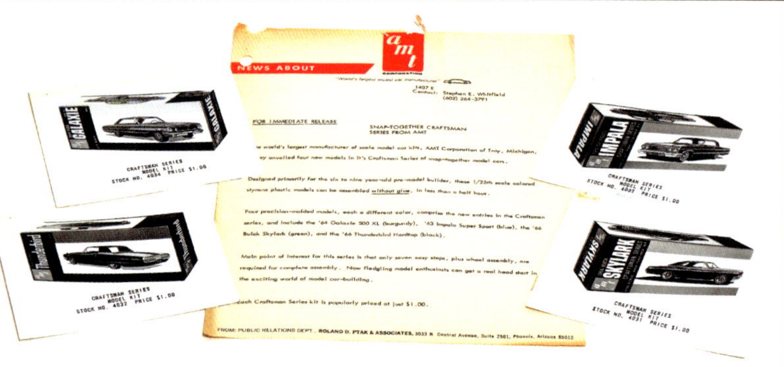
NEWS ABOUT amt CORPORATION

"World's largest model car manufacturer"

1407 E

Contact: Stephen E. Whitfield (602) 264-3791

FOR IMMEDIATE RELEASE

SNAP-TOGETHER CRAFTSMAN SERIES FROM AMT

e world's largest manufacturer of scale model car kits, AMT Corporation of Troy, Michigan, ay unveiled four new models in it's Craftsman Series of snap-together model cars.

Designed primarily for the six to nine year-old pre-model builder, these 1/25th scale colored styrene plastic models can be assembled without glue, in less than a half hour.

Four precision-molded models, each a different color, comprise the new entries in the Craftsman series, and include the '64 Galaxie 500 XL (burgundy), '63 Impala Super Sport (blue), the '66 Buick Skylark (green), and the '66 Thunderbird Hardtop (black).

Main point of interest for this series is that only seven easy steps, plus wheel assembly, are required for complete assembly. Now fledgling model enthusiasts can get a real head start in the exciting world of model car-building.

ach Craftsman Series kit is popularly priced at just $1.00.

FROM: PUBLIC RELATIONS DEPT., ROLAND D. PTAK & ASSOCIATES, 3033 N. Central Avenue, Suite 2501, Phoenix, Arizona 85012

AMT was the leader in marketing simplified assembly kits in the Wave 1 kit era, marketing them as Jr. Trophy Series and Craftsman kits. This vintage press release from AMT's public relations agency summarized the marketing approach: Designed primarily for the six- to nine-year-old pre-model builder, these 1/25th-scale colored styrene plastic models can be assembled without glue, in less than a half hour. Kit collectors have documented 26 different kit topics kits released in this series, ranging from a 1957 Thunderbird to a 1966 Buick Skylark GS.

A sampling of simplified assembly kits (typically unassembled promotionals without engines) includes these 1960s and early 1970s offerings from AMT, JoHan and MPC. Some of these kit topics were also offered as full assembly kits, while others such as the 1963 Valiant and 1964 Comet Caliente were solely in these simplified forms.

*In the mid-1970s, respected model car journalists Hank Borger and Bill Coulter decided that JoHan's Chrysler Corporation Turbine Car Gold Cup kit deserved designation as the ultimate "Grand Masters" kit. JoHan's "Frame Pak" parts tree packaging, a painstakingly accurate replication of Chrysler's unit body construction approach, separately molded front and rear subframes, finely rendered opening doors, hood, and trunk, a 21-piece Turbine engine assembly, and even separately molded vent window frames and three-dimensional styrene coil springs were all justifications for their decision. Should you attempt to locate this kit, try to find an original issue (Wave 1/***), as JoHan's many reissues suffered due to deferred tooling maintenance and other quality issues.*

Many a model kit buyer back in the day opened a Palmer model car kit, thinking it was equivalent to AMT/Revell/Monogram quality, and was faced instead with a multi-piece (separate sides and top) body and only the most generic representation of the real car . . . essentially a toy rather than a "model" kit.

Always exercise extreme caution before buying any Palmer Scale Models kit. This particular kit was better than most from Palmer/PSM, but it was still a far-from-accurate replica of the 1971 Mustang.

So You Want to Build a Muscle Car Kit

This is a topic way past the scope of this book, but just to whet your appetite, the following photos just touch on some ideas to get you started. Want to learn more? For starters, check out the back issue department at *Scale Auto* Magazine.

The GTO model car bodies shown here have been painted with factory-correct shades of actual car paint that is derived from the same paint formulas used by the real car manufacturers in their production line painting booths. These paints are now available in model car–sized quantities from a number of online resources.

Bare Metal Foil is an amazing product that is easily applied to replicate chrome trim on model car bodies. Easy, that is, if you know the insider tricks to make it work. Check the August 2016 issue of Scale Auto *magazine for all the details on how to use this self-adhesive bright metal foil.*

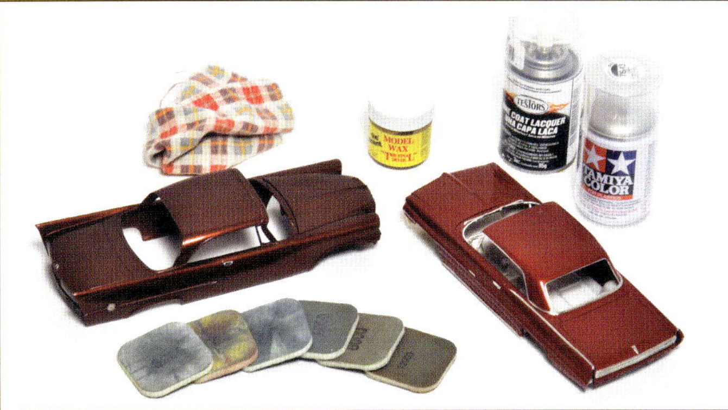

Ultra-gloss Clearcoat paints from Testors and Tamiya provide great finishes without the risks associated with and the unrealistic thickness of automotive two-part urethane paints. Then, polishing kits like the one shown here from Micro-Mark allow today's model car builder to attain shiny perfection in their paint jobs that were possible by only the most skilled builders years ago.

Many Wave 3 and Wave 4 kits include extensive underhood detailing, including plumbing for air conditioning compressors, heater hoses, and air cleaner engine nomenclature panels. In essence, all the builder needs to add is spark plug wiring. This box stock engine compartment is courtesy of AMT-Ertl's 1971 Charger R/T kit.

This 1/25th-scale 1970 Boss 302 engine compartment is factory accurate down to the last vacuum line and T-fitting. With the help of an extensive model car kit aftermarket and some ingenuity to boot, this shows what is possible for the model car builder that chooses to create a completely lifelike scale replica.

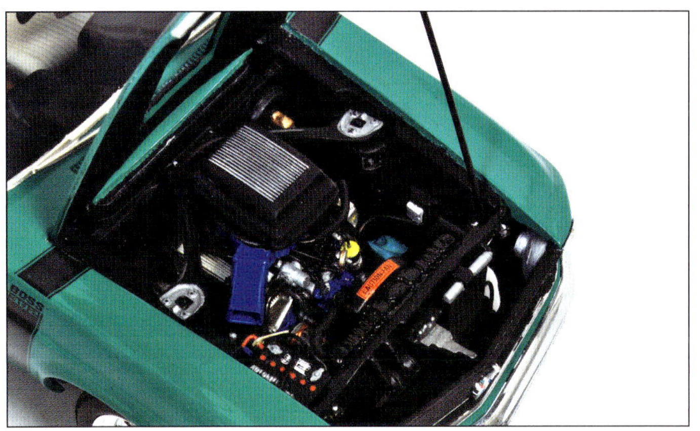

Afterword

The model car kit world of today is far, far different from the heyday of the kit business in the early to mid-1960s. Back then, a kit had to sell at least 300,000 copies to be considered successful. Some kits sold millions of copies. Today, if a new kit sells 10,000 copies during a first production run, it's a winner.

The best box art was not only visually appealing but it also engaged the builder. What kit buyer wouldn't be dreaming of becoming a drag racing driver when viewing this box art of AMT's 1970 Chevelle SS454?

So, what caused this?

First, it helps to understand that the original rise of contemporary model car kits starting in the late 1950s and continuing into the mid-1960s was a fad, and like so many other fads back then, people went on to new fads as the years progressed. Sales of model car kits grew rapidly and peaked, then dropped off just as all fads do. Moreover, in the case of model car kits, the rapid rise of slot cars and slot car racing in the mid-1960s further diverted the attention of many a model car builder.

Second, as the cultural and societal discontent of the late 1960s emerged, and then as the hostile marketplace for muscle cars (and indeed, any car with exciting styling) developed, the real cars (that formed the basis for model car kits) became far less inspiring, which made for fewer new kits, and slower sales for those that still emerged.

During the 1970s, most of the model car companies moved from those inspiring box art illustrations to pictures (often heavily doctored) of the real model cars. I'll address this more in a moment, but I believe this limited the appeal of these new kits. At the same time, as product development costs and raw materials costs increased dramatically during the stagflation era, model kit companies dropped the 3-in-1 kit customizing feature, which again limited the appeal of the new kits.

Then, concurrent with the baby boom–generation entering adulthood and focusing on careers, finding partners, and establishing families, subsequent generations of young Americans were notably smaller in terms of population, which further

The box art not only engaged the imagination of modelers, it built brand awareness. MPC was perhaps the most consistent model company for developing and evolving a year-after-year box art design language for its annual kit lineup. Every year brought a visibly new appearance, but one that developed a continuity through time such as the 1967 through 1970 kits on the left with the diagonal split backgrounds.

reduced the potential marketplace for model kits. As for those new youngsters and teens, fresh diversions such as video games captured their interests with fad-like intensity, just as the original model car fad had done two decades earlier. While building model cars required focus and a time commitment, video games seemed tailor-made for what was perceived to be the short attention span of this new generation.

In spite of all this, model kits enjoyed a period of increased popularity in the late 1980s and 1990s, when the adult hobbyist became the predominant force driving the model kit market. New and better kits, along with the emergence of several quality publications covering the hobby, drove this resurgence. But by the late 1990s, the popularization of varyingly accurate 1/18th- and 1/24th-scale die-cast models started to again limit the appeal of kits, just as maturing adult hobbyists faced many competing demands, thereby reducing their discretionary time and income to spend on the hobby.

The many economic and societal challenges of the last two decades have continued to impact the hobby. One key difference between model car kits and most other fads of the 1960s, is that model car kits remain a viable hobby and a business today. It is much different, and much smaller, for sure, but alive and vibrant nonetheless.

One step between box art illustrations and box top photos of built model cars was to use the manufacturer's brochure and advertising photography. JoHan had already been pursuing this route for its kit box art for years, but it was new to MPC for these three kits introduced in 1971½. (These kits have never been reissued in exactly these forms, and are desirable collectibles for that reason, as well as its unique box art treatments.)

Why Did the Model Car Companies Move Away from Creative Box Art Illustrations?

When the team at CarTech Books and I first discussed the possibility of this book, one of the questions I was asked was why did model car kit box art evolve away from those inspirational images of the 1960s and early 1970s. This is a question I've long shared. As I was doing contract work for AMT in the mid-1970s when this shift primarily occurred, I was present at some internal discussions of this change. I have also asked industry insiders through the years since for their views on this question. Here is what I can relay in response to the question.

First, it was the search for something new. Picturing actual built models on kit boxes had not been done to any major degree until the beginning of the 1970s. Even then, AMT, which was still the leading kit manufacturer, had largely stuck with box art developed by its crack art department staff well into the middle of that next decade. It was time to try something different, particularly since most of the kits now being produced were reissues of kits previously on the market.

The second consideration in moving toward picturing built models on box art was the evolving legal environment in the United States during the 1970s. "Truth in advertising" was becoming a mantra, and the federal government bureaucracy was becoming increasingly strident in pursuing those who violated this precept. Box art had always illustrated the kit subject

AMT Corporation commissioned your author to build these models that were later photographed in its studio for these box tops. AMT specified the kit version to be built and the paint color to be used for the exterior and interior, although sometimes they accommodated builder suggestions. Contracting outsiders for professional model car box art builds was a major cost savings, but were the lost sales worth it?

in the most appealing way. Yet the finished model often didn't look that good. There was a corporate concern that the box tops were making promises the contents inside couldn't deliver. In addition, the youngster who built the kit, or more likely his mother who bought the kit for him, was increasingly likely to complain. The solution was, of course, to show the finished model on the box top.

There was also a financial element involved. Retaining and housing a staff of highly talented commercial artists was costly for the model companies as they looked for ways to reduce costs to offset the spiking costs of styrene (a petrochemical-derived material impacted by increasing energy prices) and increased labor wages. Companies including AMT found that it could spend $30 (in 1975 funds) to commission experienced adult model builders (including your author) to build its kits to finished photo studio readiness. That was a huge savings versus the costs of carrying internally housed illustration capabilities.

These were all rational reasons for a change. In the end, much was lost. The best box art treatments of the 1960s and early 1970s visually jumped off the hobby store shelves. They engaged the kit purchaser with the idea of what might be. Yes, they generally made the product look better than it really was, but much of the appeal of the hobby back then was based on engaging the imagination and creativity of the kit builder, and the best of these artistic box arts were superb at doing just that.

Further, with the new approach of photographing real models and given the timeline for developing all-new kits, box art models often had to be constructed from early prototype kit tooling that lacked the quality and refinement of the final product. In a few extreme cases, they were even assembled from modifications of some competitor's similar kit subject. Key parts that would ordinarily be plated, such as grilles and bumpers, were painted silver or unconvincingly airbrushed in the photo studio to look like chrome. The result inevitably looked compromised at best. Not only that, the photography-based box art compositions often did a poor job of selling the kit features, and eventually this evolved toward using a few simplified bullet point statements to describe the contents (versus the previous practice of detailed side panel artist depictions of kit contents and options). With many ill winds blowing toward the model car hobby back then, the move away from high-quality box art composition and illustration only added to the downward trajectory of the model car business at the time.

Fortunately, today's kit business has once again endorsed high-quality and inspirational commercial art for the box tops of new model car kits. One only needs to look at a row of Round 2 or Moebius Models kits at the store to see the renewed impact of this kit marketing approach.

Compare the lifeless, photography-based original issue box art treatments of AMT-Ertl's 1966 Nova and 1968 El Camino (bottom left and right), with the new, artist-developed box art treatments of these same kits from the current tool owners Round 2. The top boxes restore the magic of the original box art illustration treatments of the 1960s and early 1970s. Which one would you rather buy?

Today's Model Car Kit Business

The world of contemporary model car kits is primarily adult-focused, and much, much smaller than in earlier decades. One of the most dramatic impacts on the hobby occurred in July 2007, when Wal-Mart announced that it would no longer stock and sell model car kits. Soon other big-box retailers adopted a similar policy. This was a huge shock to the model car kit industry, as sales of kits fell dramatically, and the kit manufacturers had to take drastic actions to remain viable.

One big benefit of all these changes, however, is that the merchandise buyers from Wal-Mart and the other big-box retailers would no longer dictate the topic choice and marketing of new model car kits, as they had increasingly done starting in the late 1970s. This allowed the model kit companies to become far more focused on satisfying the adult hobbyist and his or her needs and desires, and the diversity of subjects chosen for new kits improved accordingly.

Specialized kit topics like the recent introductions shown here might never have appeared if the big box retailers were still controlling the distribution and sales of model car kits as they did from the late 1970s through 2006. The model car kit hobby is a smaller hobby today but one much more attuned to the desires of the adult model car builder.

The current generation of real pony cars has superb performance characteristics and charisma, and for the most part the model car companies have produced excellent 1/25th-scale assembly kits of these topics. These kits ensure that the model car hobby will remain relevant to subsequent generations of hobbyists, including the grandchildren of those who first built model car kits in the 1960s. One inexplicable omission is the lack of full detail kits of Ford's new S550 Mustang family; so far, the only 1/25th-scale replica is a toy-like offering (top center) from Revell.

Muscle cars that were never produced as model kits, plus rare and hard to find original annual kits, have sometimes been the subject of limited production trans-kits produced by resin casters such as Missing Link, Perry's Resin Replicas, R & R Vacuum Craft, Holthaus, MCW Automotive Replicas, Air-Trax, and others. A few of these are straight reproductions of old annual kits, but most replicate topics that were never produced as 1/25th-scale styrene kits. A number of the kits pictured here are no longer available new, so when you see a resin kit you want, buy it at that point rather than wait!

Final Thoughts

At the beginning of this book, I put forward the thought that model car kits are simply the most accurate and complete way of remembering your original muscle cars, next to owning the real thing. Those of you who are already model kit collectors and/or builders know exactly why I would say this. For those of you who've never picked up a model kit or haven't cracked the seal of one for decades, I hope you can now see why I feel that way. Maybe you've even thought about the proposition yourself. All those muscle car model kits out there are just waiting for your attention.

As I was putting the finishing touches on this book, I took the time to go through my collection of *Car Craft* magazines from the mid- through the late 1960s. Many magazines covered the original supercar/muscle car movement, among them *Hot Rod, Car Life, Car and Driver, Motor Trend, High Performance Cars, Super Stock and Drag Illustrated*, and so on. Of them all, *Car Craft* seemed to be the one that was most tuned into not just the cars but also the entire muscle car culture. Going back all these years and reading each issue in detail leaves me with this one thought: the muscle car era was truly amazing on so many levels.

Fortunately, fans can relive those magical times today. Whether you do that by driving or collecting the real cars, or as I suggest here, the model car kits that replicated them, don't leave this opportunity to celebrate (again) a very special time in the American auto industry and the culture that surrounded it.

Additional books that may interest you...

SELLING THE AMERICAN MUSCLE CAR: Marketing Detroit Iron in the 60s and 70s *by Diego Rosenberg* Manufacturers poured millions into racing programs, operating under the principle of "Win on Sunday, Sell on Monday." Cars were given catchy nicknames, such as The GTO Judge, Plymouth Roadrunner, Cobra, and Dodge Super Bee. Entire manufacturer lines were given catchy marketing campaigns, such as Dodge's Scat Pack, AMC's Go Package, and Ford's Total Performance. Selling the American Muscle Car: Marketing Detroit Iron in the 60s and 70s takes you back to an era when options were plentiful and performance was cheap. You will relive or be introduced to some of the cleverest marketing campaigns created during a time when America was changing every day. Hardbound, 10 x 10 inches, 192 pages, 290 color and 145 b/w photos. ***Item # CT542***

MATCH RACE MAYHEM Drag Racing's Grudges, Rivalries and Big-Money Showdowns *by Doug Boyce* During the golden age of drag racing, fans didn't care as much about class racing as much as they wanted to see scores settled and interesting match-ups. Match races were also a great way to feature wildly popular cars that no longer had a class in which to compete, yet the fans still wanted to see them. So popular were these races that many track promoters didn't bother to promote class racing at all. Instead, they used the match races as headliners, similar to the marquee at your local arena or a billboard in Las Vegas, all resulting in putting more fans in the stands. And the drivers loved it too. Many of the most popular pro drivers quit class racing altogether just to go match racing. Softbound, 8.5 x 11 inches, 176 pages, 201 color and 96 b/w photos. ***Part # CT582***

DETROIT MUSCLE: Factory Lightweights and Purpose-Built Muscle Cars *by Charles Morris* The muscle car era, and the era that immediately preceded it, are a unique window in time; it is one that we will not likely see again. It started in the 1950s, when automakers realized that if they made their cars more powerful than brand X and won races on the weekends as well, sales would follow those victories into the dealership. This book follows the evolution of the fastest, most powerful, and exciting vehicles of the era, in both drag racing and NASCAR. From early Hudson Hornets, to the birth of the Hemi, to aluminum and fiberglass panel sedans, to lightweight special-order muscle cars ready to race from the factory, to their eventual demise, it is all covered here. Hardbound, 10 x 10 inches, 192 pages, 400 photos. ***Item # CT579***

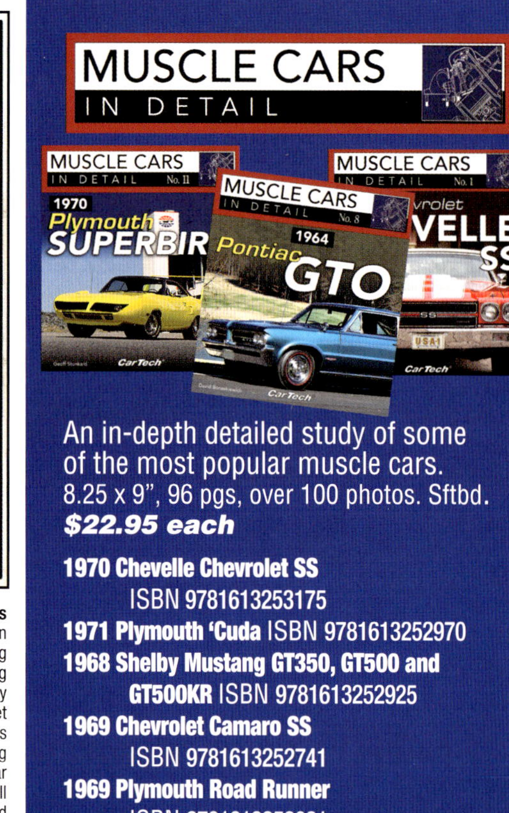

An in-depth detailed study of some of the most popular muscle cars. 8.25 x 9", 96 pgs, over 100 photos. Sftbd. ***$22.95 each***

1970 Chevelle Chevrolet SS ISBN 9781613253175
1971 Plymouth 'Cuda ISBN 9781613252970
1968 Shelby Mustang GT350, GT500 and GT500KR ISBN 9781613252925
1969 Chevrolet Camaro SS ISBN 9781613252741
1969 Plymouth Road Runner ISBN 9781613253021
1973–1974 Pontiac Trans Am Super Duty 455 ISBN 9781613253090
1969–1970 Ford Mustang Boss 429 ISBN 9781613253168
1969 Ford Mustang Mach 1 ISBN 9781613253182
1970 Plymouth Superbird ISBN 9781613253007
1964 Pontiac GTO ISBN 9781613253205
1970 Plymouth Road Runner ISBN 9781613253045

Check out our website:

CarTechBooks.com

✓ Find our newest books before anyone else
✓ Get weekly tech tips from our experts
✓ Featuring a new deal each week!

Exclusive Promotions and Giveaways at www.CarTechBooks.com!

www.cartechbooks.com or 1-800-551-4754